Tokyo, My Everest
A Canadian Woman in Japan

Gabrielle Bauer

HOUNSLOW

Tokyo, My Everest: A Canadian Woman in Japan

Copyright © 1995 by Gabrielle Bauer

Hounslow Press
A member of the Dundurn Group

Publisher: Anthony Hawke
Editor: Liedewy Hawke
Printer: Webcom
Front Cover Illustration: Cathy Pentland

Canadian Cataloguing in Publication Data

Bauer, Gabrielle
    Tokyo, my Everest : a Canadian woman in Japan

Includes index.
ISBN 0-88882-181-6

1. Tokyo (Japan) – Description and travel.
2. Tokyo (Japan) – Social life and customs.
3. Canadians – Japan – Tokyo. 4. Bauer, Gabrielle –
Journeys – Japan – Tokyo. I. Title.

DS896.35. B38 1995   952'.135049   C95-931124-6

Publication was assisted by the **Canada Council**, the **Book Publishing Industry Development Program** of the **Department of Canadian Heritage**, the **Ontario Arts Council**, and the **Ontario Publishing Centre** of the **Ministry of Citizenship, Culture, and Recreation**.

The author thanks the Ontario Arts Council for their financial assistance toward the writing of this book.

Acknowledgements

Quote p. 7 reprinted from *Ransom,* by Jay McInerney, New York: Random House, 1985.

Quote p. 31 reprinted from *The Handmaid's Tale,* by Margaret Atwood, (1985), used by permission of the Canadian Publishers, McClelland & Stewart, Toronto.

Quote p. 71 reprinted from *Touch the Dragon,* by Karen Connelly, Winnipeg: Turnstone Press, 1993.

Quote p.103 reprinted from *Metropolitan Life,* by Fran Lebowitz, New York: Janklow & Nesbit Literary Agents, 1978.

Quote p.165 reprinted from *Confessions of a Mask,* by Yukio Mishima, Copyright © 1958, New York: New Directions Publishing Corporation, reprinted with permission by New Directions.

Printed and bound in Canada

Hounslow Press
2181 Queen Street East
Suite 301
Toronto, Ontario, Canada
M4E 1E5

Hounslow Press
73 Lime Walk
Headington, Oxford
England
OX3 7AD

Hounslow Press
1823 Maryland Avenue
P.O. Box 1000
Niagara Falls, NY
U.S.A. 14302-1000

CONTENTS

THE LIE OF THE LAND

"He wondered which was worse: having a
master for whom you would cut off your
child's head, or having no master at all."

Jay McInerney

—— 1 ——

I am sitting cross-legged on the floor of a six-tatami room in the middle of nowhere, trying to see the humour in my situation, as would, say, a fly on the wall. What's a nice Jewish girl from Toronto doing in a place like this? I say this aloud, trying to put the right amount of whine in my voice. But it doesn't work. What I am thinking is that if I don't find another roof to put over my head before the day is over, I'll call the whole thing off. Take a cab to Narita airport, get on the first plane back to Toronto and tell everybody I'd simply made a mistake. It would be inelegant but forgivable. I kick myself now for having come here on a one-way ticket (as a symbol of my wish to keep things open-ended), which cost me almost the same as the round-trip fare.

There's some construction going on nearby — a highrise apartment building, by the looks of it — and my view of the surrounding greyness is partially blocked by a grid of rusty poles and an assortment of cranes, the shovel of one of them aimed at my window as though threatening (or promising) to scoop me out of my self-imposed exile. It's six-thirty in the morning, and the house is perfectly still, though I know from the past two days' experience that the quiet won't last for long. Soon enough they'll all gather in the kitchen and make friendly chit-chat about who's eating what for breakfast. Then they'll start planning the day ahead.

"Hey, Sue, wanna go shopping later this afternoon?"

"Not today, Karen. Gotta rest up. I'm working at Ginza tonight, remember?"

(In a sing-song voice) "She's the *hos*tess with the *mos*tess, so she needs her beauty rest."

"Cut it out, Jim."

"Wait a minute — I'm also at Ginza tonight. Wanna go out for drinks after work?"

"Let's do it."

"Yeah."

"Think I'll have to pass."

"Whatsamatter, Sue, you getting sensible in your old age?"

"It's the cab fare I'm talking about, guys. I can't afford it."

"Remember that cab we took back from Shinjuku the other night? Not a big deal — less than ¥2,000 each, wasn't it?"

"I don't even remember where I *was* that night, let alone how I got *back* from there."

A round of laughter.

"So, are we going out tonight or not?"

"Twist my arm a little more."

Maybe they'll even ask me to join them, although they've probably given up by now — I've refused their invitations once too often, and for no good reason. It's not their fault that they're twenty-two to my thirty-three, that they've risked nothing by coming here, that Japan is just a rest stop for them. It's not their fault that they like to cook together, to eat together, to spend their evenings huddled around the television in Sue and Trina's room. It's not their fault that they're American, or British, or Australian, and that they want to recreate the atmosphere of a college dormitory, which is where most of them have just come from.

When I arrived at Narita airport three nights ago, there wasn't a room to be had in Tokyo. It was early September, peak of the annual invasion of foreigners to Japan. As I dropped coin after coin into an oversize red telephone, I kicked myself for having decided it was unadventurous to arrange my accommodations ahead of time. I got to the bottom of my list of guest houses and cheap lodges, and was about to start calling the pricier hotels when a couple of Europe-on-ten-dollars-a-day types with bulging backpacks wandered over to where I was standing. They'd just learned about a vacancy in a guest house called Let's Go World, but couldn't use the room since they had two more friends travelling with them.

And so I found myself in the room where I am now sitting, almost comically dreary with its single naked lightbulb, walls shedding their paint, and a mattress spotted with the tarnished remains of either menstrual blood or virginal love. Whatever this is, I told myself as I unpacked, it isn't Japan.

Before going to bed I went downstairs to the communal kitchen to make myself some tea. There were several other people in the kitchen, all very young, by the looks of it.

"So what's your agenda?" a guy wearing boxer shorts asked me.

"Agenda?"

"Yeah, like what's on your plate? What did you come to Japan for? I'm Jim, by the way."

I mumbled something vague, then threw the question back at him.

"I've been studying Japanese at school," he said, "and wanted to immerse myself in the language for a couple of years. After that I think I'll go back home and do a Master's degree in economics — either that or an MBA, depending on where I get accepted."

One by one they told me their reasons for being in Japan, my spirits sinking as I listened to their bright plans, each with its tidy beginning and ending. Karen was interested in getting modelling and acting experience before returning to the Big Apple and setting up shop as a talent agent. Sue and Trina had come together from Australia, and were working as hostesses in order to make "oodles of money." That accomplished, they planned to travel around the world, and eventually find their way back to Sydney where they hoped to buy a condo together. Ron was here to learn business Japanese, whatever that was, then go back to the States and get married. In a real funk by now, I excused myself as quickly as possible and trotted up to my room, sensing that my mood would keep plummeting unless I kept my distance from this crowd.

At three o'clock in the morning I was startled awake by the floor and walls shaking. My first night in Tokyo and already an earthquake, I thought as I rubbed my eyes. But then I heard a sharp cry coming from directly below me, followed by a few grunts. Earthquakes didn't sound like that, I knew.

The following night there was a house party in Sue and Trina's room. ("You wanna chip in for some booze?" I'd been asked, and churlishly refused.) They cranked up the music — stuff I hadn't heard in decades, like Cat Stevens and The Doobie Brothers — and kept it going well into the morning. As the only dissenter among them, I didn't have the nerve to ask them to turn down the volume. I spent the better part of the night with my head under my sleeping bag, cursing the fates for having lured me halfway around the world only to deposit me in a college frathouse.

The next day I managed to get myself on a waiting list for Kimi Ryokan, a Japanese-style inn that was the starting point for many of the foreigners who arrived in Tokyo. "Keep checking," the clerk told me, so I called him ten, maybe twelve times that day. The others, who saw nothing wrong with life at Let's Go World, were baffled and a little put off by my constant trips to the telephone, my anxiousness to get out. "We're a real friendly group here," Sue told me. "I'm sure you'll get used to it here if you give it a chance. But to each his own, I guess," she added with a shrug.

That evening I went out for a walk. The narrow, crooked streets around Let's Go World quickly widened into a noisy thoroughfare flanked by boxy grey buildings, neon lights jumping up and down their facades. I crossed the pedestrian overpass, and soon found myself in another maze of narrow streets without names. On one of these, I was stopped by a man in a business suit. (Tokyoites, I would later learn, had a special aptitude for detecting newly arrived foreigners: during my first few weeks in the city, I was constantly stopped by strangers on the streets or in trains, but this happened less and less as time went on.)

"You have Yoroppa face," the man said without preamble, squinting through his glasses.

"Excuse me?"

"Yoroppa, you know? Like Paris, Milan, Lisbon — "

"Ah, you mean *Eu*rope," I said.

"Yes, yes, you have Yoroppa face. Do you come from Yoroppa?"

"I was born in France," I told him, "although it was just by chance. But yes, my parents were from Eastern Europe."

"I knew it!" he beamed. "Yoroppa face. Last year I was three months in Itaria, with my company. My name is Mr. Haruta, by the way."

On impulse, I asked him if he wouldn't mind if we spoke Japanese for a while, explaining that this was my first chance to put my six months of study to use. Mr. Haruta, though, was as eager to show off his poor English as I was my poor Japanese, so we continued our conversation with each stammering broken fragments of the other's language.

Back at Let's Go World, my spirits buoyed by the impromptu encounter, I crawled into my sleeping bag and fell asleep right away. But today, as I sit cross-legged in the hot, still air, I'm back to wondering what I'm doing here. I try to recall the heart-stopping excitement of my two previous trips to Japan, short visits that had left me hungry for more. On both occasions I had been sent by Yamaha, the company I worked for at the time, to coach a young piano student who was performing her own music in two televised concerts. I'd stolen out of my hotel every night and gone on long walks through Tokyo, high on just breathing its air.

My thoughts turn to Joel, my ex-husband (the ink still wet on the divorce papers) and off on his own adventure, trekking through foothills and mountain passes in the wilderness of Central Asia. I think of his wildly curly hair, spilling crazily on all sides of his head. How could I have left that hair? Those high spirits, that monstrous intellect?

In a paroxysm of remorse, I fish around in my suitcase, find some stationery and begin scribbling a letter of apology. I tell him that the scales have been lifted from my eyes, that I've had a change of heart and I'm coming right back home if he'll only take me. But even as I write I realize it is cowardice and not love that is pushing my pen on the page, and that if I

returned to the safety of his arms, within a week I'd be back at square one
— itching to leave.

I tear up the letter, get out of my sleeping bag and put on some clothes.
Then I tiptoe downstairs to the payphone and dial Kimi Ryokan once
again. Today, finally, there is an opening. I tell them I'm on my way.

2

Located in the heart of the riotous district of Ikebukuro (known to some as Shinjuku's poorer cousin), Kimi Ryokan was a small whitewashed building that you could easily miss as you walked by. Inside, the polished oak floors in the entrance and hallways felt cool and sensuous under my bare feet. I was given a tiny room smelling of fresh sheets, and all was quiet as I unpacked. I knew I'd come to the right place.

Kimi was different from most other *ryokan* in that it served a primarily foreign clientele, and was inexpensive enough that people could stay there for several weeks if they had to. Every morning, guests would shuffle into the dining area and eat their breakfast with their heads bent over the Japan Times classified ads, then disperse to all four corners of the city in search of jobs and places to live. The evenings were spent swapping battle stories. People warned each other about English schools that hired only young, Aryan-looking teachers, landlords who wouldn't rent to foreigners, ads for movie extras that turned out to be ploys to attract hostesses. One by one, the names and faces changed as job and housing situations resolved themselves.

I was sitting on the steps of the common room on my third evening at Kimi, getting acquainted with a few of the other guests (somehow, being antisocial didn't seem as imperative to me here as it had at Let's Go World), when a tallish woman emerged from a bedroom door, stumbled toward our group and sat down beside me. She was very pale, with blue-black hair that looked dyed.

"I feel like shit and I look like shit," she drawled, preparing herself for a yawn. The combined effect of her hair, skin and red lipgloss (with matching nails) made me think of Rose Red. "Oh, ex*cuse* my manners — my name's Charlene."

"When did you get here?"

"Last night," Charlene said. "I must have slept for almost twenty-four hours, but all I feel like doing is crawling back to bed."

"Welcome to Tokyo," Lahti said, shaking his head sadly. "It's a hard life here. I have many scars in my heart." Lahti was from Nepal, and called himself the king of Tokyo because he was on his eighth visit. "Scars in my heart" was an expression he used often, usually in the midst of recounting some racist incident that had befallen him.

"God, what I wouldn't do for a foot-massage right now," Charlene said. "Or even a back-rub."

Princess, I thought. It turned out she was from Toronto, just a few blocks away from where Joel and I had lived. Although she was a graduate of the University of Toronto law school, a year of articling in a downtown law firm had convinced her that she wasn't cut out to practice law.

"I spent the whole year in a musty library," she told us, "doing research for these tight-assed Bay Street types. Believe me, the last thing I want to do after that experience is read more law books. That's why I thought I'd try teaching in Japan — I want a job where I actually *talk* to people."

Just then we were joined by John, who was returning from his first evening of teaching. He looked flushed and bright-eyed.

"I'm floored," he said as he joined the rest of us on the steps. "Totally floored. This is the wildest night I've had in my life, and I've only been here a week." He looked around to make sure he had our attention. "I walk into the classroom, right? It's a group of businessmen, and I'm expecting them to be all shy and tongue-tied, like everyone's been telling me they're supposed to be. Anyway, I ask them about their hobbies. Standard stuff, right? Well, there's this one guy called Koji, and when it's his turn, he tells us — just like that, to a bunch of strangers — that his hobby is dragging. You know, cross-dressing. He tells us he likes to go out dragging in Shinjuku on weekend nights. And then, as if that weren't enough excitement for one evening — " he pulled a thick Japanese comic book out of his knapsack " — this is what another student brought to class." He flipped to a page on which there was a drawing of a naked man whose penis, about twice as long and thick as the rest of the man, was jutting straight skyward. "I don't know if they were trying to test me, or what, but this is mind-blowing. I can't wait to write my dad about this."

"I think it's sad, actually," a man called Howard said. "I mean, here's this society that pretends to be all squeaky clean — nobody even holds hands on the street, let alone doing anything like kissing, God forbid — and then they produce this filth for all eyes to see."

Oh no, I thought, a lecture.

"I mean, *kids* have access to this stuff," he went on. "I don't know what in God's name I'm doing in this country. It's bad enough that they were on Hitler's side during the war, you'd think they'd have gotten their act together by now. I should have gone to Israel, like my mother told me to."

"Someone told me the same thing," I said, jolted back to the conversation I'd had with an aunt of mine the night before my departure.

"Why Japan, why not Israel?" she'd asked me.

The second part of her question was easy enough to answer: the thought of going to Israel had simply never occurred to me. As to the first part, why Japan, was there any way to explain the tidal pull one felt toward this and not that part of the world? Was there any way to explain that, although I'd hardly given Japan a thought during the first thirty years of my life, when I first set foot on Japanese soil I felt as though I had come home? That when the compulsion to break free from the half-life I'd created — the half-marriage and half-career and half of pretty much everything — grew too strong to ignore, Japan emerged from my jumbled thoughts as the only, the obvious solution?

"It's the hypocrisy I can't stand," Howard was saying. "It's like their right hand doesn't know what their left hand is doing. If the men have affairs, it's nobody's business, not even their wives'. And homosexuality? My heavens, no, not in *our* society. If at least they'd admit to being as sex-crazed as the rest of us — "

"My students didn't seem to have a problem admitting it," John said.

"Yeah, well. I still think it's sad."

"He sounds like he hasn't had any tail for a while," Charlene whispered in my ear. I suppressed a laugh, and decided that she might be worth a second look.

A couple of days later, Charlene disclosed what she considered to be her worst trait. "I must have a *cha*racter flaw, or something," she told me, stressing syllables here and there as though they were in italics. "When I was working all day with all these stuffed-shirt lawyers who thought of nothing except their work and the Dow Jones, I felt like shaking them and saying, 'Get a *life*, for God's sake.' They brought out the Bohemian in me. So then I started hanging out with these artsy types — you know, unemployed screenwriters who mowed people's lawns on weekends — and after a while I just wanted to shake them and say, 'Get a steady *job*, for God's sake.' " She shook her head and rolled her eyes. "Whatever situation I'm in, I seem to want the opposite. For all I know, I'll be pining for the law library after I get into teaching."

Unlike Charlene and most of the others, who had to look for work after they'd arrived in Tokyo, I already had a job lined up. My Japanese teacher in Toronto had written to her cousin who had talked to her friend who had put me in contact with the director of a language school she attended. As a personal favour to my teacher's cousin's friend, the director had agreed to hire me as a full-time teacher, though she let me know in a letter that it was "big exception, since we Japanese usually insist on face-to-face meeting before hiring employee." I accepted the offer with a twinge of guilt, since I knew I wasn't cut out for teaching and secretly planned to look for other work after I'd settled in.

As far as housing was concerned, my original plan had been to find a place of my own as soon as I arrived. I had visions of a cozy apartment building, futons drying out on the verandahs, green tea and rice crackers with the neighbours. But it soon became apparent that I would have to defer the plan — the startup costs were simply too high. First there was the gift money, as the Japanese termed it, that you had to hand over to the landlord in order to move into a place. In almost all cases, this was two months' rent. Then there was the commission to the rental agency (unless you "knew someone," apartments could only be rented via agencies) along with two months' rent deposit, and of course, the rent for the first month — a total of six months' rent, two-thirds of it non-refundable. Had I been willing to share an apartment with Charlene, as she suggested we do, I might have been able to swing it. I preferred to wait until I could afford my own place, and decided to live in a guest house in the meantime, if I could find one that was less sophomoric than Let's Go World.

Charlene accepted the first job that was offered to her, a full-time teaching position at a conversation school called Bilingual, and she found an apartment in a highrise building owned by a foreigner. It cost her several thousand dollars to move in, but she said her privacy was worth it. "There are two things I can't live without — listening to my CDs and screwing."

It was these bursts of candour that finally made me decide that, red nails and all, Charlene was someone worth befriending. She gave me her new phone number and we promised to keep in touch.

— 3 —

Guest houses, more commonly referred to as gaijin houses by those who occupy them, are dotted all over Tokyo and number in the hundreds. Some of them have curfews, some have communal living rooms, some have shared housekeeping and cooking duties. The one I finally settled on had neither a living room nor a kitchen, which I thought would allow for a more private lifestyle.

Esther House was located in the town of Nishiogikubo in northwest Tokyo, about ten minutes' walking distance from the train station. It had eight bedrooms, each with its own sink and hotplate, two toilets and one shower. At ¥72,000 per month it cost no less than most studio apartments, the difference being that no key money or agency fee was required. There was a pay telephone screwed onto the outside wall under my window, and even with the window shut I could hear most of what was spoken into it. Though I balked at the ¥80,000 deposit required in order to have my own phone installed, I decided, as Charlene had, that I was willing to pay for my privacy.

Unlike Let's Go World, Esther House had attracted tenants of disparate ages and backgrounds. The oldest was an Australian woman of sixty who was sharing a corner room with her son and daughter-in-law. I was curious to find out what circumstances would have led to such an unusual living arrangement, so I invited her to my room for tea a few days after I moved in.

Her full name was Jeanne-Anne, but she told me to call her Jay, a contraction of her initials. "Ivrybody does," she explained, "even my kids." She was on the heels of her second divorce, which had turned ugly when she discovered that her ex-husband had sold their house without consulting her and then walked away with the proceeds.

"He's a lawyer, so he knew all the tricks. I could have taken him to court, I suppose, but I just didn't have the innergy. So there I was, sixty years old, unemployed, no savings to speak of ... It was Bruce who actually suggested I come to Japan with him and Janet. We'd all heard about the piles of money you could make here teaching English, so I thought, why not?"

When she moved into a room with the other two, it was with the understanding that she would find a place of her own as soon as she got a job — a matter of days, they all believed. But in a market where even thirty-year-olds were at a disadvantage, she was running into one brick wall after another. For two months she'd been crisscrossing the city in search of the one English school that would give her a chance, and was beginning to get discouraged.

"I guiss I was rather naive," she said into her teacup, "but I thought that with tin years' experience teaching high-school English I'd have no problem finding a job here. They tell me it's my accent, but I know what they're thinking — I can see it in their eyes, the moment I walk in the door." She paused, and her own eyes started to shine. "Can't let myself do that," she said quickly. "If I do I'm a didd duck. Innyway, you can't really blame the schools. They're running a business, and they know what their customers want."

Mark and Susan lived directly under my room. They'd gotten engaged shortly before coming to Japan, and on the spur of the moment decided to get married the weekend after I moved into Esther House. "We don't know what we're doing," Mark said cheerfully as he and Susan set off to the city hall, "but we're doing it anyway." On another occasion, when he and I were alone, he confessed that he sometimes thought of Susan as more of a best friend than a wife. "But we *did* get married, so that must mean we wanted to," he said, not sounding too sure.

Like all good Americans, Mark was a political animal, inflamed by the corruptness in Japan, America and the rest of the world. He decried the apathy of young Japanese, which I, political illiterate that I was, secretly found refreshing. "Whenever I try to talk politics to my students," he complained, "the conversation falls flat. The women are especially bad — half of them don't even know who their prime minister is. Mention Sting or Bryan Adams, though, and they're all ears."

The room to my right was being shared by a former midwife from New Zealand and a New Yorker who was looking for work as a model. They made it clear to me that they weren't a couple. "Just trying to cut costs." Ariel, the would-be model, flitted back and forth between his two personas, dashing man-about-town and brooding intellectual, and had the clothes to match both. Depending on his plans for the day, he would either breeze out of the house in cuffed pants, a plaid jacket slung over his shoulder, or drift off in torn jeans and a paint-stained white T-shirt. Even on his man-about-town days, he didn't quite cut the picture of a model — his features were too drawn, his nose too prominent — though he assured us that "interesting faces" were the coming trend in male models. Like Mark, he was a compulsive news-hound, and didn't feel right if he went to bed without having read all three of the English-language dailies, which he let pile up in a corner of his half of the room. "Just in case," he said, in case what never being quite clear to me.

Jessie, who'd had the room to herself for several months before she took Ariel in, had little patience for Ariel and his newspapers. "Stupid Yankee," she would mutter. "Thinks the world will fall apart if he doesn't hang on to last month's papers. They're a bloody fire hazard, is what they are." Rather than confront him directly (which would have been inelegant), she took to surreptitiously removing one paper from the bottom of his stack for every new one he added. "I'm wondering when he'll finally say something," she said gleefully, but he never let on that he noticed.

The worst way to deal with Jessie was to ask her a straightforward question — her barbs would then turn to poisoned arrows. I found this out when I asked her (served me right, I thought afterwards) why she'd decided to come to Tokyo.

"Dunno," she piped. "Maybe to answer silly questions."

Jessie was at her best when left to talk without interruption. "Have you ever walked into a Japanese department store at opening time?" she asked me once. "Well, I'll give you a preview. There are these two women in red uniforms on either side of the entrance. Their job is to welcome you — 'Irasshaimase, irasshaimase' — as you walk in. Up ahead near the escalator, there are two more women wearing red uniforms. Same thing — 'Irasshaimase, irasshaimase.' I ask them if they know where I can find some slippers. But it's not their job, you see. They're welcomers, not sales clerks. Onto the escalator and up to the second floor, where there are — take three guesses — two more women wearing red uniforms. By this time I'm getting kind of bored with the whole thing, so I just bow to them and say 'irasshaimase' and watch their jaw drop. Six women to welcome me, and none of them can tell me where to find a bloody pair of slippers. It's a good way to get rid of unemployment, though."

Jessie was the last person I would have figured to be working as a hostess, but that was in fact what she was doing. She wanted to have her days free so she could study Japanese full-time, though I noticed that she never actually spoke it, even when buying oranges or taking her clothes to the drycleaner's.

"It's useless to try and figure her out," Susan warned me early on. "If she thinks you may be onto her, out come the quills."

In the first-floor room facing the street lived three young men whom Jessie had nicknamed the Shadows. Days would go by without anyone seeing them, the only sign of life in their room being the clicks of what we guessed to be chess pieces hitting a board. Late one evening, when all the other rooms were quiet, the sound reverberated up through my walls. Click-click, click, click, click-click-click ... and then came Jessie's voice, piercing through the darkness. "Game's over, you bloody woodpeckers."

The following evening the Shadows moved out.

4

I was determined to love Tokyo, despite its ugliness. As I made my way through the jumble of interlocking buildings, drearily modern with their cylindrical elevator shafts or triangular verandahs or space-bubble windows bulging like giant eyeballs, or any number of inexplicable protrusions jutting out at strange angles, I tried to see not disorder but a grand design, albeit a mad one.

It soon became apparent to me that Tokyo lovers were people who carried their own vision of the city in their minds. If you were primed to find beauty, you found beauty. It was pointless to take part in the interminable arguments between Tokyo's supporters (clean, safe, charming in an oddball way) and its detractors (treeless, garish, lacking cohesion). People's opinions about the city, I suspected, had less to do with the city than with the people.

There were the hustlers, who'd come to Tokyo to make a fast buck and had little or no interest in the culture. They mistrusted the Japanese, read hypocrisy into every smile and waxed sentimental about ribsteaks. They looked forward to the day they could clear out of Tokyo with enough money to buy a house or start a T-shirt business.

At the other extreme were the worshippers, who could see or speak no evil when it came to Japan. They were very adept at picking up the language (which confirmed my suspicion that Japanese was a state of mind rather than a mere collection of words), unlike the hustlers who never quite got the hang of it. I met a man of this type during my stay at Kimi Ryokan, a Harvard dropout who was apprenticed to a sushi-chef. I spotted him on the telephone, barking out clipped phrases like a harried Japanese businessman and bowing all the while. He knew the subway system by heart and insisted that Tokyo addresses were not illogical.

During my first weeks in Tokyo, I walked long miles in my search for this or that address, turning to the sun as a guide when my labyrinthine maps failed me. Most streets had no names and most buildings were numbered according to date of construction rather than location, which one assumed was appreciated by historians. To compound the problem, most people gave directions that sounded like the clues in a treasure-hunt. ("You come to a large grey building, then turn left and walk until you see another grey building. Across the street is a small flower-shop ...")

Walking was a good way to get a feel for the city's various districts, each with its own personality. I learned how Shinjuku burst into flame when the sun went down, how Ikebukuro swaggered, how Akasaka preened. It was a novelty to feel so safe as I walked through the red light district of Kabuki-cho, passing nightclubs with signs that said "For Bad Boys Only" or "Dark Wild," amusement halls with strip-by-numbers video games displayed in the windows, groups of red-faced, lurching businessmen and various other people of the night. I marvelled at the fact that although I was wearing a sleeveless sundress, dripping with September sweat, I never got whistled or hooted at, let alone pawed.

As I made my way through the crowds in Shibuya on a Sunday afternoon, I was struck by the absence of older people. Where were all the married couples and babes in strollers? Everybody here was neatly dressed, compact and nineteen. *You're not old*, I told myself resolutely as Tokyo's youth flocked by me in a steady stream, while above our heads, gargantuan neon signs consorted with the clouds.

Tokyo was merciless in its assault on the ears, its cacophony more purposeful, somehow, than the noisemaking of most other large cities. Walking past the chattering stereo speakers posted like sentinels at every store entrance, passing cars that announced "Now I'm turning left" just as they started to round a corner, standing at the intersection and hearing a clumsy tune belched out in fat sine waves as the traffic-light turned green, I wondered at Tokyoites' seeming appetite for noise. It was hard to fathom how a people attuned to the sound of one hand clapping could have come up with the idea of talking ads on buses.

And yet none of this stopped me from turning the Tokyo I saw into the Tokyo I wanted to see. I looked for the rose among the weeds, the kimono among the sweatshirts. *This* is the heart and soul of the city, I would think as I came upon a tiny shrine, nestled innocently in the confusion of lights, sounds and buildings poking each other in the eye.

Among the various gaijin complaints about the Japanese, one of the most commonly heard is that Tokyoites are extremely rude on the train, that you have to be bleeding to death before someone offers you a seat. "I saw a pregnant woman standing in the train the other day, looking like she was going to collapse from heat-exhaustion," Jessie told me, chuckling at the recollection, "and nobody paid her any attention. Finally I tapped a man on the shoulder and said, 'Time to get up now, mister.' "

Struggling up the endless stairs in Shibuya station with a futon mattress under each arm, I too was a little annoyed when nobody offered to give me a hand. But I soon came to understand that pretending your fellow passengers didn't exist was the best way to survive the Tokyo trains. Bent out of shape by the bodies pressing against you as you fought for air on the rush-hour Yamanote, you learned to enclose yourself in a mental cocoon — to blot out the pain of an elbow digging into your back, the smell of stale eel sent up by your neighbour's belch. *I am alone on this train*, you told your-self, and came to believe it.

By taking earlier trains, I was able to avoid the worst of the crowds and sometimes even got a seat. I studied the faces, struck by how few bald pates there were. So much hair! Young men wore it puffed up on top, scraped thin at the back, a few wisps hanging coyly over their foreheads. It was thick and shiny, carefully blowdried and often permed. Gaijin hair seemed limp and lifeless by comparison. Mark, who was well on his way to baldness, the-orized that whatever substance (or lack of substance) made the Japanese small between the legs was also responsible for keeping their hair from falling out. It was an interesting theory, though it did smack of sour grapes.

Commuters did a lot of reading on the train. I would stare enviously at the businessmen absorbed in their newspapers, eyes travelling up and down the columns of Chinese characters, and think, *You're just pretending to read.* I hadn't made peace with the characters yet, and was putting off the day when I'd have to start studying them seriously. My own newspaper of choice was the English Japan Times, with its depressing classified ad section ("Wanted: cheerful foreign female, 21-25") and scaremonger headlines. "Tokyo is sinking under garbage!" said the headline one morning. I didn't quite know what to make of this, but the Aussie reading over my shoulder told me not to worry. "They've been wroiting the same article ever since I came here," he chuckled, "which was sivven years ago."

In truth, garbage was one of the more useful commodities in Tokyo, particularly for gaijin. It seemed I was the only person at Esther House who had actually bought my furniture. One of my housemates' favourite pas-times was going out on garbage-hunting expeditions, and Susan and Mark had furnished their entire room with pieces salvaged from the *gomi* pile. The Japan Times ran an article about an enterprising gaijin who had bought a large apartment complex and furnished every apartment with nothing but *gomi*. If true, this was quite a feat, since according to the article every apartment had a colour TV, stove, refrigerator, sofa and bed. Gaijin always pointed out how wasteful it was of the Japanese to throw away perfectly good appliances or furniture, and the Japanese made the equally valid point that because of their cramped quarters, they couldn't afford to hang on to items they weren't actually using, on the off-chance that these items might come in handy when they (or their great-grandchildren) finally bought a summer house in Chichibu.

When Susan and Mark invited me to go to a discotheque with some people from Esther House and a friend of Jessie's, my initial thought was that the last thing I wanted to do in Tokyo was dance the night away with a bunch of disgruntled foreigners. But, not wanting to entrench my reputation as The Standoffish One, I accepted their invitation.

We were headed for a place called Buzz Buzz ("*Everybody's* been talking about it," Jessie's friend enthused) in the heart of the Roppongi district. Roppongi is the stomping ground of Tokyo's beautiful people — the models, TV actors, would-be models, would-be TV actors — and the only part of town where gaijin are likely to outnumber Japanese, both on the streets and in the clubs.

No sooner did we step out of the train station than we bumped into a pair of blond men, swaying against each other.

"I'm so drunk," one of the men said.

"Me too. God I'm drunk."

"I'm *sooo* drunk."

"Not drunk — plastered."

"Fucking plaaastered. Yeah."

"I feel like I'm gonna get sick."

"I'm *sooooo* ... "

They stumbled onward, leaving a trail of elongated syllables behind them.

Buzz Buzz owes its name to the giant insects hanging from the ceiling, lit up by the obligatory spinning strobe-light. That night, the crowd was dominated by a large group of young boys, prep-school students by the looks of them. We squeezed through the tangle of bodies and found a small table, sticky with beer. The music thumped along — one of those snare-driven numbers that shook the table on every second and fourth beat. Jessie, Susan and Mark headed right to the dance-floor, while I stayed back with Ariel and Jessie's friend.

A beer-fight was breaking out among the prep-school boys. One of them, apparently missing his mark, flung his beer at Ariel's neck. Japanese women with wasp-waists and miniskirts that could have passed for belts were trying to get the attention of the groups of blond men milling around the dance floor. The strobe light spun dizzily, alternately lighting up black beetles, black ants and black cockroaches. The beer fight continued across our table. Ariel looked miserable and kept fingering his ruined silk jacket. My body was quaking with the vibrations from the sound.

Mark returned to our table. "-anna -o up -n -an-?" he screamed at me.

"What?"

"-anna -o up -n -an-?"

"What?"

He leaned toward my ear and cupped his hands. "Wanna go up and dance?"

Up I went to the dance floor, jostled by sweating bodies — swooning Japanese women and smug-faced blond men, all of them under twenty — and set my limbs a-swaying to the one-TWO-three-FOUR of the pounding drums. There were no kimonos here, no bashful smiles — only bugs, sweat and sneers.

This Tokyo was so much at odds with the Tokyo I carried in my mind that I feared it might come out the winner if I let it.

5

Like many similar establishments in Tokyo, Tokyu BE called itself a "culture centre" rather than a school, since it offered not only English classes but also crocheting and *sumi-e* painting and jazz dance. It was run by the giant Tokyu corporation, owner of office buildings, department stores and train lines.

"What does BE stand for?" I asked my supervisor Arai-san, a woman of about fifty who wore her hair in a high ponytail.

"It's just BE," she answered in her sing-song voice. "Like tsu be or not tsu be, haha, just like Shakespeeaah, *desho*?" She was a springy, slightly hysterical woman, the kind my mother would have called a frustrated spinster.

My first class at BE was a large and mixed group of housewives, university students, office workers and retirees. Their ages, inscribed next to their names on my class list, ranged from twenty-one to seventy-nine. As I walked into the classroom, twelve pairs of eyes followed my every movement expectantly, as though in the swing of my arms or the swish of my skirt lay the key to their future proficiency in English. I'd heard all the usual stories about Japanese students' timidity and wanted to make it clear that I wasn't prepared to do all the talking, so I told them I'd introduce myself by answering any questions they might have.

"Don't be afraid," I said. "You can ask me anything you want."

Hesitant chuckles all around.

"How old are you?" two voices sounded almost in unison.

"Well, *almost* anything you want," I told them.

"How tall are you?" a young woman asked.

"Five feet ten-and-a-half inches," I said. "One hundred and seventy-eight centimetres."

"*Heeeeeh*," they exclaimed in chorus. (I was to hear this sound — which rhymed with the British pronunciation of "fair" — every time I mentioned my height, that I was born in Paris, or that my brother was a doctor.)

"Are you married?" someone asked, and everybody giggled.

"No," I said, then added, "I'm divorced." This stopped the giggles.

"Whatto is your pahposs to come to Japang?" an older woman inquired in a brittle voice, overenunciating every syllable she didn't mispronounce.

"My purpose ..." I stalled. This was the dreaded Why Japan question all over again. I had three choices: invent a plausible reason, try to approach the truth and risk sounding like a New Age airhead ("Well, I just wanted to transcend my limitations and ...") or a pompous ass ("Japan *asked* me to come"), or admit that I hadn't the foggiest idea what my true *pahposs* was. I opted for the first choice.

"I've always wanted to have the experience of living in another culture," I said.

And so it went. From class to class, the questions were always the same. My age, height, marital status, and purpose for coming to Japan. I remembered being warned by my Japanese teacher in Toronto that it was considered rude in Japan to ask people personal questions, especially if they were well into adulthood. I was pleased that curiosity seemed to be winning out over propriety in my classes.

When I got home that night, I wrote to a friend in Toronto and asked him to have a T-shirt made, with the red words "How tall? 178 cm." on a white background, and send it to me right away. I thought it would make a good joke.

As the days wore on and the novelty of a giant-sized Canadian teacher wore off, my students lost their initial boldness and sank deeper and deeper into silence. "Teaching English to the Japanese is like bowling," a veteran teacher told me. "You keep throwing balls and they never come back." I'd never been much of a bowler, and as hard as I tried not to, I sometimes lost my patience. I found myself brimming with frustration one morning, after having asked a class three times if anybody knew the meaning of the expression "to kill time."

"Look," I said. "There are only two possible answers to my question. Yes or no. I'm not going to say another word until someone gives me an answer." The students gazed at me like stunned deer. I felt foolish all of a sudden, ashamed of my bullying tactics.

Through trial and many errors, I learned that the only way I could count on getting an answer was by addressing one person at a time rather than posing questions to the class as a group. The students had a deep-seated aversion to stepping forward and grabbing the spotlight. They seemed just as afraid of getting the right answer (and appearing to boast) as getting the wrong answer (and appearing stupid).

I also learned, the day I showed up with my "How-tall" T-shirt and got no more than a few uncomfortable smiles, that I would have to be more judicious in my use of humour. Mr. Wakabayashi, a retired biology professor, took me aside after our class and gently explained what should have been obvious to me — that I'd offended my students by implying that their questions about my height were unwelcome.

In spite of such gaffes, I was accorded more admiration and respect from my students than I'd ever experienced when teaching in Canada. I was a *sensei*, a word that means not only teacher but also doctor and respected elder. The students would snap to attention as soon as I walked into the classroom, and when the lesson was finished, nobody got up until I did. If there was a young man in the group, he'd sometimes stay behind and offer to wipe the blackboard.

"You don't have to do it," I'd say in embarrassment, unaccustomed to having people clean up after me.

"I youngest member in class," he'd explain.

Since I was a new teacher, my students were asked to evaluate me after the first four weeks. The office secretary typed up a summary of their comments and handed it to me. I read the list: "Always on time; sometimes late; easy to follow; some of your instructions are unclear; pace is too fast; you spend too much time on each point; intelligent teaching; you sometimes forget to explain things ..."

"So what do I do now?" I asked Arai-san. She told me not to worry, that the comments were better than what most new teachers got.

"Students tell me you very eregant, like from Yoroppa. I hope you continue look eregant, *neh?* Maybe students continue satisfied, *desho?*"

Tokyu BE was quite liberal compared to some of the other English schools. Janet, who taught at one of the ASA branches, showed me the list of rules she'd been given: no overcoats in the building, wear nametags at all times, no knapsacks, no open-toed sandals, pockerchiefs for men, must attend at least three student-teacher parties or else wages are docked a half-week, and above all, no socializing with students. Apparently this policy was introduced after the squabbling between male teachers (over who would get to teach a particular female student) got out of hand. Kate said that the regulation was strictly enforced, that if a teacher was caught with a student, even if they were just crossing the street together, the teacher was automatically dismissed.

At BE, the tolerance for teachers fraternizing with students had led to two marriages. David, the head teacher, had "done the right thing" after getting a student knocked up. Another teacher had fallen in love with a student he met during his first month in Japan, then proposed to her six months later. But it was Sylvana's marriage that intrigued me. Sylvana was a Canuck like myself, and just as tall. She carried herself regally and took no guff from anybody. There was something prickly about her — you felt that you had to mind your P's and Q's in her presence. I first noticed her wedding band when we were sitting in the teachers' lounge one afternoon, during a break between classes.

"I see that you're married," I said.

"Yes."

"Is your husband Japanese?"

"Yes." She sounded annoyed.

"Where did you meet him?"

"In a bar."

"How long have you been married?"

"Two years."

Something was driving me to question her more, though it was clear she was reluctant to talk. "Were there any problems with his family?"

"Why should there be any problems?"

"I mean, did they accept you right away, or — "

"There were no problems," she snapped.

She left the teacher's lounge and I chastised myself for being so nosy. Why had I grilled her like that? And why did I feel so uneasy after talking to her? Then it came to me. Sylvana had what I wanted — a piece of the East, hers forever to keep.

Marriages between gaijin men and Japanese women are a dime a dozen, but the reverse is much rarer — ten times as rare, according to statistics. "Japanese males tend to be spoiled from childhood, so the result is that Japanese men and Western women tend not to be very compatible," Ian McQueen warns in his Lonely Planet guidebook. Knowing all this, I still felt — with inexplicable certainty — that only a Japanese man would give me the key to Japan and uncover my reason for being there.

FACES IN THE CROWD

"There are two kinds of freedom: freedom to, and freedom from."

Margaret Atwood

1

I would never have met Miki, my first Japanese friend in Tokyo, were it not for my noisy housemates.

I regarded Esther House as a kind of failure on my part, and couldn't shake the sense that my life in Japan would only begin in earnest after I moved out and found a place of my own. It wasn't so much the makeshift rooms, or the lack of hot water in the taps, or the plump cockroaches that occasionally crawled out of the space between the tatami mats, that bothered me. It was the litany of complaints about the Japanese, the strains of Bob Dylan or Grateful Dead (why did expatriates always gravitate to sixties' music?) filtering through my walls, the fact that my housemates seemed determined to pretend they were back in San Francisco or Auckland. And it didn't help that Jay, having finally found a teaching job in Yokohama, was no longer around to provide the balancing effect of a different generation.

I considered it particularly unfortunate to be living next to Ariel, who had a fondness for late-night English television and an uncommonly sensitive funnybone. The corniest, most juvenile humour would send him crashing against the wall I shared with him, laughing convulsively. I would lie on my bed, trying to reconcile the erudite, intellectual Ariel who read three newspapers a day and went through books as though they were meals with the Ariel choking on his own laughter at the sight of two businessmen colliding in the middle of a street. (The walls were so thin that I could, if I wished, follow the story-line of the show he was watching.)

Lying on my bed one evening, sandwiched between Ariel's guffaws on one side and Bruce and Janet shaking out their mattresses on the other, I decided I couldn't take it any longer, put on my jacket and went out for a walk. I walked past the train station, into North Nishiogi and up to the dried-out river that snaked through it, then back and forth, forth and back along the walkway bordering the river, energized by the fantasy that if I walked long enough Esther House would evaporate and no longer be there when I returned. Finally, about two hours later, I turned back and started toward home, delaying my return by taking as many side-streets as possible. On a narrow street that paralleled the train-tracks, I came upon a neon sign I hadn't noticed before — The Jazz Inn — on the second floor of a store-front. On the spur of the moment, I climbed up the stairs leading to the sign, opened the door beneath it and stepped into a small room filled with smoke and cascading piano chords. Feeling self-conscious all of a sudden as the dozen or so patrons fixed their gazes on me, I headed for the counter at the far end of the room, sat down and ordered a beer. Seated on my right was a young-looking Japanese woman with permed hair.

I sipped my beer for a few minutes while watching the pianist banging away at the keyboard, the harsh, percussive sounds she drew from the instrument belying the small size of her hands. The woman sitting next to me lit a Menthol cigarette, and on impulse I asked her if I could have one.

"You speak so good Japanese," she said in English. "Yes, please take."

"I'm not actually a smoker," I babbled as I lit up. "Not a regular one, anyway."

"I regular smoker," she said with a smile. "I don't smoke in work place, because I woman — woman look bad if she smoking in office. But I have about fifteen every evening."

We chatted some more, each struggling to use the other's language. I learned that her name was Miki, that she was thirty and came from Kyushu. She was an architect by training but worked full-time as a draughtsperson ("Because I woman," she said), and lived alone in a nine-tatami room on the other side of the train tracks.

"Please I invite you for have coffee," she suggested. "I show you my apartment. It getting late, so we go right away. OK?" Seeing my hesitation, she added, "Don't worry. Kyushu women more friendly than other Japanese women."

As befitted an architect, Miki's apartment was uncluttered (as much as a nine-by-twelve-foot room could be uncluttered) and tastefully decorated in whites, beiges and blacks. A large draughting table stood near the single window, which looked out onto the train tracks. Miki sat me down on her sofa while she busied herself preparing coffee in the tiny kitchen.

"Do you go to the Jazz Inn often?" I asked.

"Only about once month. Usually I go home immediately after work, and continue work at home until eleven or twelve at night."

She brought out some coffee and two plastic-wrapped tiramisu cakes, plopped herself down right next to me and flashed me a warm smile. "You have hobbies?"

"Hobbies? Uh ... " I always had trouble with that question.

"I have lots of hobbies," Miki said. "Water painting one of my hobbies. I take private lesson once a month. Study English another my hobby. But recently I not enough time for study. Maybe you teach me, *neh?* Hiking also my hobby. Here, look at this." She leaned forward and reached for a photo album lying on top of a bookcase on the opposite wall. She opened the photo album to a page filled with groups of young people with mountains in the background. "See, this me here. This also me." She flipped to another page. "This another hobby, tennis. Not playing, just watching. See? This Stefan Edberg — " she grinned widely " — my hero."

"The Swedish tennis player?"

"Yes. I love him. I look every match he play on television. I also read every article about him. Sometimes information only in English newspapers, so I must to read English. *Taihen, neh?* Is too difficult, but I big fan of him — we say *dai-fan* in Japanese."

Every year in February, she told me, Tokyo hosted a week-long international tennis tournament. She always took that time off from work and spent the week in the stadium, hoping for a chance to see her idol up close. On one occasion she screwed up the courage to wait for him outside the competitors' locker room. "But when he come out, when I face-to-face him, I so shy that I can't think anything to tell him — not one word." She shook her head, laughing. "I dream about him at night sometimes. You think I crazy?"

In addition to their friendliness, Miki told me, Kyushu women were known for their fine creamy skin and long noses. "I typical Kyushu woman," she said with a chuckle, pointing to her nose, which was indeed long. "Anyway, another my hobby is Sweden."

I was beginning to understand how it was that the Japanese had such impressive lists of hobbies. The way Miki used it, the word appeared to include every leisure activity one had ever pursued, no matter how infrequently.

"Have you ever been there?"

"Oh no. Not yet. But once in few months I gather with other people who are crazy for Sweden — is like club. We talk about Sweden, look pictures, eat foods." She sighed. "Is like dream, you know?"

Her warmth and chumminess were infectious, and I found myself telling her about some of the events in my life that had prompted me to come to Japan, even admitting that I was curious about meeting Japanese men. "I don't recommend," she said, wrinkling her Kyushu nose. "Japanese men not make gaijin women happy, I guarantee — even Japanese women not satisfied."

We exchanged phone numbers before I left, and though I protested that I had no use for them, she insisted on giving me two more of her Menthols.

A few days later she called, asking me to translate a sentence in a Japan Times article about Stefan Edberg. "I can't stand suspense!" she wailed. "I don't know if good thing or bad thing. Hope you don't mind I call you."

"Not at all. What is it you don't understand?"

"This sentence, 'He ran away with it.' What it means?"

Every few days, she would call me with a similar request. "What means 'looking somewhat haggard'?" or "Is written 'He outdid himself.' That good thing or bad thing?"

And so, out of the unlikely combination of a group of noisy tenants and a woman's insatiable thirst for information about a tennis star, a friendship took hold. Esther House didn't seem quite as oppressive anymore, and Tokyo now had a face.

2

Mr. Shimoda was a retiree in his late sixties and one of my most advanced students at BE. A former engineer, he'd made his fortune by developing a hydraulic braking mechanism which he'd patented and sold to a major railway corporation. As far as I could see, his main reason for enrolling at BE was to display his near-perfect English, to boast of his wealth (" ... and on the *third* floor of my house ... ") and to drop names. Now that he was retired, Mr. Shimoda spent most of his time on his two hobbies: hunting and "taking portraits of beautiful women." He seemed to have targeted me as his next victim, and there was nothing I could say to make him give up the idea. "Come to my house next Saturday at three," he told me after our third class, in a tone that would allow no argument.

The following Saturday I found myself in Mr. Shimoda's living-room, smiling stiffly while he trained his lenses and filters and strobe-lights on my face. As he adjusted the position of my elbows on the armrests of his blue velvet *fauteuil,* he flashed his bejewelled watch in front of my eyes, back and forth, forth and back, so many times that I finally had no choice but to ask him where he'd gotten it.

"Oh, you mean this?" he said off-handedly. "It's just a little gift from the former king of Kuwait. He's, aaah, a long-standing friend of mine."

"Is that so?"

"Yes, we go back a long way, the king and I. We've been hunting together for years."

"Is that so?"

"Oh yes. I remember the night he gave a party in my honour ..."

After the photo-session, Mr. Shimoda gave me the grand tour of his house, drawing my attention to the Persian rugs, the *sumi-e* originals on the walls and the baby-grand piano, polished to such a fine shine that we could see our reflections in the wood, just like the woman in the Pledge commercials.

"And this," he told me as we entered a den-like room on the second floor, "is my karaoke machine. Top of the line, by the way. It's the first of its kind, I'm told — it's not even on the market yet. But since the president of the company is a dear friend of mine — a former hunting partner, I should add — he gave me this prototype as a gift. Anything you'd like to sing? I have English songs, French songs, and of course, Japanese songs. But my specialty is Latin music. I have a huge collection ..."

Before I could answer, he pulled out a disk and set the machine to work. *"Para bailer la Bamba ... "* he crooned into the microphone. "Or how about this one?" He pushed a few buttons. *"Viénen los gitanooooos ... "*

"If the music is too high," he explained, "you just turn this knob and the whole thing slides down a few tones, without changing speed. You can adjust it to suit your range. It's like the machines they have in karaoke clubs, only even more sophisticated. Would you like to hear a Japanese song?" He quickly inserted another disk into the machine. *"Awai kuchiiii-izukeeeeeh ... "*

When the grandfather clock struck five, I ducked out of Mr. Shimoda's house under the pretext of having to meet a friend for dinner. I was relieved that he hadn't insisted I try out his machine. Even though I had taught music to children for several years — or perhaps because of it — the thought of sharing my singing voice with people older than twelve gave me the jitters.

I knew, however, that I couldn't postpone my karaoke debut forever. Karaoke machines were everywhere in Japan — not only in bars and private houses but also on street-corners, at the base of Mount Fuji, even in taxi-cabs. If you had the misfortune of stepping into such a cab, I was told, the driver would badger you to sing until you finally dropped a coin into the machine, which of course was the sound he *really* wanted to hear.

Opportunity knocked on my door again at the end of the month, when I got a phone call from my former supervisor at Yamaha. His real name was Toru Koyama, but in Canada he'd gone by the name of Tom. He was transferred back to Japan shortly after I went to live in Tokyo.

"Remember Mr. Inoue?" he asked me.

Tom's father-in-law was not the forgettable type. I'd met him twice before, while in Japan with the Yamaha group. A successful doctor by day, he was a party-'til-you-drop animal by night, and claimed to wake up fresh as a daisy no matter how much he'd had to drink. Like many educated Japanese, he combined a near-encyclopaedic knowledge of English, vocabulary with the inability to put together a complete sentence. "I xenophilic," he'd beamed at me the first time we met.

"Mr. Inoue and his family are in town for the next few days," Tom told me, "and they'd like to take us out to a karaoke club."

The following evening I found myself riding in the back seat of a limousine, along with Tom, Mr. Inoue and his daughter Hanako.

"Where's your wife?" I asked Mr. Inoue as we cruised along.

"Why would I want bring wife to club?" he said with a conspiratorial wink. "Is hostess club, you know."

The limo rounded corner after corner and navigated through narrower and narrower streets until it finally came to a stop, in a part of the city I'd never seen before, and we all disembarked. Mr. Inoue led us to a side-door and into an elevator. "This is a *very* exclusive club," Tom whispered to me as we rode up. "You can be sure the evening will cost well over $500. But don't worry, he can afford it."

The next thing I knew, we were in a small, dimly lit room, far away from planet Earth. Dragon claws holding gilded balls protruded from the dark stuccoed walls, and open-mouthed dragon heads — dark green, with streaks of red and gold — hung from the ceiling. Red and green track-lights bathed the room in an eerie glow. That sudden transition into another realm, upon entering a room, was something I was beginning to recognize as thoroughly Japanese.

A middle-aged man escorted us to our table. It was one of only three seating areas, each one backed by a semi-circular partition.

"How good to see you again," he told Mr. Inoue. "Shall I get your bottle?"

A pair of women, all atwinkle in their sequined mini-dresses, stood by our table as we took our seats. The younger one wore a velvet headband from which red feathers fanned out in all directions. The hostesses disappeared for a few moments, then came back with a tray of bite-sized foods. The manager brought out Mr. Inoue's *otobin* — the "private bottle" he was accorded as a regular customer — and poured some whiskey into four glasses.

"So how have you been, Tina?" Mr. Inoue asked the younger hostess. "She from Philippines," he whispered to me in English. "She look younger than thirty-two, don't you think?"

Tina gave an expert pout. "I've missed you these past few weeks," she said in Japanese. "You *know* you're my favourite customer, don't you?"

"Favourite customer?" he laughed. "A wrinkled old man like me?"

The other hostess, who looked to be around forty, sat down beside me. "My name is Salamía," she said. "I'm also from the Phillipines. Tina and I both came here two years ago."

"Where did you learn your Japanese?"

"It's not hard," she shrugged. "I just picked it up after I came."

"You didn't take lessons?"

"If you want to do well as a hostess," she said, "you have to learn the language. It's as simple as that." She shrugged again.

"*Obatarian*," Mr. Inoue chimed in. Salamía made a face at him.

He turned to me. "Do you know the word? It means old hag." He burst into peals of laughter. "You're an old hag, Salamía, don't you know it? You shouldn't be working here anymore." Salamía smiled graciously between pursed lips.

Tina edged up to Mr. Inoue. "Let me feed you," she pouted. "I've got some *delicious* eel for you." She picked up a strip of glistening eel with her chopsticks and brought it to his lips. "Eat that for me, will you?"

"Come closer," Mr. Inoue said with a wink.

She sidled up to him. "Is this better?"

"*Much* better, hahaha," he told her cleavage.

All the while, Hanako was staring demurely at her hands. "My mother and I," she said suddenly, "we're the quiet ones in the family. My father is the lively one, as you can see." She looked embarrassed.

"So what do you think of all this?" Tom asked me. "It's not every foreigner who gets to visit this sort of place."

I wasn't sure what to think. On the one hand I was charmed, as I had been the previous times I'd met him, by Mr. Inoue's infectious good cheer. On the other hand, some feminist demon was pushing me to label hostess clubs as sexist institutions that ought to be outlawed. Just as I was pondering how to answer Tom's question, Salamía got up and traded places with Tina, who now sat beside me.

"Won't you try some?" she asked sweetly, dangling a sliver of eel in front of my lips. "Open wide, theeere we go. How do you like it?"

"*Oishii*," I nodded in approval.

"Your Japanese is so *good*," she chirped. "Here, have some more. And how are you doing with your drink? Maybe just a little bit more, *neh*?"

Meanwhile, Hanako had walked up to the karaoke booth at the opposite end of the room. Her selection came on and she started to sing. It was a sad, dignified song, and she sang it in a crystal-clear voice, without smiling once.

"My daughter is also *obatarian*," Mr. Inoue told me as Hanako walked back to our table. "Eh, Hanako? Thirty-six years old and still not married."

"Will you sing for us, please?" Tina asked me, pouting in the same way she'd done for Mr. Inoue.

"I'm too shy," I said stupidly.

"Shy? A nice-looking woman like you? Go on, I'm sure you'll enjoy yourself once you're up there."

As Tom took his turn at the microphone, Tina continued to lavish her attentions on me.

"Here, try some *daikon*, won't you?" She fed me a piece of pickled radish. "Can you eat *all* types of Japanese food?"

I nodded.

"Even sea-urchin?"

I nodded again.

"You're really like a Japanese, aren't you?" She patted my knee. "Where did you get those *gorgeous* pants? They're silk, aren't they?"

Sexist? I wasn't so sure anymore. Tina and Salamía were all abuzz around Mr. Inoue, but they were paying no less attention to me. I was being treated like a queen, just as he was being treated like a king. And I had to admit it — I was beginning to find all this attention just the tiniest bit, well, flattering.

Suddenly I saw it clearly — how irresistible these dens of illusion would be for men who got only brisk efficiency from their wives, whose marriages were little more than business deals. If I, with my feminist leanings, was falling under the spell of a hostess club, what chance did these men have?

Mr. Inoue leaned across the table and put a hand on my shoulder.

"You make me happy if you sing," he wheedled. "You make me young man again."

"I can't, I'm too shy."

"*Obatarian*," he winked at Salamía. "I think our guest needs some more whiskey." She obediently refilled my glass, then went off to get a new bottle.

I looked at the English song-list as I gulped down the whiskey. "But I don't know any of these songs — "

"Stop making excuses," Tom said.

"Alright, alright," I said with a burst of Dutch courage. "Tell the manager I'm going to sing 'Yesterday.' "

I got up, staggered to the microphone and waited for the sound to come on. Under the scrutiny of friends, strangers and bug-eyed dragon-heads, I sent my shaky airwaves into the microphone. When I got to the "Why she had to go" part, my voice thinned to a hoarse whisper. I kept my eyes glued to the video monitor, where the lyrics floated by against a back-drop of fair-haired lovers cavorting in a meadow.

The applause was wild. They whistled and cheered. The guests at the other two tables joined in the fanfare as I made my way back to the table.

"That was great," a stranger boomed out at me.

"Sing another one."

"Siiiiing."

"We want more English songs!"

"Siiiiiiiiing."

It was then that I realized what my mistake had been. I had thought I was expected to sing well. Karaoke, I realized, was not about singing well. It was about singing badly. It was about getting up and performing, whether you were a rock-star, an office worker or a bow-legged engineer. This was one arena in which the usual excuse of *hazukashii* just didn't wash. Shy or not shy, you were expected to be a good sport and provide your share of the evening's entertainment.

I perused the song-list again. I Left my Heart in San Francisco, Autumn Leaves, Moon River ... The only songs I felt confident about getting through were the Christmas carols. What the hell, I told myself, Christmas is only two months away. I went back up to the microphone and delivered, with much more authority this time, what was no doubt the season's first rendition of Rudolph The Red Nosed Reindeer.

Once again, the patrons and staff broke into applause, whistles and cheers. I lingered at the microphone for a few moments, savouring the adulation. This was it — my fifteen minutes of fame, just as Andy Warhol had predicted would be everybody's due in the future. It was good to know that in Tokyo, the future could be bought for just $500.

All at once it was time to leave — the shop was closing. Tina and Salamía disappeared behind a back door. "Come again soon," the manager beamed at Mr. Inoue as he stored his whiskey-bottle in a cabinet. There was a round of bowing, and then we all filed into the elevator. Just as the door was about to close, Tina and Salamía stepped in behind us. They were both wearing faded jeans and sweatshirts.

"God, I'm tired," Tina said dully, to nobody in particular.

They both looked tired. Minus the sequins and feathers, they were just working women, going home after a hard day at the office. The spell had been broken. All their fawning and pouting, it was suddenly clear, had been nothing more than work for wages.

The difference between Mr. Inoue's perspective and my own, I mused as the elevator shuttled us back down to Earth, was not in the way we'd been treated by the hostesses. It was that while I was relieved to see them drop their act, Mr. Inoue, I felt sure, would have wanted the illusion to continue past closing time.

—— 3 ——

To hear it from my younger students, the Japanese mother-in-law had quite a bit more clout than her Western counterpart. She was accused of being bossy and meddlesome, and especially eager to impose her will on her hapless daughter-in-law who, bound by the age-old tenet of deferring to one's elders, was powerless to stand up for her rights. Word had it that some frustrated young women in Tokyo had started a group called Women Against Mothers-in-Law, which one supposed was the Japanese answer to North American groups like Toughlove or Women in New Roles.

Traditionally, the *chonan* or eldest son is expected to live under the same roof as his parents even after he gets married, and to provide for them in their old age. Although the multi-generational household is dying out in urban areas, the spirit of the tradition prevails. Many young women, aware of the duties expected of a *chonan*'s wife, give eldest sons a wide berth in their search for a husband. Those women unfortunate enough to be saddled with live-in mother-in-laws complain of being bombarded with advice on how to cook for their husbands, how to discipline their children, and the various other do's and don'ts of running a proper Japanese household.

One week I told all my students to bring photos of a family member or friend to the next class, to use as a starting point for free conversation. The following week, when I asked Kazuko — one of my more diligent and spirited students in an upper-intermediate group — to show us the picture she'd brought, she produced a small photo of two elderly people. "These are my mother- and father-in-law," she told us. "I've known them for over thirty years." Kazuko had a large family, and in previous classes had always talked proudly of her assorted children, nieces and nephews, so her choice of picture was puzzling. I didn't remember her ever mentioning her parents-in-law.

"Their house is very close to ours," she continued, "only a fifteen-minute walk. Every morning at nine o'clock they come over and have breakfast with me. Or rather, I prepare some food for them but don't eat it myself, since I usually have my breakfast at seven-thirty, right after my husband leaves for work."

"How long do they stay at your house?" a student asked.

"All morning," she said. "Sometimes we even have lunch together."

I asked her if it wasn't a little tiresome to spend every morning with them, and she said no, she didn't mind doing it and actually enjoyed their company.

"It's my duty to take care of them, but also my pleasure. I'm always happy to see them."

"But every day?" I asked. "Don't they ever stay at home and let you have a rest?"

"They come every day except when it's pouring rain." Kazuko paused for a moment and went on. "Every morning, the first thing I do after waking up is go to my bedroom window and check the weather outside. If it's sunny, then I'm happy. And if it's raining hard ... then I'm *really* happy."

Kazuko smiled down at her hands, looking embarrassed but pleased. She had managed to unburden herself without uttering a word of complaint. I couldn't help feeling sorry that this art would surely die out in the next generation of emboldened daughters-in-law.

Stories such as Kazuko's gave glimpses into the spirit of *akirame*, or resignation, that is the legacy of Japanese women from far back in time. The Japanese — women in particular — are keenly aware that their destiny is shaped by forces outside their control. Whatever hardship comes their way is *shiyo ga nai*, "it can't be helped," an expression that they seem to use as casually as how are you or have a nice day.

One morning we were having a discussion about education in an advanced class called Cross-Cultural Communication. Most of the students were older women who had spent some years abroad with their husbands and families. Chieko, a graying woman whose softly wrinkled face spelled kindness and hard times, had often spoken to us about her youngest son, a troublesome teenager who skipped classes and spent hours alone in his room. "It can't be helped," she would say with a sad smile whenever she talked about him.

"I think I know when the trouble started," she told us that morning. "It was during a math class one day in early spring, when he was in fifth or sixth grade. The weather was exceptionally clear and warm, and my son was a bit restless. He looked out the classroom window and there was Mount Fuji, perfectly framed and much sharper than he'd ever seen it. It's rare to get such a good view of Mount Fuji from Tokyo and he was quite excited. On impulse, he asked the teacher if she could stop the class for a few moments so that all the students would get a chance to catch the view. The teacher got angry at him and scolded him for disrupting the class.

"When he came home from school that day he seemed upset. I asked him what the matter was, and he told me the story. He couldn't understand why the teacher had scolded him, since it was obvious that he hadn't meant to be disruptive — he'd just reacted spontaneously to a beautiful sight and wanted to share it with the others.

"Since that day," Chieko went on, "he has never been the same. He lost his confidence, somehow. I think he felt he couldn't trust his instincts anymore."

I remembered my own mother, marching indignantly into the principal's office after she learned that my teachers were trying to get me to write with my right hand. Chieko, of course, would never have thought to make a fuss. She only knew how to grin and bear and think *shiyo ga nai* while each day brought a new wrinkle to her face.

Polished pearls like Chieko's Mount Fuji story were few and far between, and didn't quite make up for the daily tedium of teaching the lower-level students, who would gaze at me with anxious faces while I talked myself hoarse. For some teachers, this type of class was a challenge. For me it was merely exhausting.

Many of these "beginners" had been coming to BE for several years (in addition to the six years of English they'd been required to take in school) and were still unable to make themselves understood. Having studied a bit of linguistics, I knew that Japanese was a so-called sound-poor language, meaning that the number of different phonemes, or individual sounds, was very low — just over one hundred compared to about three thousand in English and one thousand in Chinese. Consequently, if you were a Japanese attempting to emulate English sounds, your tongue and lips would be struggling to perform entirely new motions. If you weren't paying close attention, your muscles would revert to their old habits and channel the sounds into their closest equivalents in Japanese, which were usually not very close at all. Thus, "colour" came out as "karah," "learn" as "rahn" and "seafood" as "sheehude." The result of all this was that my students were more likely to be understood by each other than by me.

During one class, a young housewife called Naoko announced that the previous weekend she'd had dinner with a holenah for the first time. I smiled blankly as I tried to figure out what a holenah might be (for some reason it made me think of a species of whale), when another student came to my rescue. "Was it an American?" she asked Naoko, giving me the clue I needed. I asked the students if anybody else had ever dined with a foreigner, and the discussion continued.

I didn't fare quite as well with Atsuko, a breezy society lady who came to class in tailored suits and a high chignon. In mid-October, she took two weeks off to visit her sister in California. It was her first trip abroad, and she'd been excited about it for weeks. But when she came back, she looked more despondent than relaxed.

"Six years," she said, staring at her hands. "I coming to Tokyu BE for six years. All my teachers tell me I making good progress, and I believe it. But I go to America and I can't even order my own food at MacDonald's. So my teachers all tell lie to me, now I realize." I tried to protest, but she shook her head and went on grimly. "I go to MacDonald's across street from my sister's house, and ask for hisshu-bahgah. The cashier look me like I crazy, so I try say it again, but still she don't understand. Finally I have to point my finger to picture on wall."

"What *is* a hisshu-bahgah?" I asked unthinkingly.

Atsuko didn't answer. I looked at her face, and saw that her lips were trembling. *Fish-burger, you idiot*, I thought to myself, but it was too late.

I never saw Atsuko after that day, nor did any of the other teachers or students. I was afraid she would complain to Arai-san about my tactless question, but I never heard a word about it. Like Chieko, whose son had been unjustly scolded by his teacher, Atsuko didn't complain — she simply disappeared.

— 4 —

"Excuse me, but does the next train go as far as Nishiogikubo?" I asked the woman standing beside me in my most careful Japanese.

Shinjuku Station, with its fourteen platforms through which passed local, semi-express, express and super-express trains, its overlapping loud-speaker announcements and computerized bulletin boards, its underground network of walkways and restaurants and stores that rivalled a mid-size prairie town in sprawl, still held me in awe and confusion after two months in Tokyo.

The woman looked startled. "Excuse me, my English not so good," she answered.

"It's OK, you can tell me in Japanese," I encouraged.

"You speak Japanese?"

I was getting used to this type of conversation by now. Apparently, a lot more proof than actually speaking the language was needed to persuade the natives that one could.

A yellow train was coming toward us, and the woman gave a nod to let me know it was the one I wanted. We both boarded the same car but sat some distance apart. When I stood up to get off the train, seven stops later, I saw her get up too. As I started down the stairs leading to the exit gate I felt a light tap on my shoulder.

"Excuse me."

I turned around and there was the woman again, looking embarrassed. Her hair was cropped short and she wore a baggy grey sweatsuit. She looked fifty-somethingish but somehow youthful.

"Do you live Nishiogikubo?" she asked hesitantly.

"Yes, I do."

She introduced herself as Teruko. "I like foreigner," she said. "I want make foreigner friend." (She pronounced it "holenah," as my student Naoko had done.)

I told her I was equally interested in making Japanese friends, and asked her if she too lived in Nishiogi.

"I own two houses," she said, "one of them in Nishiogi. I live Nishiogi house in weekday, Kokubunji house on weekend. You want come and bisit my house?"

I told her I didn't have time just then, but would be glad to go and see her some other time. She told me she had been on her way to Kichijoji to do some shopping, but when she saw me get off at Nishiogi, decided on impulse to follow me out and introduce herself. We exchanged phone numbers and went our separate ways.

A couple of days later she called to invite me for supper. "I lonely," she said simply. "Always eat alone. Please come my house, *neh*?" One more stereotype shot down, I thought, startled by her directness. I had a hunch she might have stories to tell.

Since it was largely obscured by vegetation I had a bit of trouble finding Teruko's house, her quaint instructions adding to the challenge. She'd told me to look for a narrow footpath amid some shrubbery a little way past the laundromat with the orange sign, then walk along the path until I came to a small courtyard encircled by a few houses, one of which was hers. I stood there in confusion for a few moments until I saw her waving from inside.

"You know *nabe*?" Teruko asked as I put on the fake leather slippers she offered me, which of course were several sizes too small. "I cook *nabe* tonight."

Her house was cramped and messy — dirty, even. A film of dust coated the countertops and lampshades, and the walls were dotted with grease stains. She led me into the living room and told me to sit down.

"You know *kotatsu*?" She showed me to a low table in the middle of the room. Though I'd heard of the word, this was the first time I'd actually seen one. She told me to plug in the electric cord so the heat would start radiating from the box-like stand upholding the table.

"I hope you don't mind the mess," she said in Japanese as she went off to the kitchen to bring our food. "Nobody ever died from a little dirt, *neh*?"

I laughed, once again struck by her deviation from type.

Teruko came back into the living room with a giant tray of cabbage leaves, tofu and raw chicken strips, and an electric pot filled with water. As we waited for the water to start boiling, she got right to the point.

"I have failed," she said. "My whole life has been a failure. And now, in my old age, I'm paying the price." She eyed me intently for a few seconds. "I have no idea what to do with myself. I often get depressed — very depressed. Sometimes I wonder why I continue to get up every morning.

You understand what I'm trying to say, *neh?*"

She had a very pretty face, I noticed for the first time. She might well have been a head turner in her younger years.

While we cooked and ate our *nabe*, Teruko told me the story of her life. She spoke matter-of-factly, almost without pausing except when I stopped her to ask the meaning of a word.

Hers was a shotgun marriage, arranged by her father after he tore her away from the man she was in love with, a lowly bean-cake maker. The day before her wedding, her mother took her aside and gave her a single piece of advice about married life: a ship can have only one captain.

"I was never able to follow that advice," Teruko told me, "which is why my life has been a failure."

"What do you mean?"

"A Japanese woman has to have *enryo*, restraint. Otherwise she can't live in harmony with her husband, or with the rest of her family."

She and her in-laws were at each other's throats from the start. If they asked her to help out at one of the four Chinese restaurants they owned, she'd refuse. If they asked her to cook an *udon* noodle dinner, she would spitefully cook *soba* instead — or nothing at all. She was brimming with resentment about her forced marriage to a man who was turning out to be an abusive drunkard, and was unwilling to go the usual route of suffering in silence.

She gave birth to three sons. The oldest son was a misfit with a strong depressive streak. He often contemplated suicide in his youth, until he was recruited by the Jehovah's Witnesses and found a way to depart the material world without actually killing himself. He was thirty years old now and lived in the house next to Teruko's, though he hardly ever saw her except when she handed him his monthly allowance. "But he doesn't believe in money," she said wryly.

"And the other two?"

"One is a salary-man in a small company, and the other is in Australia."

"Surely they must give you some pleasure."

She considered this for a moment. "No, I don't get any pleasure from my children. We hardly ever see each other. I guess it's like my marriage — failed marriage, failed children."

"And where is your husband now?"

"He's in the hospital, with terminal cancer. I go to see him for a couple of hours every day, though I sometimes ask myself why. He means nothing to me. When I look at him, all I see is a piece of rotting flesh."

She went to the kitchen and brought back an electric teapot and a couple of grease-coated teacups. Her mood seemed brighter all of a sudden, as though telling me her life story was a formality she'd had to dispense with, like a comment about the weather.

"Anyway," she shrugged, "I've had a few bright spots in my life. Like now — " she leaned over conspiratorially " — I have a lover. A foreign lover. Australian. And he's younger than me." She paused for effect. "*Eighteen years* younger."

"Does your husband know about it?"

"No, of course not. When my husband dies, I plan to take my boyfriend to Hawaii for a couple of weeks. He's never been there, and I know he'd love to see it. I haven't told him yet, though. Just little hints. You know, to keep him guessing."

Our legs toasty under the *kotatsu*, we sipped green tea and listened to the night sounds for a while — the trill of a cicada, a child's wail, the squeaking of bicycle tires.

"Sometimes I think he's just after my money," she said softly, just as the same thought was crossing my mind.

Teruko shuffled back and forth between her houses, picking up mail and phone messages, doing her laundry in one house and sorting it in the other, or just "checking up" on things. She seemed to need the pointless, manufactured activity in order to get through each day without giving in to the despair that periodically assailed her.

When she came to visit me, I noticed, her mood was usually brighter than when we met in her home. At Esther House, she had the chance to breathe in some of that rarified holenah air she so craved. She would sprint up the stairs in her dirty sweatsuit, hair dishevelled and skin sallow against the pink of her lipstick, and plunk herself down on my tatami floor (never on my sofa-bed—in this she was thoroughly Japanese), ravenous for my companionship. We almost never spoke English, since she really couldn't manage it, though she would occasionally take a deep breath and, with pea-cock pride, utter a badly mangled version of a word like "inheritance" or "funeral."

"Do you know what happened last night?" she told me one evening while we snacked on the rice-and-seaweed crackers she'd brought along. "For the past year I've been renting the second floor of my house in Kokubunji to a couple, an American man and a Japanese woman. Anyway, last night I went to the house to pick up some sheets, and just as I was about to walk in I heard a strange noise. At first I thought it was a cat meowing — I really did — but then I listened some more and realized it was the woman making, ah, sex noises. I've never heard anything like it in my life. I was shocked." She didn't look shocked at all, only fascinated. "I didn't think Japanese women made such noises — *I* certainly didn't when I had sex with my husband. Did you?"

I dodged her question. "Surely she's not the only Japanese woman who makes noises during sex."

"But you should have heard it! She was screaming like a mother giving birth. And then, when I went inside, I heard the bedpost banging against the wall — *gatan, gatan, gatan* — and I could actually *see* the walls shaking." She shook her head in awe.

"Tell me," she said after a pause, "is there something ... well, *different* about foreign men? Is there something they do that gives women so much pleasure?"

I laughed. "What about your Australian boyfriend?"

She lowered her eyes. "We hardly ever have sex, actually. And no, he doesn't make me scream like that. You should have heard her — it was so loud, I was afraid everybody on the street would be able to hear it." Once again she shook her head at the memory. "*Big* shock."

I looked at her wide, eager eyes and sensed the curiosity that lay beneath them, the hunger for lurid details, the latent raunchiness.

You wanna be shocked, lady, I thought suddenly, *OK, I'll shock you.* And I told her about a case my brother had encountered while interning at St. Joseph's Hospital in Toronto. A man had showed up at the emergency room with the tail of a dead mouse sticking out from between his legs. When my brother asked him, as nonchalantly as he could, how the animal had come to be there, the man explained that he and his lover had been engaging in a practice called mousing, which consisted of having a live mouse (it had to be a particular species, bred for its small size) inserted into one's rectum, and savouring the sensation as it burrowed around until it met its death by asphyxiation. According to the patient, the practice was not uncommon. Usually the mouse didn't get very far and was easily extricated, but this had been a particularly tenacious animal and the patient's lover had been unable to remove it.

Teruko looked at me intently while I told her the story, but she didn't seem particularly shocked. When I was finished, she sat in thoughtful silence for a few moments, then asked, without a trace of irony, "What for?"

I often wondered what fuelled our friendship, what drew me again and again to Teruko's unkempt home and slapdash hospitality, and her to my drab little room in Esther House. It was only much later that I realized that what held us together, what propelled us into a lasting friendship, was the alienation we both felt from our own cultures, the irrational longing to inhabit each other's worlds.

5

*"Tokyo is a candy-store, and while I'm here, I intend
to eat to my heart's content."*
"Tokyo is a man-desert, and I'm a thirsty woman."

According to Charlene, who relayed it to me in scornful tones over the telephone, the first statement was made by a male teacher at the English school where she worked. The candies he was referring to were of the almond-eyed, silky-haired variety. I came across the second statement in the Tokyo *Journal*, a slick monthly magazine catering to English-speaking Tokyo residents. It was a quote from an American woman who was fed up with the lack of dating opportunities for Western women living in Tokyo.

With almost two months behind me, I too was beginning to notice the inequities in Tokyo's dating scene. For gaijin men, the situation was ideal — they were in limited supply and in constant demand. Tall ones, short ones, fat ones, skinny ones, classically stunning and classically ugly ones — just about every Western man was able to find a Japanese girlfriend in record time. Not a day went by when I didn't see a gaijin man with a fresh-faced Japanese girl hanging on to his arm and looking up at him with doe eyes.

I sometimes wondered what the women saw in these conquest-seeking men. Charlene, on the other hand, wondered what the men saw in their Japanese girlfriends. "These women are such *airheads,*" she told me in her italicized drawl. "They run around the office acting like five-year-olds just to get the teachers' attention. It makes me want to *vomit,* the way they walk with those mincing steps and talk in those ridiculously high voices."

As to why the Japanese women worshipped gaijin men, part of it had to do with a general admiration, in Japanese society, of all things Western. Western men, like Western movies, Western fashion or Western music, were cool. A gaijin boyfriend was a status symbol. On the train to work one morning, I struck up a conversation with a British man who told me he'd answered a Japanese woman's personal ad in the Tokyo Journal. After a few dates, he began to notice that she seemed more interested in driving him around the city in a car packed with her buddies than in seeing him alone. "It started to feel like all she wanted to do was show me off to her friends," he said.

But it went deeper than that. Many young Japanese women looked to gaijin men as a way to escape the confines of their predictable future as Japanese wives. By hooking up with a Western man, they were also buying into the cultural ideal of the West — a relationship that would give them romance, sexual fidelity and a chance to spread their wings.

It was hardly surprising that, surrounded by such a bountiful supply of eager women, gaijin men sometimes went a little crazy. They found girlfriends within days of their arrival in Tokyo. They traded up — plainer ones for more attractive ones, older ones for younger ones — and competed with each other to see who could get the prettiest one in the shortest time.

Stuart, a BE teacher from Vancouver whose cocky demeanor was a magnet for the female students, would boast of his exploits between classes. "Take a look at this," he'd say to us, pinning a note to the bulletin board. It was usually written on pink stationery and said something like "Mr. Stuart, I so much enjoy your teaching. Every class I watch your cheerful face. I would like to have dinner with you. Please say yes."

Jeffrey Addleman, BE's youngest teacher and not quite so much of a lady-killer, always rose to the bait. "So what's your secret?" he'd ask Stuart with undisguised admiration.

Relationships between gaijin men and Japanese women worked well, it seemed to me, because both parties got a better deal than they would with a partner from their own culture. The man got more pampering and less argument. The woman got more independence and more of the flowers and compliments she upheld as a romantic ideal. They were mirrors for each other's fantasies as they walked arm in arm, equally triumphant as they displayed their conquest to the world.

This state of affairs left many foreign women railing against young Japanese women for having an unfair advantage in the playing field. They accused these women of stunting themselves like bonsai trees in order to appeal to the male fantasy of a childlike woman (something that they, of course, would never stoop to doing). Gaijin men saw it differently. "Do you know what that idiot had the *gall* to say?" Charlene told me, referring to the same teacher who was bent on satisfying his sweet tooth. "He said he prefers Japanese women because they're lighthearted and fun to be with, and that the gaijin women who come to Tokyo are — get this — too *serious* and full of hang ups. Can you *believe* it?"

For all their complaints about the dating scene in Tokyo, most Western women I knew had no particular interest in trying their luck with Japanese men. Some claimed to find them unappealing as a group, while others were not above the occasional one-night stand but would never consider a long-term involvement. The general consensus was that a Japanese man, with his addiction to work and reluctance to show affection, didn't have much to offer a Western woman.

Young Japanese men, on the other hand, seemed eager to date outside their culture but didn't quite know how to go about it. Unlike gaijin men, who knew they were in high demand, Japanese men felt at a disadvantage in the game—they assumed their overtures would be met with rejection. "Japanese men are hated all over the world," a friend of Miki's told me. He had spent four years in America studying law, and hadn't been as successful with the local women as he would have liked. He confessed that after managing to get a date with an American woman, he was on a high for weeks and all he could think of was "I did it, I did it, I did it!"

Insecurity aside, Japanese men were also aware that the culture gap might be too wide for a long-term relationship to flourish. Among the men who'd actually tasted the fantasy, the feeling seemed to be that, in the words of a young man interviewed in the Tokyo Journal, "Western women are much better in bed than Japanese women, but I would never have a serious relationship with one — they make too many demands on a man's time."

It was the reverse of the gaijin man-Japanese woman equation: both parties got less of what they wanted than with a partner from the same culture. The woman got less time and less affection, the man less patience and docility.

The result of all this was that when it came to dating and mating in Tokyo, Western women got the short end of the stick. Gaijin men were too busy chasing Japanese women to notice them, and Japanese men were either too wrapped up in their work or too shy. There were exceptions, of course, but many of the gaijin women I met in Tokyo had gone for months or years without any romantic involvement.

Valerie was a two-year veteran at Tokyu BE, a boisterous woman with an all-American smile and intense blue eyes. Two years of manlessness had made her, as Jeffrey put it, "as horny as two women rolled into one."

"Do you know what really burns me up about this city?" she told me one afternoon in the teachers' lounge. "You go to a party, you meet a cute guy, and the vibes are great, right? He's acting real flirtatious and you're thinking maybe he'll ask for your phone number, then along comes this cute little thing called Sumiko or something, and he says By the way, I'd like to introduce you to my girlfriend, and you're like, pffffft ...

It was hard not to be rankled about the unfairness of it all. I would browse through the travel section of the Kinokuniya bookstore and find books called "Bachelor's Japan" or "A Guide to the Single Foreigner in Tokyo." There were pages and pages of advice to gaijin males on the prowl, but hardly a word to us females. Tokyo had very little, these books seemed to be saying, to offer the Western woman in search of romance.

Charlene vented her anger over the telephone lines. "I have *zero* respect for these men," she told me. "They're such *losers*. All they want is some bimbo to fawn all over them."

"I know what you mean."

"Besides, I think it's *racist* to limit your dating choices to one group of people."

"I'm not sure I agree with that," I told her. "If it's alright to have a preference for bearded men, or tall dark types, or musicians or executives or whatever, why isn't it OK to have a preference for Japanese women?"

"Preference is one thing, but most of these jerks won't even *consider* a non-Japanese woman, even for a one-night fling."

I had no doubt that Charlene would find a way to track down the exceptions.

One evening in early November, I bumped into Janet and Bruce in the Shinjuku train station. They were on their way to Maggie's Revenge, a pub that advertised itself in the Tokyo Journal as a "robust Australian bar; enjoy and be noisy!"

"We're going for our monthly dose of homesickness medicine," Janet said with a laugh, and invited me to join them.

No sooner had we sat down and ordered our lagers than we heard a commotion at the other end of the room. We looked over and saw a bearded gaijin sitting by himself in a corner, banging on his table with a beer mug. Suddenly he got up and staggered to the centre of the room.

"*Three years*," he said thickly, steadying himself against the counter. "I've been in this city for three fuckin' years and I still haven't found a Japanese girlfriend."

"No worries, mate," someone snickered. "I've got one for you, a pretty one with tits."

"Shut up!" he bellowed.

"Take it easy, mate," Bruce called out to him.

He turned in our direction, gave us a suspicious stare, then grabbed his beer mug and walked slowly toward our table.

"Mind if I have a seat?" he said, looking down at us with bloodshot eyes. Without waiting for an answer, he pulled up a chair and sat down.

"I'm Nat," he said. We told him our names.

"Three years," he said softly.

He took a swig of beer. "All my mates've got girlfriends," he told us. "I got this one mate, he's so ugly he'd scare away a cockroach, y'know what I mean? And even *he's* got one."

None of us said anything.

"*Fuckin' tired of it!*" he yelled suddenly.

"Take it easy, mate," Bruce told him.

"What the fuck's the matter with this city?"

"Maybe you're trying too hard," Janet said.

He shook his head slowly. "Three fuckin' years and all I've got to show for it are some goddamn pictures of Tokyo Disneyland."

Disagreeable though he was, I could understand his frustration. He was like many Western women in Tokyo — forever on the sidelines.

6

She was one of five students in my Wednesday morning class. From the very beginning, I sensed a special quality in her. For starters, she was beautiful. Her face was a study in Oriental harmony — classic almond eyes, reticent nose and porcelain skin, with hardly a wrinkle to betray her thirty-nine years. Though on the tall side for a Japanese woman, she was slender enough to look fragile. She dressed with flair — rumpled linen jackets, silk pants, body-hugging turtle-necks — and there was a dignified bearing in her step. During class, I sometimes caught her giving me warm, almost maternal looks. Hitomi was her name.

As I try to recreate her on paper, I come up against the certainty of being unable to do her justice. If I mention that she used a fountain pen and always carried a handkerchief in her purse, no doubt she'll seem stuffy. If I talk about her happy-sad smile, the look of kindly resignation in her eyes, she'll sound like the long-suffering type. No matter how the words land on the page, they'll fall short of capturing the essence of a woman in whom traditional Japanese sensibilities, avant-garde chic and aristocratic manners coexisted with a total lack of affectation.

Since there were four other students in the class I didn't get much of a chance to talk to her privately, though I soon discovered that if I walked into the classroom a few minutes early I could almost always find her sitting there, back straight and features set in that trademark happy-sad look of hers. Our chance to get to know each other finally came about halfway through the fall semester, when the other students happened to be absent on the same morning. A few minutes into the lesson, Hitomi suggested that we forget about the textbook and have an hour of "free conversation" instead.

I learned that she came from a family of musicians and painters, had been married to an architect for fifteen years, and had no children.

"May I ask why not?" I blurted out, instantly regretting the question.

But she didn't seem to mind.

"My husband say he doesn't want bring children in a too much crowded world," she said quietly.

"And did you feel the same way?"

"Well, I understood his feeling ..." She was thoughtful for a moment, then smiled and said, "I think that real reason is my husband loves his work too much."

She's probably right, I thought. (I had always suspected that people who claimed they didn't want kids because of the terrible shape the world was in were using the sorry state of the world as a foil for other, more private reasons.)

"I'm so glad we had a chance to talk," Hitomi told me at the end of the hour. "I wanted to become your friend from beginning of class, but was too shy for suggesting it. Will you come my house for supper this Saturday?"

The following Saturday I found myself sitting in the living room of Hitomi's ultra-modern house, which her husband, Kazuo, had designed himself. It was small, but full of light and wood and interesting angles. In short order, I discovered two of its most delightful features — a heated living-room rug and a heated toilet seat. With restrained wifely pride, Hitomi showed me some of Kazuo's creations — a pewter lamp that looked like it belonged in a museum of modern art, space-age scissors, a CD holder that fanned out like a peacock's feathers. Everything in the house was stylish and eye-catching, just like Hitomi herself in her angular blue tunic and peach silk blouse. When Kazuo rang the bell and stepped in, I wasn't at all surprised to see that he was strikingly handsome.

Hitomi had invited another friend of hers, Yoko (who was also thirty-nine and married to a man who didn't want children), and the four of us sat down to eat. The long rosewood table was set like the tables in five-star restaurants, with rows and rows of forks, knives and spoons for each setting, along with black lacquered chopsticks. I stared in astonishment as Hitomi brought out the platters of food — sashimi sprinkled with ice cubes and diced vegetables, curried eel in a cream sauce, slices of chicken breast topped with fresh mangos and a ginger glaze. Clearly, Hitomi was one of those people who turned everything they touched into gold.

"I love cooking," she said shyly when she saw my look of amazement. "I specially like to experiment with combination Japanese and French style." She went on to tell me that she always tried to think of the most appropriate foods to serve to a particular group of guests — the foods that were most likely to make conversation flow and create amicable feelings. She seemed to have hit the bull's eye that evening, since Yoko and I got along famously and made plans to get together the following weekend.

Hitomi continued to flood me with her quiet generosity. One Sunday she insisted on taking me on an architectural tour of Tokyo. Predictably, her taste in buildings was as impeccable as her taste in everything else. She introduced me to stylish constructions like the Watari-um museum of modern art and architectural oddities like Tokyo's narrowest house — hidden jewels I'd have never thought to find amid the jumble of post-modern kitch I usually came across on my jaunts through the city. She met me for lunch in airy sandwich bars in Harajuku and lured me to her own kitchen to sample her latest creation, which could be anything from bacon fritters to salmon-and-cheese soufflé. If I happened to mention that I liked the music playing discreetly in the background — usually jazz or alternative pop — the next time we saw each other she'd hand me a cassette copy of the music, with the title of every song written in meticulous capital letters on the cardboard insert. At such times, I was filled with what the Japanese call *kokorogurushisa* — a feeling of thankfulness bordering on discomfort.

While she took pride in her Japanese heritage, she wasn't afraid to be critical of her own people. She disliked, for example, the tendency of the Japanese to put themselves down. "If a friend give compliment about my dress," she once told me, "I make effort I don't follow Japanese habit to answer 'Not at all, far from it, it's such an ugly thing.' I think Western way is better in this case, just accept compliment and say thank you."

Although we started out conversing mainly in English, as time went on we found ourselves speaking more and more Japanese. I knew she was eager to use the English she was learning at BE, and had the feeling she'd made the switch for my sake. "No, no," she assured me when I asked her about it, "it's much more relaxing for me to speak my own language." My selfish interest in practising Japanese made me accept her words too readily, though in my heart I knew otherwise.

During the first few weeks of my friendship with Hitomi, I found myself inadvertently shying away from Teruko, whose casual manners and goggle-eyed curiosity about Western sexuality now struck me as more vulgar than bracing. I had to wait a couple of months, until Hitomi's spell over me had worn off a little, before I could once again appreciate Teruko for who she was.

I became a regular guest at Hitomi's dinner parties and got to meet a number of her friends. Many of them were women in their late thirties or early forties, married and childless, leading busy lives filled with jazz ballet classes and trips to Europe. For the most part, these women seemed genuinely content with the path they had chosen. It appeared that Japanese women were just now discovering the joys of a "child-free" existence, some fifteen years behind their North American sisters in the so-called Me

Decade. Government officials were alarmed that if the trend continued, the next fifty years would see a giant increase in the number of senior citizens with no children to pay and care for them. According to Hitomi and her friends, the decision to go childless was often motivated by the dread of having to enter a child in the frantic race for the right kindergartens, the right grade schools, the right cram schools, all in the hope that the kid would eventually make it to one of the better universities and a better station in life. To a growing minority of married couples, the financial burden, the stress, the shame if the child didn't make the grade, were not worth the trouble.

In early December, under the pretext of breaking in the year-end party season, Hitomi invited me to have dinner with her and Kazuo at one of their favourite hangouts. She admitted that Sushi-sei, as the place was called, was in the top price range for sushi restaurants. "We want you to have a real sushi experience," she declared.

They'd made reservations ahead of time, which had me feeling just a shade smug as we cut through the lineup and made our way to the sushi counter. The restaurant was just the kind I liked — small and cozy, with lots of wooden cross-beams and sliding doors. Kazuo introduced me to the head sushi chef, who stiffened for an instant as he took in the length of me, then broke into a huge grin from which he never quite recovered.

"I hear you're from Canada," he volleyed in rapid-fire Japanese. "It's an honour to have a Canadian at my counter. The last time we had a Canadian guest was back in spring — he was some kind of journalist, I think. He had this sheet of paper near his plate and took notes while he ate. He kept asking me, 'What's this?' 'What's this?' 'What's this?' with a deadly serious face, as though someone had just died." He broadened his grin. "I tell you, the guy was irritating. 'What's this?' 'What's this?' 'What's this?' To be honest, I felt like giving him a *bakudan* just to shut him up. Do you know what a *bakudan* is? I don't know the English word, unfortunately."

"Bomb," Kazuo supplied.

"Oh yes, bomb. It means a piece of sushi with a large chunk of *wasabi* mustard hidden between the fish and rice parts. In former times, sushi chefs used to give *bakudan* to their enemies and watch them choke, heh heh." As fast as his lips were moving, his hands were slicing fish, patting rice balls into shape and placing assembled pieces of sushi on our trays. "I'll bet you don't eat *kujira*, do you?"

"*Kujira?*"

"Whale," Kazuo obliged again. The sushi chef waved a hunk of gleaming red meat at me. "This is *kujira*," he beamed.

"Well ..." I was torn between curiosity and learned guilt.

"I know, I know," he boomed, "you think it's wrong to eat whale meat, *neh?*" He gave a snort of mock derision. "For us Japanese, it's a delicacy. I can't understand you Americans — "

"She's Canadian," Hitomi interjected.

"American, Canadian, whatever. When you dropped the bomb — " he splayed his fingers as though dropping an egg " — you didn't say *those poor people*, did you? But when it comes to the whales, you're forever crying *poooor, poooor things, isn't it terrible?*" Laughter danced in his eyes as he spoke. "*Poooor, poooor whales*," he repeated for effect.

By this time I too was laughing. "Sure, I'll try some," I said, mostly to surprise him. I chewed the raw whale meat under his watchful eye, easing my guilt with the thought that a true philosopher will try anything once. I found that it didn't taste all that different from raw tuna, though I knew better than to tell him that.

"You're a strange Canadian," he told me when I nodded my approval.

Pieces of sushi continued to materialize on our trays, along with refills of cold *sake* in our cups. One by one, I sampled my favourites, all of them fresh and fragrant — scallop, sweet shrimp, *anago* eel and finally the hand-rolled *makizushi*. I wondered who had come up with the curious notion that it was impossible to fill up on Japanese food.

Kazuo dismissed my tipsy protestations as he went to pay the bill, while the chef made a great show of shaking my hand across the counter. "Come again, come again," he said with cheflike geniality, looking right and left to make sure he was being properly watched by the other patrons.

We slid open the entrance door and stepped out into the cool night air. Before I could formulate a suitable expression of gratitude, Hitomi looked up at me and said, "Thank you for accepting our invitation."

7

Not being a particularly touchy-feely sort of person, I hadn't expected that I would feel quite as starved for physical contact as I did by the time November rolled around. I no longer dreaded the sardine-can train rides into Shibuya every morning, but found myself — I realized this with a shock — almost looking forward to them. Being squashed by a half-dozen people was a shoddy form of body contact, but it was preferable, evidently, to none at all.

Around that time, I was invited to spend a Sunday evening with the Mikami family, an upper-middle-class couple and their twelve-year-old daughter. A mutual friend in Toronto had written to them about my arrival in Tokyo, and they made it a point to have me over for a home-style dinner every few weeks. Both parents were doctors — he a psychiatrist and she a family practitioner — and Yuki brought home report cards that predicted an equally high-powered career.

Because they treated me casually and went about their usual business when I was there, I didn't feel I was imposing on them as much as I might have otherwise. The television was kept on while we ate, Mr. Mikami chewing silently while he took in the six o'clock news, and as soon as dinner was finished Yuki would bound up the stairs to her room and Mrs. Mikami would hand me a dishtowel so I could dry while she washed. Sometimes she even asked me to check Yuki's English homework. What I enjoyed most about those evenings was the sense of being granted an off-the-record, intimate glimpse into the life of a Japanese family, though the relaxed Mikamis could hardly be said to typify a Japanese household.

At the end of that Sunday evening in November, the three of them saw me out to the hallway and clustered around me while I put on my shoes and jacket. As we exchanged our goodbyes, I impulsively flung my arms around Yuki and held her in a tight hug. Yuki jumped back, her face taut with alarm and confusion, and Mrs. Mikami burst out laughing. She told me not to be offended by her daughter's reaction, that Japanese children past the age of about ten were not used to being touched by older people.

"Not even by their parents or relatives?" I asked Miki a few days later. We were sitting in her apartment, looking at her family pictures: children and adults lined up in neat rows, sometimes smiling, sometimes not, hands by their sides or clasped symmetrically in front of them.

"*Kimochi warui,*" she said with a shudder. "Bad feeling. I be scared if my mother kissing or hugging me, I think."

"What about your friends?"

She laughed. "No, I never touching my friends. If I touch them they think I strange. Last time somebody touch me was my boyfriend, but that seven years ago."

"Honestly? You never miss it?"

She shook her head resolutely. "You never miss bowing, or sitting *seiza*-style?"

Until then, I hadn't thought to question the prevailing Western view that physical contact was a universal human need, that people withered and died if they went too long without being touched. But most Japanese I knew hardly seemed in danger of withering and dying. Though by Western standards they might be a little repressed, their sense of community, of connectedness, was hardly the weaker for their lack of physical demonstrativeness. There were other ways to satisfy the desire for connection, and perhaps what Miki got from her chummy female friendships and assortment of hobbies was in some way equivalent to a backrub or a squeeze.

What I had a harder time accepting as healthy was the strength of her fantasies about Sweden and Stefan Edberg, her investment in the improbable. And it wasn't only Miki. I had a thirty-six-year-old student for whom Elvis was clearly more alive than her husband. As often as she could, she made the pilgrimage to Graceland where she would spend a week soaking up the magic with like-minded compatriots. Another Japanese woman I knew had spent her year-long stay in Toronto pining for Kurt Browning, the figure-skating champion, videotaping his every televised performance and writing him love letters. She showed me one of them, a string of soupy sentences that sounded nothing like the articulate woman of twenty-seven that she normally was:

> *Even other people may doubt you, but I know you're the best.*
> *Always you smile at camera, even if make mistake and fall.*
> *When you gave me that piece of paper with autograph*
> *(remember?), it was the best day of my life, and I will carry it*
> *with me always ...*

I couldn't recall any of the friends I'd had, even as a teenager, being so passionate about their idols as were these women — solid, hard-working women who could hardly be accused of self-delusion in other aspects of their lives. There was, I suspected, something fundamental that these women needed but could not get in their real lives, a yearning for which the only reasonable expression, other than despair, was intense fantasy.

Meanwhile, at Esther House, the tension was gradually building. Nobody had come to blows yet, but the daily sharing of two toilets, one shower and one telephone among a dozen ill-assorted people was taking its predictable toll on everybody's nerves. The collective mood brightened somewhat when, toward the end of the month, a very tall Nordic woman showed up at our doorstep, surrounded by brimming black suitcases. We made a great show of welcoming her, sensing that she might break up, at least temporarily, the web of petty grudges that had started to form between us.

Birgit Sorensen was from Stockholm, and had come to Japan to do some modelling and get away from her homeland, where she claimed to be dying of boredom. She was a classic Swedish beauty, with ramrod-straight blonde hair and legs that went on forever. I got a taste of what it was like to live in her skin when I took the train into Shibuya with her one morning. Over six feet tall in her high-heeled lace-up boots, hair gleaming against her black leather jacket, she drew all eyes toward her. Teenage girls whispered to each other while sneaking glances in her direction, *obaasan* gave her head-to-toe scrutinies, and older men forgot to close their mouths as they gaped without shame. I heard the word "beautiful" float up in a guttural whisper as we breezed by a pair of businessmen (with Birgit you didn't walk, you breezed), and was all too certain they weren't talking about me.

Within two weeks of her arrival, Birgit had gotten a hefty contract modelling sunglasses for an eyewear company. Ariel, who'd been pounding the pavements in search of modelling work for more than two months, had trouble disguising his resentment. "Guess I should dye my hair blond," he said. "And maybe my eyes, while I'm at it. I don't know what the fuck I'm doing in this city — there's no appreciation for *interesting* faces, just the washed-out Aryan look."

"Don't give up," Birgit urged him, and with the magnanimity afforded by success, promised to put in a good word for him if one of her employers ever needed a male model.

Birgit floated from contract to contract, from party to party, each experience another opportunity to toss off a casual boast. Loved by Japan but herself indifferent to the country, she skimmed the surface of her adventures, none of them meaning very much to her since her life was already well mapped out: at the end of the year, she'd be returning to Stockholm to get married to her six-foot-four fiancé, and presumably have a batch of six-foot-eight kids in boring old Sweden and never give Japan another thought.

By this time, all of us at Esther House had caught on to the cheating games played by Tokyo commuters, and Jessie was a particularly enthusiastic player. The Japanese called the practice *kiseru*. A *kiseru* is a traditional Japanese pipe with a metal bowl and mouthpiece, joined by a flexible bamboo tube. Like the hard metal pieces at both ends of the pipe, commuters' entry and exit stations are fixed, unbendable. But what happens in between is as flexible as the pipe's tubing. If, for example, your daily commute is from station A to station Z, twenty-five stops further, you can do the honest thing — buy a monthly train pass allowing you to ride between A and Z — or instead, buy an A-to-B pass and a Y-to-Z pass, which is a lot cheaper. You use the first pass when getting on at A, the second pass when getting off at Z, and nobody is the wiser. There are many other variants of the game. Some people go as far as studying the ticket-clerks at different stations to find out which ones are likely to be sleeping on the job and therefore unaware that the rider is flashing them a pass for an entirely different train-line.

Jessie took it upon herself to coach Birgit in the art of *kiseru*, but the apprentice soon overtook the master. Unlike the rest of us, Birgit didn't have to use her wits to play the game. She had only to breeze through the turnstile, draw herself up to her full six feet and train her brilliant blue eyes on the ticket puncher, and he would become so flustered that it was all he could do to keep from falling off his chair. As the weeks wore on, she got bolder and bolder. From expired train passes, she went on to use telephone cards, packs of cigarettes, and finally nothing but her smile. She never got caught.

I, on the other hand, got caught after only three or four tries — dragged by the arm into an office where I was made to pay a fine of three times the normal fare and given a sober talk in Japanese of which I understood nothing but the last sentence, "Please don't do that anymore." After that incident I stopped playing *kiseru*. There was something about the officer's tone of voice — its unexpected gentleness, perhaps — that made me lose my interest in the game.

I thought that Miki would be excited at the opportunity to meet a bona fide Swede, but when I asked her if she wanted to meet Birgit, she seemed oddly resistant to the idea. "I too shy," she said vaguely, and after a pause, "I not ready yet." Not ready, I guessed, to face the possibility that the real Sweden was nothing like the Sweden she'd invented for herself, the Sweden that had fuelled her fantasies for the past ten years.

Reality, illusion ... I didn't know which was better anymore. I saw myself, unhappy and striving, and I saw Miki, content to hear her idol's footsteps in the corridors of her imagination, her cravings less insistent because they didn't need to be satisfied.

8

Some of the gaijin I was meeting in Tokyo were as captivated by Japan and its people as I was. But even the most die-hard Japanophiles admitted to growing weary of answering, or dodging, the same old questions about age, marital status and ability to ingest raw fish. In our more generous moments, we attributed the predictability and persistence of these questions to the old saw that a culturally isolated people such as the Japanese could hardly be expected to behave with international sophistication.

True to form, Jeffrey Addleman had compiled a list of Snappy Answers to Stupid Questions (as they used to do in Mad Magazine, he said) and was urging the rest of the BE teachers to try them out on our students. My three favourites follow.

"Can you eat sushi?"   "It's quite good with ketchup."
"Are you married, Mr. Jeffrey?"   "No, but I'm living with him."
"Can you use chopsticks?"   "No. Can you?"

Part of the problem is semantic. In Japanese, the "can you" question form has alternative meanings of "do you like" or "are you accustomed to." Foreigners who didn't know this accused the Japanese of being condescending and ignorant. "What do they mean, *can* you eat sushi?" these gaijin would ask each other in consternation. "Do they think we're physically incapable of opening our mouths, stuffing a goddamned piece of fish inside and chewing?"

Semantics aside, the knee-jerk questions betrayed a discomfort around foreigners that seemed particularly strong in the Japanese. This was hardly surprising if one considered that most Japanese had been raised on a diet of clownish TV gaijin, glamorous movie gaijin, frenetic rock-star gaijin, and almost no contact with the real product. They were unprepared for the droves of Japanophiles intent on proving that foreigners could master it all

— language, tea ceremony, calligraphy — that no turf was sacred. "I remember a grade-school teacher telling me that foreigners really *couldn't* eat sushi, that they'd get indigestion if they did," an embarrassed student once told me in defence of the question.

Can you sleep on *futon* mattress? Can you read *hiragana* alphabet? Yes, yes, I answered proudly, suspecting it was no they wanted to hear, the no that would bolster their faltering belief in their own uniqueness.

Susan and Mark wanted to take a weekend trip to the Izu Peninsula before the cold weather set in. I took on the challenge of making *ryokan* reservations for them, though my telephone Japanese was still shaky.

"Can they speak Japanese?" one innkeeper asked me.

"Not very well," I told her, "but they're quite familiar with Japanese customs."

"Can they eat Japanese food?"

"That's not a problem. They like all — "

"Can they use Japanese-style toilets?"

"Yes, of course."

"And we don't have any Western-style beds ..."

It wasn't dislike of foreigners that had prompted the innkeeper's questions, Hitomi assured me when I told her the story, but fear that her modest accommodations weren't good enough for Americans and that she would fail as a hostess. "We Japanese have *rettokan*," she told me. "In English you say inferiority complex, I think."

Westerners, as we all know, play their own part in perpetuating the us-and-them myth. The Western media still haven't tired of portraying the Japanese business executive as a faceless robot, an economic animal hell-bent on taking over the world. Many gaijin I knew in Tokyo went on and on about Japanese timidity, propriety, enslavement to the group. I too resorted to this sort of cheap trick, finding that the easiest way to wake up dead soldiers in a classroom was to turn the conversation to cultural differences. "Is it true that Japanese mothers never boast about their children?" "Is it true that a salaryman should never refuse his supervisor's invitation to dinner?"

Another topic that used up class time was the old cliché that logic was Western, intuition Japanese. "We Japanese are not logical," more than one student insisted to me. "Look at your electronics industry, your clockwork trains," I would counter. "Isn't that evidence of logic?" But they weren't about to give up their romanticized view of themselves.

Was it because of this strong cultural identity, I wondered, that individual Japanese seemed satisfied with such weak personal identities? "I am a typical Japanese" was a self-assessment I heard time and again, along with the sentence starter "We Japanese," as in "We Japanese believe in the after-life," or "We Japanese enjoy the sound of raindrops."

"Is it a good thing to be a typical Japanese?" I asked a student.

"Yes, good thing."

"Why?"

"We Japanese all want to be same."

I didn't quite buy that. "All people want to be unique in some way, don't they?"

"Japanese person just want be little bit unique, just little bit different, like have special hobby or sport, maybe own motorcycle. But we get nervous if not typical Japanese."

My students seemed surprised that I was planning to stay in Japan over the winter holidays. "When are you going back to your country?" they would ask. Canada is not *my* country, I'd think to myself, saddened to be regarded as a guest rather than a long-term, possibly permanent resident. On the other hand, I realized it had probably not occurred to them that someone who had North America at her doorstep would choose to make her home in Japan. The majority of young Japanese dreamed of finding freedom abroad. That a North American might seek freedom in their close-knit, decorous society was surely baffling to them.

The questions followed me out of the classroom and into the streets of Harajuku, where an ice-cream vendor asked me if I thought Sting was a greater artist than Bruce Springsteen, into a Shinjuku watering hole where the bartender asked me if all American high-school students used drugs, into the trains, the stores, everywhere. It was the insatiable curiosity of a satellite culture about a dominant one, the curiosity of an island people about the mainland.

Misled by the naiveté of some of their questions, I was unprepared for the shrewdness of others. In late November, I went to interview for the position of English editor with a scientific publishing company. The publisher showed me into his office — a tiny, windowless room filled with papers stacked in teetering piles — and let me rattle on about my credentials while he sucked on his Lucky Seven.

"Which you like better," he asked suddenly, "coffee or tea?"

"Coffee," I said. "Why?"

"You like collecting things, like old newspapers, postcards?"

"No, not really."

"You wait for red light before crossing street, even if no cars?"

The questions continued, each one more puzzling than the last.

"You no good for this job," he said finally.

"But I have a science degree, and editing experience — "

"You not patient person. You get bored with this job. Is very detail, how you say ... *routine* kind of job. To do this job well, you must be the person who love small details. You must be the person who don't have too much strong ideas. You must follow our company's system of editing, even if you think you find better way. You not this kind of person, I think."

He knows all this, I thought, just by asking a few loopy questions? As he shook my hand and showed me to the door, I had the sense of having been outwitted.

A few days later, I went for an interview at a small agency that set up English classes for business executives. I was hoping to drop some of my teaching hours at BE and replace them with company classes, which sounded like less work for more money. Just like my previous interviewer, the owner of INTEC, a pale, thin man of about seventy, dismissed my credentials with a wave of his hand. He wanted to know about my interests, lifestyle, goals. I tried to gloss over the gaps in my work history, the abrupt shifts of focus, from Spanish to science, science to music, music to Japan.

"You're obviously a restless person," Mr. Sato told me in his near-perfect English, "and my impression is that you get bored easily. Maybe you'll change your mind about Japan in six months and decide to leave. When we hire people, we like it to be for at least two years, preferably longer."

"But I have no intention of leaving Japan," I told him.

"Maybe not," he said, staring right at me. "But you might get bored with the job. You need mental stimulation, don't you?"

It wasn't a question one could answer no to.

"This job requires a lot of patience," he continued. "Many of our students are slow learners. You're not a patient person, are you?"

This style of interviewing — focusing on personality rather than credentials — was one I would encounter again and again in my interviews with Japanese companies. Instead of looking for people whose experience was a perfect match with the job description, they seemed to favour candidates whose personalities were well-suited to the work they'd be doing. I wondered if this might not be one of the reasons that job hopping was so uncommon in Japan.

It looked like Mr. Sato was going to turn me down, when all of a sudden a tall woman flounced into the room, almost blinding me with her sartorial splendour: lime-green miniskirt, opaque stockings of the same colour and a woolly sweater in a violent shade of pink. She looked to be in her early forties, though it was hard to tell — her face was curiously unwrinkled from chin to eyebrows and deeply furrowed on the forehead. I took in her long straight hair, parted in the middle and slightly greasy, her heavy makeup and false eyelashes, and thought, *frozen in the seventies*.

And then she started to talk: about her Masters' thesis in linguistics, about books she'd been reading, about the lack of serious, committed teachers in Tokyo. It turned out I had read some of the same books she had — *Iron and Silk, The Remains of the Day.* That bit of serendipity got us into an animated discussion about books versus films, films versus plays. I stared at her in astonishment, unable to reconcile the sober, high-toned remarks about Kazuo Ishiguro's "tasteful, minimalistic book" with the fuchsia lipstick bleeding past her lipline, the powder-coated eyelids and eye-popping garb.

"I like her," Vivian told Mr. Sato. ("He's my boss," she whispered to me, "but he trusts my judgment.")

And so I found myself with two new evening classes — IHI salespeople on Wednesday and SECOM scientists on Friday. The IHI group was in good spirits the first week, livelier and more responsive than any of my housewife classes. I gave them my standard ask-me-anything-you-want introduction, which one student countered with "Are you looking for Japanese boyfriend?"

Finally, I thought — a different kind of question. There were possibilities, and my mood brightened.

SMALL VICTORIES

"What I am now is an interesting deformity.
I am not Asian and never will be. Even if I
forget it sometimes, no one else does."

Karen Connelly

1

It was my first meal in a Japanese home. Although many more were to follow, it never got any better than Miki's sukiyaki. She'd invited two other friends, Chiemi and Naomi, both single women who still lived with their parents. The obligatory can-you-guess-my-age's were exchanged and a ranking was established: Naomi was the senior member of our party at thirty-five, next came thirty-four year old Chiemi, then myself and finally Miki. They waited expectantly for me to marvel at how young they looked, which I was able to do without lying.

I excused myself to go to the bathroom and Miki mumbled an apology about its small size and lack of a bath or shower. I told her I wasn't planning on taking a bath, but the joke didn't catch.

"If I take apartment with bath, I pay about ¥20,000 more rent," she explained when I returned to the room. "So I going to *sento* about five times in one week."

The public bath was a seven-minute walk from her place, she said, and cost ¥400 per visit, which meant that her net monthly savings were closer to ¥12,000, or $120.

"Do you think is strange I have no bath?" she asked me, looking embarrassed.

"Not at all," I said reflexively, surprised nonetheless that a professional architect working six days a week would have to budget so carefully.

"If I man, I get much more high salary for same job," she said, as though guessing my thoughts. "Maybe two times more high." There wasn't a trace of bitterness in her voice. Half-wages and daily treks to the *sento* were a small price to pay, she seemed to be saying, for the freedom to do what she wanted.

She brought us each a giant bottle of beer and we got into position around her low wooden table, the three of them kneeling *seiza*-style and I extending my legs under the table with the abashed explanation that sitting

Japanese-style caused instant cramping in the soles of my feet. "Don't worry," they reassured politely, "with friends any sitting style OK." Plates of cabbage, sliced leeks, tofu and beef strips were laid out around an electric frying pan. Miki turned on the pan, lined it with oil and poured in the beef. She sprinkled *shoyu* sauce over the meat as it simmered, then added a cup of sake and several heaping spoonfuls of sugar. "This is Kyushu style," she said with a hint of pride.

As we waited for the meat to cook they told me about themselves, as eager to shake the dust off their English as I was to hear them speak Japanese. Naomi was the worldliest and most fluent of the three. She'd spent a year teaching Japanese in England, where she'd made the happy discovery that her name, composed of the characters for "straight" and "beautiful," also happened to be an English name.

"I *ki ga oi* type," Chiemi sighed to me, Naomi explaining that this meant someone who had so many interests and ambitions that they couldn't decide which one to pursue. In addition to being a semi-professional dancer, Chiemi also worked as a part-time administrator at a culture centre, was collaborating with a friend on a new method of teaching Japanese to foreigners, and dreamed of becoming a licenced colour psychologist, whatever that was.

Miki's ambition was to design wheelchair-accessible buildings based on Western models. For the past few years, she told us, she'd been toying with the idea of going to study architecture in Stockholm, which she saw as a model of progressive city planning. The stumbling blocks were huge, though: no architecture courses were offered in English, and she didn't speak a word of Swedish. But it had to be Sweden — America or England wouldn't do — which led one to suspect that ramps and large toilet stalls were only a small part of her motive.

Marriage appeared to have as much bearing on their plans as the Second Coming. I asked them if they'd ever given the matter any thought.

"You know Japanese men?" Chiemi asked me, as though the question answered itself. Miki and Naomi groaned in assent.

"She *like* Japanese men," Miki told the others on my behalf.

"*Heeeeeh?*" They looked astonished.

"Japanese men so boooring," Naomi said. "How you can like?"

"I can't explain it," I told them, embarrassed to have my secret divulged so quickly, "but I'm curious." They looked at me incredulously. I mumbled something about romance being the most interesting way to gain insight into a culture, though it would have been more accurate to say that I was boning up on the culture so I'd be ready for the man, if and when he showed up.

"Maybe you should try *o-miai*," Naomi laughed. "You know *o-miai*?"

"Yes," I said, "but I don't think foreigners are allowed to participate."

O-miai's literal meaning is "seeing-meeting." What you saw was a prospective candidate's resume, given to you by a *nakodo* or matchmaker. Vital statistics were age, height, weight, name of Alma Mater — university, one hoped — and annual salary. The man was also given your resume, in which you'd been careful to include such accomplishments as calligraphy or graduation from a French cooking course. If both parties agreed to it, the *nakodo* gave the man your phone number. You then arranged to meet, and although you were theoretically under no obligation to like him, parents got exasperated with daughters who were too fussy, especially if they were nearing the end of their eligible years. If you did like him, and he you, you were free to arrange further meetings. Proposals usually occurred after four or five dates.

The meat was browned all over and Miki added the tofu and vegetables, a few more sprinkles of *shoyu* sauce and another half-cup of sake to the simmering broth. The beer had loosened our postures and I settled in for what I knew would be a delicious meal and good gossip-fest.

"Have you ever tried *o-miai*?" I asked Miki.

"Just I try last month," she admitted, glancing ruefully at her friends.

"*Hontooooo?*" they squealed. "How it was?"

"*Damè*. No good at all. He fat, he *hage*, how you say *hage* in English?" She pointed to her head.

"You mean bald?"

"Yes, yes, bord. He bord, just little hair on side, also can't do conversation, only talk about he buy new washing and drying machine. After ten minutes I want leave."

Chiemi and Naomi's faces were taut with suppressed laughter.

"I return my home, telephone *nakodo* and tell her it was *damè*. She say she understand my feeling, when she arrange *o-miai* she not yet meet man, but few days later she met and thinking he *terrible*, so when I call she say solly, solly."

She took a final sip of the broth and pronounced it ready. With her chopsticks, she transferred a few pieces of meat and vegetables into her bowl, instructing me to do the same. The others followed suit.

"You like?" she asked expectantly as I chewed. The meat was dripping with flavour, tender and moist. I told her I'd never tasted anything more delicious.

"Lots of *o-miai* men is bord," Chiemi said. "I also heard story if a man can't find woman by *o-miai* system, he try make lots of money and buy house, then he get photo of himself standing with house in background, attach photo with resume. He thinking maybe women like him more because he have house."

"Yes, I hear same story. So if I see man put house on resume, I know he bord!" Naomi was doubled over with laughter.

The sky had turned purply-black outside, the air was thick with fragrant vapours, laughter was bouncing crazily off the walls and I felt myself being drawn into their world, light-years away from my own, spiralling up, up, up ... Bang! There it was, the all-too-rare but unmistakable wash of feeling that, for want of a better term, I privately thought of as a Travel Orgasm. It was this, and only this, that made travel worthwhile.

"You know *mazakon*?" one of them asked me.

"Mazawhat?"

"It comes from English words," Naomi said, wiping her eyes. "Mother complex, I think. It means grown-up man who still controlled by mother. Lots of Japanese men *mazakon*."

"Actually," I told them, "in English we usually call such men Mama's boys." Chiemi reached over to her purse, pulled out a notebook and wrote "mama's boys" in it, which prompted me to dig out my own notebook and scribble "mazakon" in a wobbly hand.

"Are you sure you want meet Japanese man?" Chiemi asked me. "You crayyyzee, I think."

"You want to know why *o-miai* system didn't go well for me?" Naomi said, straining to compose herself. "I tried about four or five times, *nakodo* gave me man's resume, but she also friend of my parents, so they asked to see it too. Then if I didn't like man after I met him, my parents get angry with me. They ask me, 'Why you don't like him? He comes from good family, works for Mitsubishi and gets ¥5,000,000 salary.' If I say I just didn't like him, just didn't like his personality, that not good enough answer for them. They continue angry with me, tell me I make stupid mistake to refuse such good man. So I *atama ni kita*, you know what means? In English you say fed up, I think. So I fed up and thought, no more *o-miai*."

They went on to tell me that computer-dating services were on the rise, especially in the large cities, for precisely that reason: unlike a *nakodo* or parents, computers didn't make you feel obligated. And you could make requests (the most popular one being no eldest sons) that would be awkward when dealing with a human go-between.

As the evening wore on and the girl-talk grew thicker, I learned that Miki was the only one who'd had any experience with men at all — the other two admitted that there had been no men in their lives, ever. I was to meet several more women of this type, women who had what it took but had never been taken. They were a minority, no doubt, but unquestionably a larger group than in the West. By and large, Japanese people paired off through the established channels, like work or *o-miai* — or not at all. Chance encounters at laundromats, grocery stores, museums or swimming pools, planes or trains, bookstores or coffee-shops, were not part of the dating culture. I once asked a group of students, young men who clearly had women on the brain, if they would consider approaching a woman at a party and asking for her phone number. Discussion ensued and a consensus was reached: no, they wouldn't, not if they didn't know anything about her beforehand. If they happened to meet her a second and third time, and if the host could give them some information about her, then maybe. But they'd still be very shy about it. The result of all this timidity was a large number of people with little or no dating experience. To compound the problem, the women were as choosy as Hollywood starlets, demanding that their potential suitors have *sanko* or "three heights," meaning bodily height (the standard minimum being 175 centimetres, with a recent push for 180), education at a high-level university and high salary.

And if real men couldn't live up to their standards, the disenchanted women fell back on their long-standing foreign idols, on their fantasy lives. In their ardor for Western movie-stars, my three friends were a match for the giddiest American teenager. "Do you like Mickey Rourke?" they questioned me, hardly waiting for my reply. "Yes, yes, Mickey Rourke! He great, *neh?*" "How about Michael Douglas?" "Harrison Ford!" "Patrick Swayze!" "Yes, yes, Patrick Swayze! " How could a balding Mitsubishi-man stand a chance?

As I looked around the table at the three vibrant women, it struck me as a shame that a whole side of them was being unexpressed. But they seemed to feel differently. "If I must to choose either three good friends or one good lover," Miki said emphatically, "I choose friends." She brought out another round of oversize beer-bottles, and our shouts of *kampai* rang out in a declaration of sisterhood.

2

It was the trifling incidents, the random drifts of day-to-day life that were gradually giving me the sense of belonging rather than watching. No longer vast and exotic, Tokyo was splitting up into manageable chunks, and I was starting to feel territorial about Nishiogi, its tidy streets aglow in the light of storefront signs and lanterns mixed with slabs of fading sunlight. The vegetable vendor would smile as I walked by and sometimes wave a sprig of chives in my direction in hopes I might be tempted, the jeweller's wife knew me by name and never missed a chance to offer me tea and belabored English phrases, the man who sold coffee beans would start grinding up my favourite blend as soon as he saw me step inside his shop, and even the old grouch in the stationery store would do his best to stop scowling when I walked in. I knew where to get *anko* cakes with the freshest and most finely pureed bean paste filling, an impossibly tiny store owned by an aging couple. The first time I stopped by I left my umbrella behind, and the woman called out "Gaijin-san!" to me, then drew in her breath and started to laugh self-consciously. I knew that Mr. Owner and Mrs. Customer were standard forms of address in Japanese, but evidently Mrs. Foreigner sounded just as ridiculous in Japanese as it did in English. I introduced myself to the couple, and they too became *kinjo no tomodachi*, my neighbourhood friends.

I no longer moved aside for the steady stream of cyclists whizzing by me, no longer worried about being run over by the cars and trucks that grazed my sleeves as they passed. Shin Midori street was drawing me in, little by little, allowing me to become a participant in its orderly confusion.

One thing that I missed, during those leisurely walks to and from the train station, was the freedom to munch on a snack as I strolled along. Eating on the run, Hitomi had told me, was still considered bad manners in Japan, despite the proliferation of fast food joints and vending machines. (It always amused me, when walking by the Baskin Robbins in East Shinjuku, to see young office ladies sitting demurely on the pink stools, nipping at their ice-cream cones like pigeons.) In time I got up the nerve to break the taboo on occasion, but never with impunity. I would scurry along, throwing furtive glances in all directions, and when I was pretty sure nobody could see me, tuck my hand into the bag of jellybeans hidden in my purse and hastily transfer some to my mouth.

When I first came to Japan I was a conscientious camera toter, a diligent note taker. By November I had stopped using my camera and even my journal showed gaps of several days at a time. The compulsion to record was giving way to the craving for immersion. I wanted nothing more than to be a cog in the wheel, an unnoticed, unremarkable participant in the life of my street.

One Saturday morning, while standing on the platform waiting for the train to Shinjuku, I noticed two kimono-clad *obaasan* arguing about the train schedule. The departure times for the various trains were posted on a large board in the middle of the platform, and the old women were pointing to the numbers in seeming confusion. I looked more closely and realized what the problem was. I walked up to them and told them in what I hoped was suitably polite language that since it was Saturday, they should be looking at the weekend times listed to the right of the regular schedule. They shrank back in surprise, covered their mouths with their hands and broke into an effusion of nervous giggles. As I was walking away I heard one of them say, "Imagine! A foreigner explaining the train schedule to us. It's just too funny." It was a small victory, but it made me feel that much less of a tourist.

On another occasion I was riding a crowded train and the man sitting next to me got up from his seat. A young mother pointed to the empty space and told her pre-school daughter to sit down. She was about to climb on but then looked up, noticed me and burst into tears. She moved back toward her mother, grabbed onto her leg and continued to stare at me with bulging eyes. The mother seemed embarrassed and gave me a sheepish look. She kept on urging her child to sit down and the child kept shaking her head, staring at me and crying. After a few minutes of this I pulled out a compact mirror from my purse and showed it to the girl. It had two sides, a regular and twofold magnification. "*Ookii*," I said and pointed to her enlarged reflection, then "*chiisai*," as I flipped the mirror and she saw her true-to-life self gazing back at her. After we had repeated this procedure a few times, she looked up at me again as if reconsidering her initial misgivings. Then, very slowly, she pulled a candy out of her coat pocket and offered it to me. I made a big show of unwrapping it and popping it into my mouth. "*Oishii desuka?*" the little girl asked shyly. "*Oishii*," I said, delicious. It seemed we'd made a small step toward *kokusaika* or internistionalization, the hot new buzzword on the lips of every politician and businessman in Tokyo.

One evening I answered my ringing phone and was greeted by a timid voice I didn't recognize. It sounded like a teenage boy. My telephone Japanese was still shaky, so I went through my usual routine of stating that I was a Canadian and would he please forgive me for not speaking too well. He didn't answer, and I asked him if he was sure he had the right number. "I just wanted to talk to someone," he said hesitantly, "so I dialled a number at random." I thought of hanging up the phone, but he sounded sincere and somehow sad, so I told him that if he spoke slowly and could put up with my limited Japanese I'd be glad to talk to him.

"I've been kind of unhappy these days ... " he started to say, then fell back into silence.

"What's the problem?" I asked after a few seconds.

"It's not one thing in particular, it's everything." More silence.

"For example?"

"Well, my parents are on my back because of my grades, but my grades are poor because they're on my back, do you know what I mean? And ... "

"Yes?"

"And my older brother is so good at everything he does, so I tell myself what's the use, even if I work harder I'll never do as well as him. And do you know the word *ijimerareko*?" I didn't, but could figure it out: child who is tormented. He must mean scapegoat.

"Lately," he continued, "I've become one of the *ijimerareko* in my school. I don't know why, but ... "

Life was no bowl of cherries for this kid, that much was clear. It was hard to think of something to say that wouldn't sound like an idiotic adult platitude. The best I could do was tell him that young people who were loners or outsiders or otherwise on the fringe often ended up leading the most interesting lives later on. It occurred to me as I spoke that what I'd observed to be true in the West might be less true in a country where *deru kugi ga utareru*, the nail that sticks out gets hammered in. I wasn't sure my words were of any use to him, but knowing that somewhere in the great megalopolis of Tokyo there was a troubled Japanese boy with whom I'd communicated gave me the sense of playing a part, however modest, in the drama of the city. And this, the travel guidebooks admonish, is the gaijin's fatal mistake: believing it's possible to fit in.

— 3 —

Just as the expression *shiyo ga nai* was a constant refrain in the conversations of my Japanese friends, the term "human rights" cropped up all the time in our discussions at Esther House, especially when Mark was one of the participants. If you slipped on the pavement, then it was not fate or bad luck but someone's fault (either the municipal government or the manufacturer of your shoes or your stress-producing job), and it was your right to have the wrong righted. Mark was always carrying on about how this or that right was being violated in Japan. Some of the rights he concocted were quite exotic — the right to personal space on trains, to round-the-clock bank machines, to public vehicles without loudspeaker announcements.

Though he'd always had a penchant for using long, obscure words in conversation, I noticed that in the past couple of weeks he'd started lacing his speech with the most astounding locutions — eudemonic, serpiginous, myrmidon, and many others I couldn't catch. He tossed the words off coolly, without giving them any emphasis, as though their meaning ought to be evident to anyone with just a little education.

One rainy evening Susan and I were sitting on the floor of their room having a bed-time snack of rice-crackers and peanuts.

"Is it my imagination," I asked her, "or has Mark been trying to expand his vocabulary these days?"

"It's not your imagination," she sighed. "It's English — his latest hobby."

In the three months I'd known Mark, I had seen him go through a folk music phase and a photography phase, putting his heart and soul into each endeavour.

"See that thing over there?" she said, pointing to a monster-sized book on their shelf. "That's his new Webster's unabridged. He bought it last month at a book sale. He's been studying it diligently ever since, ten new words every day. The worst part is he insists on trying them all out on me before taking them to the outside world." She shook her head in mock resignation.

Just then the door opened and Mark stepped into the room, glistening with raindrops and looking very tired. "I've had it," he said as he tossed his jacket and briefcase on the floor. "The vituperative appellation has been used for — " At this we burst out laughing, and Mark gave us a puzzled look.

"So have a seat," Susan said to him, "and tell us what's bugging you."

"It's that word," he said, grabbing a fistful of crackers and slumping down on his bed. "You know the one I mean?" We didn't.

"There are people from just about everywhere in the world living in Tokyo, right? We've got Australians, New Zealanders, Americans, Canadians, Brits, Germans, Swedes, not to mention Israelis, Iranians, Filipinos, Ghanans ... " We waited for the punchline.

"And the Japanese still insist on lumping us all together as *gaijin*." He made a face as if to spit out a lemon seed.

"Well," I said, "I see your point, but you can't expect them to refer to all non-Japanese as Australian-or-American-or-Ghanan-or — "

"That's it!" he exclaimed. "What's wrong with simply calling us non-Japanese?"

"Come on, kid," Susan said. "When was the last time you referred to someone as a non-American or non-British?"

He considered this. "I agree that nomenclature is a bit of a problem, but the word gaijin has got to go. *Outside person.* I don't know about you guys, but I for one find it mephitic."

"I think he means offensive," Susan whispered to me.

"Why don't you write a letter to the editor?" I suggested. Clearly he needed to unburden himself to a wider and more sympathetic audience. "You can send it to the Japan Times, or the English *Yomiuri*."

A couple of days later I answered a resolute knock on my door and there stood Mark waving a typewritten page in my face.

"Have a look at this, if you don't mind," he said, "and tell me what you think. Feel free to use your editorial skills, by the way."

As soon as he left I started to read, with increasing amazement, the letter he had composed. What follows is a portion of it.

" ... It is a travesty of democratic principles that in this crepuscular phase of the twentieth century the word gaijin should continue to be bandied about in flagrant disregard of the multitudinous diversity of Tokyo's inhabitants. There are Americans, Canadians, Australians, New

Zealanders, Iranians, Israelis, Ghanans, Brazilians, Norwegians, Filipinos, Thais and a plethora of other peoples in this great metropolis. The entrenchment of the word gaijin in the face of such vertiginous variety is a Pharisaic practise against which I cannot but inveigh, and I would venture to opine that my sentiments are echoed across the entire checkered panorama of non-Japanese people residing in Tokyo ... "

How could I possibly edit such an piece? As self-parody it was brilliant, but I suspected Mark didn't see it that way. I contented myself with changing the odd preposition. The letter did eventually get printed in the *Yomiuri*, though he lamented that they'd taken out the best parts.

When Mark wasn't around, Susan would sometimes complain to me that his negative attitude about Japan was starting to wear her down. She was doing her best to get something positive out of her stay in Tokyo, to learn something about the language and the traditional crafts, but was finding it difficult to get into the spirit of things with a husband who never stopped bad-mouthing the place. If it wasn't the word gaijin, it was the whaling industry, trade barriers or the rudeness of subway riders. Mark was the only foreigner, as far as I knew, who wasn't captivated by Japanese women. "Airheads, every one of them," he was fond of saying. "Talking in those silly high-pitched voices, covering their mouths with their hands and looking embarrassed all the time. Whenever I ask them a question in class, they start blushing and giggling as though I'd asked them to take their clothes off." I couldn't quite put my finger on it, but I often felt there was something forced, something false in his indignant tirades. It seemed to me that the lad doth protest too much, that he couldn't possibly be so repelled by what every other red-blooded gaijin was powerless to resist.

Over the course of the next few months, Mark had several more flare-ups of indignation about the various injustices in Japanese society. The throwaway mentality, insensitivity to the environment, and suppression of individualism all came under the attack of his hyperbolic pen. Some of his letters got printed, others didn't. And his vocabulary continued to grow.

4

"You're as young as you feel," I told myself over and over as I rubbed elbows with the hordes of young people pouring out of their offices at lunch-hour Shibuya, swaggering down punky Takeshita street, milling around in Yoyogi park. That was the trouble — I didn't feel very young. In my more honest moments, I faced up to the fact that my thirty-three years of age had quite a different meaning in Tokyo than they did back in Toronto.

If you were thirty-three in North America and your life wasn't going quite the way you wanted, you still had the chance to jump ship and board another one — to start a new career, a new relationship, or simply to toss off old chains and savour your independence. This was, in fact, what I had done. The irony was that the place I'd chosen to start my new life was not prepared to let me do it, at least not in the way I had envisioned.

America is obsessed with age, people often say, but I found this to be even more the case in Japan. The Japanese have a term — *nenrei ishiki*, or age consciousness — which reflects the emphasis they place on a person's age. This consciousness begins at home, where older siblings are called "older brother" or "older sister" while younger ones are called by their individual names, and is carried over to the workplace. My SECOM and IHI students always specified whether a colleague of theirs was a *sempai* (older co-worker) or *kohai* (younger co-worker), and prefaced their stories about friends and acquaintances with statements like "She's six months older than me but graduated a year earlier," or "He entered university at the same time as my younger brother."

"*Nenrei ishiki* feeling even between good friends," Hitomi told me. Yoko, she explained, was only four months older than she was, but they still used different language when speaking to each other — Hitomi's speech was more deferential while Yoko's was more casual and chummy. Even twenty years of close friendship hadn't erased their ingrained awareness of who had emerged earlier from the womb.

Not surprisingly, *nenrei ishiki* was especially significant in man-woman relationships. A woman's eligibility for marriage was said to end at age thirty in the big cities, a few years earlier in small rural communities. Although Japanese women of my age tended to look much younger than I did, they already perceived themselves as *obasan*, middle-aged women, for whom it was no longer appropriate to entertain thoughts of romance. I watched these women — my students, fellow teachers, my growing circle of friends — and was struck by how many of them seemed to have given up on the possibility of change in their lives. If they hadn't managed to snare a husband or embark on a bona fide career, then it was time to throw in the towel, to play out the rest of their lives as dutiful daughters, or doting aunts, or poorly paid office ladies who had nothing to look forward to except more of the same. I was baffled by people like my student Yuki, an attractive woman of thirty-four who spent her days helping out in her parents' furniture store and her evenings watching soap operas. Though a restless energy sometimes leaked through her complacency, she proudly and somewhat stubbornly refused to do anything to change her situation. With her haughty, wordless stare, she challenged my right to pass judgment on her life. "Don't you ever think of doing anything else with your life?" I tactlessly asked her one afternoon. She glared at me for a moment or two, then changed the subject.

Another constraint facing older women in search of a mate is that single men are not being "recycled" in Japanese society the way they are in the West. While divorce has been increasing by leaps and bounds in Japan, the age distribution of divorcing couples differs sharply from the Western pattern. Couples split up either very soon after marrying — at the extreme, the "Narita divorce" at the airport following the couple's honeymoon, during which the bride was presumably disillusioned with the groom — or after the kids have all grown up and settled down. Very few people will disrupt a young family, as they do in America, in order to bail out of an unfulfilling marriage. The result, of course, is a much smaller pool of single men in their thirties and forties.

While Japanese men are not, in principle, stamped with an expiry date, they too seem to hit an invisible wall once they hit a certain age. Among my students, probably half of the men over thirty were unmarried, most of them not out of choice. They complained of women's shopping-list mentality, of their own timidity, of being too busy to juggle their work with the kinds of relationships young women were starting to insist on. In the changing cultural climate of the nineties, there seemed to be a clash between the men's concept of marriage — as a more or less utilitarian arrangement — and the women's new, Westernized expectations. In *The*

Japanese Mind, published in 1983, Robert Christopher quotes an Italian priest and long-time resident of Japan as saying that "Japanese think anyone over thirty who is still unmarried is a little bit crazy." Things had apparently changed a lot over the past few years.

Considering the premium placed on youth, I would have expected the Japanese to be coy about revealing their ages. I found the opposite to be true. Perhaps because they aged so gracefully, they took more pride in *looking* young than in *being* young. In the classroom, on the train, at the stationery store, I was constantly being lured into games of "Guess my age."

"Thirty-two?"

"No, higher."

"Thirty-six?"

"Higher."

"Forty?"

(*Trying to conceal pleasure*) "Higher."

And then, out of politeness, I had to reciprocate — to let them guess how old I was, which was what they'd wanted to know in the first place. Unaccustomed to reading foreign faces, they were usually wide off the mark. After only three months in Japan, I'd had my age estimated at twenty-two, thirty-nine, and just about everything in between. But even the lower figures did little to cheer me. Under my black cloud of self-preoccupation, I was convinced that only those who guessed high saw me with clear eyes.

And so I continued my lunch-hour jaunts through Shibuya, each day bringing a sharper bite to the air and an additional twinkling light or miniature Santa doll to a store window. On one occasion, while crossing one of the giant intersections where pedestrians converged from all directions, I collided with full force into another walker, lost my balance and fell to the ground. I saw a purse fly into the air, then heard the clatter of hard objects hitting the pavement.

"Can't you watch where you're going?"

At the sound of the shrill, British-accented voice, I glanced up and met the gaze of a stocky blonde woman. She looked very young, maybe twenty-two.

"I'm sorry, I — "

"Just help me pick up my stuff, will you?"

She kneeled down beside me and we began collecting her things, an uninterrupted procession of shoes grazing our fingers as we reached for her mascara, lipstick, nail-polish and hand-mirror. We dusted ourselves off and somehow fell into step as we made our way toward the cluster of fast-food restaurants in East Shibuya.

"You have time for a chat?" the woman asked, swallowing the final T. By some wordless understanding, we headed to the bench in front of the Haagen Dasz parlour and plopped ourselves down on it. For a few moments we sat in silence while we caught our breath.

"I'm bloody pissed, if you want to know the truth," she said suddenly. I mean, Shin — that's my husband — well, he *knows* how much Christmas means to me, but he hasn't made any plans for it. Didn't do anything last year either. You'd think it might occur to him to take the day off, right? But no, never. Just because it means nothing to *him* — "

"I take it he's Japanese?"

"Right. Don't know what ever got into me to marry the bloke." She looked up at me briefly. "Don't mind me, OK? I'm not making any sense, not even to myself. Maybe it's 'cause I'm pregnant."

I couldn't help it — thinking of her unborn child, half east and half west, I felt a pang of envy. I said nothing.

"I waited a week before telling him. I just had this *feeling* he'd say something to piss me off, y'know what I mean? And do you know what he told me when he found out?"

"What?"

She didn't answer right away. I turned to look at her, and found that her face was contorted in an effort to stave off tears.

"It's all right," she said finally. "Forget it."

She got up abruptly, and left me sitting on the bench in a surreal daze, the question she'd left behind her still ringing in my ears.

The following Wednesday evening I told the story to my IHI students, who were just as intrigued as I was.

"Maybe he want she stop working."

"Maybe he want baby to go to Japanese school, and she want move back to Great Britain."

"Maybe they not really married, and he tell her to go get abortion."

It was still the norm, they told me, for women to stop working when they found out they were pregnant. It was also not uncommon for a woman to spend the last few weeks of her pregnancy in her parents' home, the rationale being that she needed more care and attention at this time than her husband was able to provide. The students listened goggle-eyed while I told them about the "fathering" phenomenon — the his-and-hers breathing classes, the husband hollering words of encouragement to his wife during childbirth, aiming a video camera at her parted legs all the while. Mr. Tsurushima, who'd recently announced that his wife was pregnant, looked distinctly alarmed, as though he were worried this sort of thing might catch on in Japan within the next nine months.

That same Friday, I described my encounter with the British woman to my Cross Cultural class at BE, and asked them to write an short essay called "Shin's request." The women started scribbling, Kikuko looking particularly intent as she bent over her notebook. I collected the essays and read hers aloud.

> When Susan came home and told Shin she pregnant, suddenly he realized how big thing he did. When he got married her, he thought: I'm so modern, so trendy, because I got a foreigner woman. However, now he imagined about his little half child, and he got scared. Because really in his heart he wants the Japanese child. So he told Susan, if he is a boy, let's call him Hiroshi. He didn't shout but he spoke very seriously. And now Susan get scared, because he didn't ask her, or discuss about the name, just he told her: let's call him Hiroshi. Suddenly she realized her life with that man, she saw the future in front her eyes, she understood her life in future is "no picnic," in the slang idiom. She understood she make big mistake.

When I finished reading, the other women broke into applause.

"Don't you think it can ever work, between a Japanese man and a Western woman?" I asked Kikuko.

"Maybe a few months, maybe a few years, but not whole life, no. Young Japanese women a little more modern, I think, but Japanese men still not ready for change." The other women nodded sagely.

"Do you know what change my life more than anything else?" she asked in a lighter tone.

"What?"

"*Remocon*," she said, and at my blank look, added, "You know, the box for change TV channels without getting up. Anyway, the reason it change my life — when we first got television, my husband used to ask me I sit near him while he watching. When he want to watch different program, he shout 'channel two!' or 'channel four!', and I must get up and change the channel. *I* was the *remocon*."

We all laughed, and then she turned serious again. "And now I free, I don't have to change the channel for my husband. You probably think is strange — " she turned squarely to face me " — but I sometimes miss the old days. Do you understand what I mean?"

"Yes, I think — "

"No," she said softly. "You can't understand. I'm Japanese, and you're Canadian. I'm old, and you're still young ... "

For a moment I had an image of the gulf between us, deep and wide. And then I thought of the last word she'd spoken, "young," and smiled warmly at her.

5

While chatting with Jeffrey in the teacher's lounge one afternoon, I happened to mention that I'd had a few Hebrew lessons as a child. He almost fell off his chair.

"So *you're* a member of the Tribe?" he asked in disbelief.

"Officially, yes."

"This is awesome," he said. "A fellow Jew. Though I wouldn't have thought it."

"Why not?"

"Oh, I don't know," he said. "You just don't ... " I knew what was coming.

"Don't look Jewish, and don't act Jewish, right?"

"You said it, not me. But to be honest, yes."

"What am I supposed to act like? Stuff cheese blintzes into my mouth all day and say *oy vey* between mouthfuls?"

"Very funny," he said. "Anyway, this is so exciting. Don't get me wrong, I like Japan and everything, but I sometimes feel like the man from planet X. My Japanese friends draw a total blank when it comes to Judaism."

We chatted some more. It turned out he'd set himself the ambitious goal of keeping strictly kosher for the duration of his stay in Tokyo. I hadn't realized how traditional he was, having been misled by his enthusiastic pursuit of Japanese women. But as I listened to him talk now, I realized that these women were just a game for him, that he would no sooner consider marrying outside his own faith than he would stealing jewellery from his mother.

"Hey, why don't we go to the synagogue together?" he suggested. "There's a Chanukah dinner coming up at the JCC, and — "

"Before you get too excited," I said, "I should tell you that the last time I stepped into a synagogue was so long ago I can't even remember."

"Come on," he coaxed, "Aren't you a little curious about the Jewish scene in Tokyo?"

"No, not really."

"The Jewish *singles* scene, perhaps?" he added with a wink.

Why not, I thought. It would be interesting to see how it felt to walk into a synagogue after all these years. Who could tell, it was possible I might have some blinding revelation of faith that would send me crawling back into the fold. I'd read stories like that, about people rediscovering their roots in far-off places. Not likely, I thought, but possible.

On the appointed evening, Jeff and I took the train to the upscale district of Hiro, where the Jewish Community Centre was located. But as soon as we stepped inside, we were no longer in Hiro, no longer in Tokyo, for that matter, but somewhere in Brooklyn or Chicago or Teaneck, New Jersey. It was like a warp in place and time. The hundred-or-so people assembled in the lobby were all shaking hands and saying *shalom* and *hag sameach* and how's the rag business and have you heard about Rhonda and the twins, and I was starting to feel a little dizzy with culture shock. I looked around the room and saw not a trace of Japan. No Chinese characters, no sliding doors, no *sumi-e* paintings on the walls, only men wearing *yarmulkes* and prayer shawls and women in splashy print dresses and snippets of thick New York brogue cutting through the Babel of sound. Jeff, excited as a puppy and clearly in his element, dashed off to talk to a young man he thought he recognized from his Cornell days. For me it was the same as always — a longing to belong mixed with the smug relief of standing apart.

I wandered around the room, eavesdropping on some conversations and joining in others. What struck me again and again is how none of these people, even the ones who'd spent large chunks of their lives in Japan, had allowed the country to seep into their blood. They'd figured out how to make their lives as un-Japanese as possible. Like homing missiles they'd zeroed in on the closest equivalents to the amenities they were used to back in Long Island or Philadelphia: the international grocery store that featured a Kosher section, the lunch counter that served falafel, the pharmacy that stocked Ex-Lax and Tylenol and Crest toothpaste. Their gestures hadn't softened, they still talked and laughed in primary colours. None of this was any cause for shame, of course, but after having spent three months in Japan and absorbed some of its muted tones, coming here felt to me like a regression of sorts. It didn't look like I'd be having any paroxysms of faith after all.

As the room continued to fill I spotted the odd Japanese face, always female, always accompanied by a Jewish man. One such couple especially caught my attention: he, tall and thin and wrapped in his prayer shawl, and she, a tiny thing with a pixie-face and ramrod-straight hair that grazed her waist, looking adoringly into his eyes. Both wore wedding rings. She must have converted to Judaism, I realized, since most practising Jews would insist on it before agreeing to such a marriage. A Japanese Jew seemed an incongruity to me, a clash of ill-matched flavours. I couldn't imagine her dancing the *hora* or chuckling at a Woody Allen movie or teaching her children to stay away from shellfish and pork. Not with any conviction, at any rate. (I was later to learn that Woody Allen movies were extremely popular in Japan, but I suspected this had more to do with the Japanese passion for Americana than with their appreciation of the subtleties of middle-class Jewish neurosis.)

I struck up a conversation with a young Israeli who worked part-time in the synagogue as a garage attendant. He told me they held conversion classes for these women, who on the whole were model students and had no trouble adapting to life as the mistress of a Jewish household. When I expressed surprise at this, he said that it made sense if one considered two things: the casual attitude of most Japanese toward their own religion and the fact that Japanese women were trained from babyhood to adapt and to serve. And that many would do anything to hook up with a Western man, I thought privately. Still, it was hard for me to picture the daily life of such a couple: "Pass the gefilte-fish, *o-negai shimasu.*" I just couldn't see it.

Just as the dinner bell sounded I ran into Jeff and we walked up the stairs to the synagogue, which had been converted to a dining hall for the occasion. He hadn't eaten any meat since Rosh Hashanah in September and was dying to sink his teeth into some dripping flesh. "Two whole pieces!" he exclaimed when his food was served to him, and dove into the chicken with such gusto that I felt sorry for him and gave him a piece from my plate. I, after all, could eat non-kosher chicken or beef or even *butaniku* any day of the week.

Seated to my right was an older man who appeared to have come by himself. He introduced himself, and I learned that he was a visiting engineering professor at Sophia University. He looked to be in his late sixties. "If you want to know the truth," he said, lowering his voice, "I only come here for the food and the company. I'm not much of a Jew, actually." He lowered his voice even further. "A card-carrying atheist, if you really wanna know." I really didn't wanna. People who stripped naked in front of total strangers made me nervous, no matter how sympathetic I was to their views. I reluctantly continued my conversation with the professor, whose questions were getting more and more personal.

When the meal was over he handed me his business card. "Tokyo can be a very lonely place," he said. "Maybe we could go to a movie or something." When he asked for my number, I told him I didn't have a phone and that the communal phone in the gaijin house was being repaired. Undaunted by my transparent excuse, he pointed to the phone number on the card. "Call me when you get lonely," he said suggestively.

This was a first for me — being courted by a senior citizen — and to my shaky, age-obsessed ego, the ultimate insult.

"Do I look old?" I asked Jeff as we made our way back toward the bus stop.

"What's old?" he said. "Don't worry, you don't look a day over fifty."

"I'm serious, Jeff. I mean, do I look middle-aged?"

"Not to me you don't. But why the concern all of a sudden?"

I told him what had happened. "This is the first time I've been asked out by anyone over forty."

"Think of it as a milestone," he said, giving me his trademark wink.

A few weeks later I heard through the grapevine that my erstwhile suitor was known to show up at practically every social gathering in town that included foreigners. He went to choir rehearsals, though he couldn't sing. He went to the international dances, though he couldn't dance. And he went to the monthly meetings of the Tokyo Adventure Club, though one could safely presume he had no interest in rock-climbing. What brought him to all these events, I was told, was his endless appetite for picking up (or trying to pick up) young women. I felt a little better after hearing that.

6

December brought with it an earthquake rumour that swept through the entire gaijin community of Tokyo, and it brought Tyler Bigley to Esther House. In time I would find myself wishing that Tyler had been the rumour and the earthquake a reality. But more on that later.

It started with a short newspaper article and a bulletin on the English language news. There was a geologist, some maverick whose alleged predictions of the 1989 San Francisco earthquake had fallen on deaf ears (why do these clairvoyant types always come out of the woodwork *after* the fact?), and whose seismographic equipment and sixth sense now pointed to the "great likelihood" of an earthquake in Tokyo on December third or fourth. The rumour flew from gaijin to gaijin and by the first of the month panic reigned.

Advice was passed along, getting progressively distorted as in a game of telephone: store up on water, store up on water and juices, keep two weeks' supply of liquids in a safe place away from your home, pack your bags and leave the city. Sylvana, ever the believer in intuitive predictions, was trying to convince her husband to take her to Kyoto during those two days.

Curiously enough, none of my students had heard a thing — apparently the Japanese media hadn't breathed a word on the subject. When, for the sake of argument, I presented them with the evidence, they looked bored and not in the least bit alarmed. "We've lived through many earthquakes and we've lived through many rumours," was how one of them put it to me.

December third came and went, as did the fourth, without incident except for Tyler's appearance on the scene. Sitting at my desk the evening Tokyo was slated to cave in, I heard some crashing noises coming from the room next to mine on the left, which had been vacant since the time I moved in. The next evening, and the next, it was the same. Boom, blam, blong, as if someone was being axe-murdered in there, though I couldn't hear any voices. On the following night the noises started later, after I'd already curled up under the covers. I clambered out of bed and knocked on the door of room six. The door swung open and there stood a short but muscular man, the sort detective writers would call swarthy, all disheveled and sweating like a pig, pantingly introducing himself as Tyler Bigley from Australia. "Sorry about the noise," he said, wiping his forehead. "No worries, it's just me doing my exercises." He pointed to a barbell and some weights in back of him.

A couple of nights later I was compelled to knock again. "No worries, I'll stop if it's bothering you," he said cheerfully. But the following night he was at it again. Pretty soon he began cranking up his stereo as he worked out. "Tyler, it's midnight, could you please do your exercises earlier?" I asked him in exasperation. "Now don't start getting all worked up," he said, cheerfully as ever. "No worries, I'll try to be quieter." And so on.

Coinciding with his arrival, cigarette butts began appearing mysteriously on the communal dirt pathway, directly below the window of his room. This bothered Susan in particular.

"Tyler," I heard her confront him once, "Have you been throwing your cigarette butts out your window?"

"Maybe once or twice," he answered, breaking into a cackle.

"Why don't you just use an ashtray?"

"Well," he said sheepishly, "Sumiko — my girlfriend — has been on my back about smoking, y'know what I mean? She doesn't like the smell, so I've been smoking near my window and blowing the smoke outside. Must've accidentally dropped the butt a couple of times, heh heh. No worries, though, I'll try to be more careful about it."

The butts continued to accumulate below his window, and Susan continued to sweep them up. "Could you *please* use an ashtray?" she would implore him periodically. "No worries, I'll be quitting soon, so there won't be any more butts," he would say and let out his hyena laugh. The day a glowing butt fell on Susan's head, though, she dispensed with her customary tact.

"Tyler," she yelled upward, "will you come down here this minute and throw out your filthy cigarette?" After that he took to having his smokes in the communal bathroom, and his girlfriend was never the wiser.

Just like Tyler, Sumiko became known to me by sound before sight. About a week after Tyler moved in I found myself listening in on a classic pre-feminist-era sex act, from foreplay (thirty seconds) to intercourse (three minutes of metronomic thumping interspersed with an occasional "Tyyyylller ..." drawled out theatrically by a breathy female voice) to afterglow ("That was great, Sumiko, heh heh"). All this came through my useless wall in hi-fi realism.

This sequence, I learned over the ensuing weeks, never deviated by as much as a second or a breath — as if they were rehearsing a movie scene, trying to get it just right under the scrutiny of a fussbudget director. Even the background music, a lusty Kate Bush number, was always the same. "I know they're winding down when the chorus kicks in for the third time," Jessie joked. And when they weren't copulating, they were arguing. "Tyler!" Sumiko would scream. "If you don't change, I can't marry you!" As often as not she would burst into tears, and as often as not their fights would continue through the night while I stuffed my ears with cotton and vainly tried to sleep. "Face it, Sumiko," I heard him tell her once, "You're just not the intellectual type." I hoped, for the sake of Australian women, that *his* type was a dying breed.

Late one evening, while listening in on a particularly vitriolic argument between Tyler and Sumiko, I got a call from Joel. I described my living situation to him with as much humour as I could manage, but felt something weakening inside me.

"Joel," I asked cautiously, "How would you feel if I were to come back?"

"Like, when?"

"Oh, I don't know, maybe in time for the holidays ... "

"Seems like you're not too happy in Japan," he said after a pause.

"It's not that, exactly. I mean, it's been interesting from the start, I've enjoyed learning the language and getting to know the people, but nothing really *spectacular* has happened, and the gaijin house is driving me insane. It's not what I came to Japan for."

"Maybe you haven't been getting enough nookie," he suggested.

"Joel, we don't *all* need it as much as you do."

I was disgusted by my own spinelessness. So many times I'd tried to leave this man, going off to Banff the first time, and when that didn't work, to Los Angeles. If even Japan wasn't far enough, then what was left? Mars, perhaps? At least a year, I'd told myself when planning the trip. Would I end up bailing out once again, adding another half-finished project to my long list?

We left the question hanging. But I didn't seem to be packing my bags, and on Christmas day I was still in Tokyo. The owner of Esther House gave us all the same present, an abridged New Testament translated into Japanese and bound in grey leather. Word had it that he was a devout Christian, and no doubt he selected his gift with the idea that it would allow us to kill two birds with one stone: improve our Japanese and get back onto the right path.

Susan and Mark had a party in their room, a pot-luck dinner with lots of gourmet cheeses and wines and not a Japanese dish in sight. Jessie gave

us a drunken rendition of a song she and Mark had composed, "I've Got
The Gaijin Blues," accompanied by Mark's folksy strumming. When I jok-
ingly said *itadakimasu* before starting on my food, Jessie shot me a baleful
look, as if to say "Just today, let's forget where we are, OK?" The mood of
the party wasn't entirely to my liking but it was better than the alternative,
sitting alone in my room, and better still than the other alternative, slinking
back home to Joel in defeat. I had the sense of having escaped a great danger.

7

With the Japanese new year just around the corner, classrooms — especially those where housewives predominated — started to buzz with talk of the preparations for Shogatsu. Straining to get their words right, students told me of the rigours of preparing the holiday foods collectively known as *o-sechi*. Some of these foods, such as the *mochi* rice-cakes, could be prepared in advance and preserved. Older students waxed sentimental about the good old days before the advent of *mochi*-making machines, when people had to use their own strength to pound the rice. They swore that hand-pounded *mochi* were much tastier than the machine-made variety.

"How you make fruitcake?" or "How you make turkey stuffing?" they would ask me, surprised when I told them that there were as many versions of these recipes as there were cooks. Shogatsu recipes, it seemed, were a lot more standardized. There was some variance from region to region ("Osaka way" or "Tohoku style"), but almost no person-to-person variation within one region.

" ... then you must slice carrots diagonal way," a student would explain to me, "add *shoyu* and *mirin*, three cup and one cup, and finally half cup *wakame*."

"Have you ever tried it with leeks?" I would venture, thinking that leeks might make a tasty addition to the mixture she'd described.

"Oh no," she'd answer soberly. "That is *not* the way to make ... "

Although I wasn't particularly sentimental about this time of year (neither Chanukah nor Christmas having been properly stamped into my psyche), the threat of holiday loneliness loomed large. Through the gaijin grapevine, I heard that an English school called HSC (High Speed Conversation) was holding a week-long intensive course at a resort near Mount Fuji. Figuring that working through the holidays would be the best antidote to self-pity, I offered my teaching services to the school, and was told that I would have to undergo a day of training at HSC's Tokyo headquarters.

Out of the eighteen of us who showed up for the training, fifteen, we were told, would be selected as teachers. Ninety students had registered for the course, and each teacher would be in charge of a group of six. The course's brainchild, Mr. Matsumoto, was a short, thick-set man who continually clasped and wrung his hands in what appeared to be an effort to rid himself of nervous energy. He handed out the course materials, asking us in turn to read aloud from the introductory comments: " ... Japanese are fundamentally serious people. If they spend seven days pleasantly and look happy, they will conclude this is not a good school. On the other hand, if all students look exhausted at the end of each day, they will regard the school as excellent ... Though I am sure you have a good teaching method of your own, in this school you are requested to teach your students under OUR ways instead of YOUR ways. I, as a man in charge of this course, will show you our method ... "

With a pained look on his face, as though in anticipation of our stupidity, Mr. Matsumoto told us about the program's main selling point, a technique called stopwatch drilling. Using a stopwatch, teachers were supposed to ask sixty seconds' worth of rapid-fire questions to each student in their group. The students were required to answer in full sentences that precisely matched — "precisely" was the key, he stressed — the teacher's sequence of words. The object was to get through as many question-answer pairs as possible within the sixty seconds. A week of this sort of drilling, he asserted, would make the students fluent in English.

We spent the morning practicing with each other, I and a British woman called Julie exchanging glances when things got particularly amusing.

"John, did your father buy a boat yesterday afternoon?"

"Yes, Bruce, my father bought a boat yesterday afternoon."

"John, did your brother buy a paperback book at the auction last week?"

"No, Bruce, my brother didn't buy a book at the auction last week."

"John, did your — "

"Stop!" Mr. Matsumoto barked. "Bruce, why didn't you correct John?"

"Correct him?"

"*Yes*, Bruce," he said with a smirk. "John, do *you* know what your mistake was?"

"Uh ... I didn't repeat 'paperback'?"

"That's *right*, John. Did you hear that, Bruce? Exact repetition, that's the key — haven't I told you already? Are you deaf?"

"Thoroughly unpleasant, isn't he?" Julie whispered to me.

Later in the morning, John once again forgot to correct his partner's inaccurate answer. Mr. Matsumoto marched up to him, grabbed his shoulder and shook it back and forth several times. For a split-second John looked confused, then he turned to face Mr. Matsumoto squarely.

"Nobody," he said, his voice shaking, "touches me that way." With that, he got up from his chair and walked out of the room. In quick succession, two other trainees followed suit, the rest of us staring dumbly at their departing backs. "So much for the selection process," somebody muttered.

During the afternoon, we got to practice stopwatch drilling with volunteers whom Mr. Matsumoto had rounded up from among the office workers. He gave them felt pens and nametags, and told them what names they were to use. "Akira, you're Art. Kaoru, you're Karen. Joji, you're George. And you, Kokiji — " he pointed to a man of at least seventy who, his body racked with Parkinsonian tremors, was trying to lower himself onto his chair " — you're Cocks."

I kept my head down, laughter pressing against my ribcage, while Mr. Matsumoto spelled out C-O-C-K-S to Mr. Kokiji. I didn't dare look at Julie, whose turn it now was to do the drilling.

"Karen, did you bake a cake for your mother last week?"

"No, Julie, I didn't bake a cake for my mother last week."

"Cocks, did you watch the news on television last night?"

"Yes, ah, yes, ah, ah ..." Kokiji answered in a gravelly voice, then looked around in all directions, as though trying to figure out where he was.

"Ask the question again," Mr. Matsumoto hissed. Julie looked from him to Kokiji uncertainly. "*Now*."

"Cocks — "

It was too much for me, and I let out a giggle.

Mr. Matsumoto wheeled around to face me. "Is there anything you find amusing?"

"No," I said automatically. "I just — "

"Just pay attention to the training," he snapped, and would no doubt have dismissed me had there been more than fifteen of us left.

Another feature of the program was the sentence contest, in which students had five minutes to write down as many sentences as they could think of on a given topic. "Long sentence not important," Mr. Matsumoto instructed. "Correct sentence important." To demonstrate the technique, he told our group of volunteer students to write on the subject of "my family," set his stopwatch to five minutes, and yelled "Go!" The students began scribbling furiously — all except for Cocks, who was putting all his effort into gripping his pen tightly enough so that it wouldn't slip out of his hand.

When the five minutes were up, the students took turns reading out what they'd written. Some of them had made the mistake of being too ambitious, and had come up with such sentences as "My little sister is very cute, although she has temper and sometimes makes my father angry."

"No points, no points," Mr. Matsumoto would cut in, clearly pleased at the opportunity to show off his English knowledge. "You forgot to write 'a' before 'temper,' so no points."

The winner was George, who was no more proficient in English than any of the others but had obviously caught on to the system. "Very good, George," Mr. Matsumoto beamed. "Twelve points, no mistakes. Will you read it again, so the other students can learn?"

"I have a brother," George began. "I have a sister. My parents live in Kanagawa. My father works hard. My mother likes to cook. My brother likes to drive. My sister likes to read. I like to eat. I work at HSC. I am poor at English. My sister is good at English. My brother has a girlfriend."

The following week we all convened at the HSC resort, which was perched atop a hill overlooking the town of Fujinomiya. Mount Fuji loomed large and majestic some five miles away, sometimes shrouded in mist, sometimes naked in its snow-capped symmetry. The winter air was crisp and bracing, its pine-scented freshness a reminder of everything I was missing by living in a big city.

Teaching the course turned out to be quite painless, since we no longer had Mr. Matsumoto breathing down our necks and flying into a rage every time we slipped up. The students were forbidden to use dictionaries during classes ("Dictionaries are a clutch," Mr. Matsumoto insisted), and we were supposed to reprimand them if we caught them speaking or reading Japanese, which of course we never did. Every day, a student from each class was assigned meal duty, which meant setting the table before each meal and initiating the verbal sequence that had to take place before we could start eating.

"Are we ready?"

"Yes!"

"Then let's begin."

I'd have expected to hear a snicker or two, but the students were surprisingly cooperative, both at meals and during the stopwatch drills. I couldn't help wondering why ninety adults of apparently sound mind would have elected to spend the equivalent of $2,000 for such a tense, highly regimented week. This was Shogatsu, after all, the most important holiday of the year.

Some of the students, it turned out, had been sent by their companies (*"Shiyo ga nai,"* they sighed to me), but many had come of their own accord. It wasn't that they didn't like to celebrate Shogatsu, it was simply that they liked studying English even more. And some of the unmarried students hinted that they had other reasons for enrolling in the course.

By the end of the week, the students were no more fluent in English than they had been on the first day — some, in fact, got lower scores on their proficiency tests on the last day than on the first — and only one couple had formed. But I heard not a word of complaint.

A couple of hours before we were due to return to Tokyo, Mr. Matsumoto had us assemble in the teachers' lounge for a final meeting.

"Last night I gave a questionnaire to all the students," he told us. "They filled it out and gave it back to me this morning." He handed us each a complete set of questionnaires and told us to study them carefully.

"Look carefully at question three, 'What was your favourite part of the course?' and question five, 'Do you plan to take this course again next year?' I think you'll be surprised by the answers."

Sure enough, the majority of students said they intended to return, and almost all of them gave top marks to the stopwatch drills. The drills were the backbone of the course, its gimmick and selling point, so it was understandable that the students should wish to justify their questionably spent money by giving them accolades. It was harder to understand why so many of them planned to take the course again. Could they possibly be unaware that they hadn't made one iota of progress during the week?

"Now we will calculate the percentage," Mr. Matsumoto said. "What is the total number of students?"

"Ninety," we replied in chorus.

"And how many of them said they plan to come back?" A few teachers started counting.

"Fifty-six," someone said after a few moments.

"You see, you see," he said excitedly, "Fifty-six students say they want to come back. Fifty-six students — that's more than sixty percent." He brandished a questionnaire and waved it in the air. "And what did ninety percent of the students say they liked best?"

We stared at him in silence.

"Answer me!" he barked. "I said, what did ninety percent of the students say they liked best?"

"Stopwatch drills."

"Yes, that's right," he said triumphantly. "During the training session, some of you seemed to think the stopwatch drills were not a good method. Well, the students say it's the best part of the course. It proves my point, doesn't it?"

The only thing it proved to me was that in Japan, like anywhere else, there was a sucker born every minute.

I returned to the city later that day, to the same old room, the same old neighbourhood, the same old housemates, students and friends that I'd left a week before. But something had changed. It wasn't that I felt happy or even content — there was still a gaping hole in my life, waiting to be filled by I wasn't quite sure what — but that, inexplicably enough, Tokyo now felt like home.

A CHANGE OF SEASON

"There is no such thing as inner peace. There is only nervousness or death."

Fran Lebowitz

—— 1 ——

It was always a challenge to pump some life into my business classes, whose participants suffered not only from timidity but from exhaustion. I struck gold during my first IHI class after the new year, when I brought up the subject of the American legal system. The normally reserved group of salesmen exploded into sentence fragments.

"I hear story, one man sue his mother!"

"Statistics in newspaper say in America fifteen times as many lawyers, how you say, each capital — "

"Per capita."

" — per capita as in Japan."

"If man in America have accident, he pretend he sick to get the money from insurance company. I hear this story from American teacher. In Canada is same?"

It was rare to see students so excited, and I didn't want to stop the flow by reminding them of verb tenses and articles. They were all very young, too young to look as haggard as they did, and clearly they lacked sleep even more than English conversation skills. But orders were orders, and under their boss's watchful eye they filed meekly into the conference room every Wednesday evening for their two hours of English instruction. Under my tutelage they were expected to lose their peach-fuzz and acquire "international" polish. For my part, I considered the class a success if they managed to stay awake.

"Has an IHI employee ever sued the company?" I asked, knowing full well how unthinkable this was.

"Sue company is like sue father!"

"How about insurance? Have any of you collected insurance money for, say, stolen property or repairs after a car accident?"

"I had small car accident just few months ago," Kawai-san said. He was a soft-spoken man with a passion for moving vehicles, and the envy of the other students because he owned not only a car but a motorboat, which he kept in his parents' garage.

"It was other driver's fault, I think," he went on. "He bump into my car from behind. Both of us go outside and look at damage. I estimate about ¥40,000, so I told him and he pay me right away. No lawyer, no insurance company, just he pay me directly. When I got car fixed it was costing ¥45,000. I had his phone number, so I thought maybe I call him, but then I think, why make so complicated? So I lost ¥5,000, not so terrible."

"Did the other driver actually have insurance?" I asked him.

"Of course. But probably he decide not necessary to use. Japanese system ..." he hesitated. "I think maybe Japanese system is better, not so much people care about exact money, but easier system than in America." He went on to explain that while ordinary Japanese citizens did sometimes use lawyers, they tended to view them as a last rather than a first resort.

The Japanese reluctance to litigate is reflected in the discrepancy between the number of former law students (many) and the number of practicing lawyers (very few). The great majority of law students go on to become salarymen, just like everyone else, or civil servants or entrepreneurs. Lawyers are respected but not much needed in a society where people are more intent on avoiding conflict than on exercising their rights. If a thief is apprehended, he is just as likely to be given a stern lecture as a fine or prison sentence. It is assumed that citizens are cooperative, self-monitoring, repentant if they behave badly.

Even the most devoted Japan-bashers among my compatriots couldn't help being impressed with some of the things that happened — or didn't happen — in Japan. Where else in the world could you leave your bicycle unlocked near the train station, as I did morning after morning, and count on finding it intact when you got back in the evening? Where else, if you found a cheque lying on the street and were kind enough to return it to its owner, would you be given a reward of five to fifteen percent of the cheque's value? (This is still very much a cash society, I learned, and apparently the Japanese haven't yet caught on to the idea that a cheque can be cancelled or destroyed without anybody losing money or face.) And where else could you borrow your train-fare from the man in the police-box, who would ask you to kindly return it the next time you were in the neighbourhood?

Quite understandably, the Japanese were proud of their honesty, of the awesome safety record of even their largest cities. One way of bringing a class discussion to a grinding halt was to ask my students if they'd ever been mugged, robbed or otherwise harassed. Even the oldest students had nothing to contribute to this sort of conversation. Sometimes their refusal to believe there could be a bad apple in their midst was carried to extremes. When I told a group of students about having had my wallet stolen on the Yamanote train, they insisted, after they'd recovered from the shock, that "it had to be a Korean."

Against Arai-san's sing-song protestations, I'd been slowly and steadily whittling down my teaching hours at BE. I was now down to Mondays and Fridays, and felt as though a weight had been lifted from my shoulders, my only regret being that I was no longer teaching Hitomi's Wednesday morning class. Shortly after classes resumed in January she gave me a call.

"We members of class had meeting together," she told me in her earnest way, "and decided we want to have conversation lesson from you. Our idea is you teach us once a month, every time in different house. We are seven members want to study, so we pay you three-thousand yen each person for two-hour lesson. Is OK for you?"

Was it OK for me? Close to $200 for a couple of hours of chatting with my favourite students and a chance to visit their homes? It was absurdly generous, and I told her so. She said she'd discuss the matter with the others and get back to me. A couple of days later she called again.

"We members of class had another meeting," she said, "and we thought, you so honest because not wanting to charge too much money. We very impressed, so we decided to pay you more. We pay ¥3,500 each instead of ¥3,000. Is OK for you?"

Although they took their own honesty for granted, they insisted on rewarding me for mine. There was nothing I could say or do to change their minds, short of refusing to teach them. We held the first class in Hitomi's house, and it was much more like a party than a lesson. For many of the women, it was the first time they would be speaking English in a room that didn't have blackboards and desks, and they were clearly excited about it. They wanted nothing to do with textbooks or grammar drills — only free conversation. And these women liked to talk. Ayumi let off some steam about her workaholic husband, Sachiko complained about her errant teenage son, and the others were eager to commiserate and offer suggestions. The women all agreed that this was a marvellous way to learn English. After the lesson was over, Hitomi served us a festive lunch of sushi, homemade crab-cakes and *gomadofu*, a sesame-based tofu dish I'd once told her I liked. Then it was fruit, chocolates and steaming coffee, and another two hours of gossiping with the ladies that amounted to a Japanese lesson for me. For this I was getting paid?

2

If instrument cannot perform this function correctly, I remembered reading in the instruction manual of my Roland drum machine, *it is probably due to operator idiocy.* This had been my first glimpse into the world of Japanese English, some ten years before I first set foot in Japan. As I made my way through Tokyo it popped up at every turn, this talent for coming up with howlers when ordinary mistakes would have done just as well. It was hard to fathom how such names as Calpis (a carbonated beverage which no self-respecting gaijin would drink after saying the word out loud), Pocky pretzels or Creap coffee whitener could have been dreamed up by Japanese marketing moguls, time and again, without conscious intent. And when I stumbled upon street-signs like "Sauce with the Oyster" — not a restaurant, of course, but a men's clothing store — or "PMS" (short for Pulse Music System), I wondered if the whole Japanese-English phenomenon hadn't been masterminded by some zany gaijin who was having a good laugh at Tokyo's expense.

Chewing gum wrappers promised peace of mind, pretzel boxes a cheerful disposition, and soft-drink cans the fountain of youth, all in earnestly florid English. When I joked about these blurbs to my Japanese friends, they insisted that it wasn't the words but the *feeling* that mattered. It was beside the point, they explained, that "some afternoon, a leaf invited me to a path of the wood" had little to do with vanilla-wafer cookies. But the "feeling" contained in the inscription on a box of Koeda chocolate-sticks eluded me as thoroughly as its madcap humour eluded my friends.

"A lovely and tiny twig, Koeda, is in the forest. The sentimental taste a heroine's treasured chocolates born is cozy for the heroines in the town ... now another heroine comes out. Listen! ... A lovely and Koeda is always the love of the heroine. Now another heroine comes to the forest.

The sentimental taste is cozy for the heroines in the town. Koeda is a tiny twig, Koeda is a heroine's treasured chocolate born in the forest."

In their translations of English into their own language, Japanese copywriters are no less inventive. The early James Bond movie "Dr. No" was apparently introduced to Japanese audiences as *O-ishasan Wa Shiranai*, "The Doctor Doesn't Know," with hardly a viewer knowing the difference. More recently, the movie "Don't Kid Yourself" was released in Japan as *Amaeru-na*, meaning "don't act like a spoiled child." I figured that if subtitles were translated with the same flair, it was hardly surprising that the same movie provoked such different reactions in Japanese and Western audiences.

One phenomenon that older Japanese grumble out but nobody seems able to control is the influx of English words into their language. This is easy enough to understand when there is no exact Japanese equivalent for a word, as with *buzzah* (buzzer), *shiriaru* (cereal) or *torendii* (trendy). But the incorporation of English extends far beyond such functional adaptations. Listening to Miki and her friends talking to each other in Japanese, I was more likely to hear "drive" than *unten*, "nervous" than *kincho*, "gorgeous" than *goka*, even though the Japanese words were perfectly capable of conveying the desired meaning. Here again, they explained to me, it was in their "feeling" that English words had the edge — they were moodier, more evocative than their Japanese counterparts. While *unten* simply meant driving, "drive" called up images of cruising along a winding road of an early Sunday afternoon, on the way to meet a lover under the shade of an acacia tree ...

Not satisfied, apparently, with merely borrowing English words, the Japanese never tire of inventing new ones. It was only when I made her look into her dictionary that Miki acknowledged, with real surprise, that "skinship" and "womanship" were not part of the English language. "But "friendship" real English word, *neh*?" she asked hopefully, disillusioned that expressions she'd assumed to be Western were in fact home-grown. Another Japanese English speaker was disappointed when I drew a blank at his sentence, "you must dress according to TPO." He'd been sure that this acronym for "time, place, occasion" was a standard term in American business circles.

In all likelihood, the linguistic playfulness with which the Japanese use English stems from the nature of their own language. Like the flecks of glass in a kaleidoscope, Chinese characters can be tossed around into an almost limitless number of combinations. This has led to a proliferation of words that are contractions of other, more basic words. For example, the phrase *shobai no saino* (talent for business) can be shortened to *shosai*, made up of the first characters of each constituent word. From *chokusetsu* (direct) and *honyaku* (translation) comes *chokuyaku*, "direct translation." Coined in the same spirit is the word *sekuhara*, hilarious to my Western ears but excusable if one considers that it would take at least ten syllables to articulate "sexual harassment" in Japanese.

Whoever said that the Japanese have an underdeveloped sense of humour was obviously not familiar with some of their more outlandish linguistic concoctions. An amalgamation of *mado* (window), *kiwa* (edge), and *zoku* (tribe), *madogiwazoku*, or "window–edge tribe," refers to employees who, no longer deemed useful at the office, are given a desk near the window, often without a telephone, from which they can stare out at the scenery. Similarly, the word *hotaruzoku*, "firefly tribe," has been created to describe those husbands who are forbidden by their wives to smoke anywhere in the house except on the balcony.

Through trial and a couple of embarrassing errors, I discovered that the tendency to use milder and milder words to avoid offending minority groups (as in "coloured people" to "negroes" to "blacks" to "people of colour") is just as evident in Japanese as it is in English. A good example of this is the evolution of the word "blind." Though it was once correct to refer to blind people as *mekura* (literally "dark-eyed"), the word came to sound harsh and was supplanted by the more neutral *me ga mienai*, meaning "eyes can't see," which gave way to the still less objectionable *me ga fujiyu*, "eyes are unfree." The implication seems to be that what is unfree today might become free in the future — a hopeful sentiment, which unfortunately does little to alter the reality of being unable to see.

Spring was in the air and my students were still tongue-tied. In an effort to elicit some strong opinions, I asked the more advanced classes to write short essays in letters-to-the-editor style. The topic could be anything, I told them, as long as it was a complaint of some kind. We would submit the best letters — pseudonymously, if they wished — to the English *Yomiuri*, the slim daily newspaper where Mark had made his mark. That seemed to inspire them. An engineer with a passion for wine wrote of being ashamed that the Japanese followed trends rather than good taste in their choice of wines. "Why can't we Japanese people enjoy the feeling of quaffing true spirit wine ... " An office worker complained that graffiti were threatening to ruin the face of Tokyo. "On a date with your boyfriend," she wrote, "you are trying to kiss each other with fresh feeling. In such a time, if you find 'fuck you' on wall you are leaning against, what will become to your kiss, easy to be break new loving time?" A student who was engaged to a single mother wrote against the ostracism of single parents in Japan, ending with some thoughts on his own upcoming marriage: "I am looking forward to the happy perplexings with new family, little peaceful everyday but also shocking maybe, and man is not give up easily." He had a glorious future as a copywriter for Koeda, if only he knew it.

My own struggles with the Japanese language were giving me a measure of sympathy for my students' off-the-wall efforts. I would scan through my electronic dictionary and find a dozen Chinese-character words that were all pronounced *kosei*: fairness, offensive, correction, rehabilitation, public welfare, future generation, junior pupils, fixed star, proofreading, constitution, composition, hardness ...

People whistled in admiration when I used the Japanese words for myopia or subconscious, though I tried to explain to them that anybody could look up a complicated word in the dictionary, that the real challenge of Japanese lay in finding the appropriate terms for everyday concepts such as coming, going, taking, getting, and especially giving and receiving. The characteristically Japanese psychology of duty and propriety is reflected in the complexity of the language centred around the exchange of favours. Not only are there different verbs for giving and receiving depending on whether the exchange is with a superior, an equal or an inferior, but the act of giving or receiving something neutral or negative, such as an injection or a parking ticket, requires still another set of verbs. So while I had no trouble describing the symtoms of a chest cold in Japanese, I had to think long and hard before asking Hitomi for a second helping of herbed potatoes. The choices were daunting: May I have some more potatoes? Might I get you to serve me some more potatoes? I am sorry to be causing trouble, but would you allow me to humbly receive some more potatoes?

After five months in Tokyo, I was becoming proficient at figuring out the japanized pronunciations of English words. I could guess, for example, that the words floor, club and drum would turn into *furoah, kurabu* and *doramu*. But the reverse — tracing japanized words back to their source — was still giving me trouble. I often found myself caught in tug-of-war conversations due to my inability to understand what the Japanese presumed was my own language.

"Do you have a hakk'su at home?"

"A what?"

"Hakk'su, hakk'su, you know hakk'su?"

"I'm sorry, I don't understand — "

"You don't know hakk'su?"

"I don't think so, no."

"You never hear about hakk'su machine?"

"Oh, you mean a *fax* machine? No, I don't have one."

On one occasion, my inability to understand a japanized pronunciation prevented what could have been a tense confrontation with a student. It was during the first session of an intensive workshop I'd reluctantly agreed to teach for four Saturdays in February. Sitting in the front row of the classroom was an apple-cheeked woman of about twenty, staring gauzily at me and occasionally breaking out into a beatific half-smile. When it was her turn to introduce herself to the class, she stood up shakily and bowed in several directions. "My name is Mayumi," she said, the smile never leaving her lips, "and I can't see very well — in fact, I'm almost blind. I studied history and German language in university, and my favourite is, ah ... *Hit*torah!"

The other students looked uneasy.

The following lesson she asked me point blank: "You like *Hit*torah?" I still didn't know what she was talking about. Then it came to me: history, German ... Though I was tempted to walk right out of the room, I hung on until the end of the month, watching the other students cringe when Mayumi approached them, barely able to conceal my own distaste for her, the smiling young woman with the dark inner landscape.

— 3 —

Weather-wise, the winter was turning out to be much more pleasant than I'd expected. The bitter cold my students loved to complain about didn't rate a mention by my Canadian standards. The temperature never dropped below freezing, not even in the middle of the night, and the sun shone relentlessly. Joel had faded to a distant memory, Canada was as remote as the North Star, and I was exactly where I wanted to be, under Tokyo's brilliant blue sky, inhaling its crisp mid-winter air.

I'd been accepted into an upper-level Japanese course at the Tsuda language institute. Since half the classes were to be given by teachers-in-training, the six-month program was free of charge. A comparable course taught by full-fledged teachers might have cost about $1,000. In Tokyo, I was beginning to suspect, anything was possible if you kept your ear to the ground. The students hailed from all parts of the world and were a particularly lively group, tossing up jokes and questions irreverently — just the sort of students I would have wanted in my own classes. "Whazzat word mean?" "Is there a Japanese equivalent to 'get off my case'?" "Do native speakers *really* use the causative-passive form?" The trainees, though, were more flustered than pleased by our merriment. Jokes and questions derailed them from their meticulously crafted lesson plans, and they didn't seem too comfortable ad-libbing.

Especially entertaining in our group was Aviva, an Israeli woman who ran a trading business with her husband. I'd sometimes wondered how a Japanese would fare in Israel, a country where yes means yes and no means no, where not speaking your mind means not having a mind. Predictably, Aviva and her husband were having hilarious difficulties in Japan. "When we first got here two years ago," she told us in her halting Japanese, "we ran into one frustration after another. We'd be negotiating with some managers and they'd end the discussion with something like '*chotto muzukashii desu ne* ... ' So my husband and I would tell them, 'You say it's a little difficult, eh? Don't worry, even if it's a little difficult, I'm sure we can reach an agreement.' And they'd look at us as if we came from another planet."

Then there was Joanne, a thirtyish woman from Vancouver who wore body-hugging clothes and long scarves that flapped behind her as she flounced into the classroom, always ten minutes late. Like me, she had a bit of a thing for the local men, but she was much more outspoken about it. "Those sexy eyes," she would sigh to me. "That smoldering look beneath the tight lids and droopy eyelashes ... Can't say I like their hands, though. Too spindly. Give me a large, coarse, tobacco-stained hand and I'm a happy woman." She had only two more months in Japan, and was determined to find herself a boy-toy for the remaining time. "Trouble is," she said, "they're so bloody timid, I feel like shaking them sometimes. I've lived in Spain, Italy, South America, London, you name it, and believe me, this is the only place where I've gotten such a wishy-washy response from the men." She told me about a man she'd met some weeks before, at an international food fair where she had a gig serving drinks. "He wasn't hard to look at, let me tell you. You know the kind I mean? Smooth olive skin, piles of hair on his head, slit-eyes ... He seemed attracted to me, and we exchanged phone numbers. When I didn't hear from him after two weeks, I called and asked him if he wanted to meet me. He said yes, *aitai*. So I said OK, when? He kept repeating *aitai, aitai*, but wouldn't give me a specific date. Too shy, he said. Can you believe it?" But she wasn't about to abandon her quest. "Let's you and me go hunting sometime," she suggested.

Around this time, Esther House was given an extra shot of adrenaline with the arrival of Claire, a manic Frenchwoman who could not get through a complete sentence without breaking into peals of laughter. It was that rippling laugh of hers, even more than her fresh-looking skin and gamine haircut, that made her seem a good decade younger than her forty years. She'd lived in China, Thailand, India, Korea, never staying in any one place long enough to settle in, and unlike many other so-called free spirits, didn't appear to be running away from anything. "If I'm struck by lightning tomorrow, hahahahaha," she told me in her fluent but slightly accented English, "*je m'en fous*, hahaha, it's fine with me. I've had such a *ball* on this planet so far, I can't tell you how much fun it's been, hahahahahahaha." Such relentless good cheer would have been an irritant had it been anything less than authentic.

Somehow she ferreted out my preoccupation with aging, and never missed an opportunity to tease me about it. "Have you found a new wrinkle today?" she would ask, poking me in the ribs. "Did you say you were thirty-three? Or was it thirty-five or thirty-six?"

"Do I *look* thirty-six?" I'd answer dispiritedly, falling right into her trap.

"Hahahahahahaha," she would gurgle. "You're *so* much fun to tease, hahaha. Anyway, what the hell difference does it make, how old you are? And what's the point of crying about it? *Ça sert à rien, n'est-ce-pas?* Hahahahahaha ... "

She'd come to Tokyo with a tall, baby-faced Swede named Fredrik, fifteen years her junior, who didn't seem to do much except look stunning. They'd met in Korea and were just friends, she claimed, though she seemed to stiffen when Jessie paid him more than routine amounts of attention.

Claire was not about to tone down her exuberance in order to harmonize with her milieu. She tore up and down Shin-Midori street on her beat-up bicycle, making vroom-vroom noises as she rode, calling out to me at the top of her lungs when we crossed paths and taking great pleasure if she succeeded in embarrassing me.

"What about When-in-Rome?" I asked her once.

"*Qu'est-ce-que ça veut dire, ça?*"

"You know, adapt to the local culture and all that?"

"*Oui d'accord*, in some countries I've tried to do that, like in Spain or Brazil, and I had a grand time. But this country is so full of dead soldiers — they need to see examples of people who are still *living*, hahahahaha. We're all going to die anyways, might as well celebrate our turn on earth, *n'est-ce-pas?* Hahahahahahahaha ... "

One Sunday Claire knocked on my door and persuaded me to go to the *sento* with her and Jessie. "We're gonna have a *good* time," she piped. I was a little apprehensive, fearing that Claire's "good time" might jeopardize my reputation at the bathhouse, where I was a regular customer. Against my better judgment, I packed up my soap, shampoo and hairbrush and went along with them.

As soon as our clothes were off, Claire ran to the whirlpool and jumped in with a noisy splash. Jessie and I followed her in. Claire submerged herself in the foaming water, making gurgling noises and blowing bubbles, then popped up like a Jack-in-the-box, exploding with laughter. The Japanese bathers sat at the edge of the pool, averting their eyes, frozen with embarrassment. Claire went under again, spewing out a stream of water from her mouth when she resurfaced. She and Jessie started to splash each other, trading insults along with the water.

"You filthy Aussie!"

"I'm from *New Zealand*, you bloody Frenchwoman!"

"Will you kindly tell me what the hell difference there is, hahahahaha?"

Claire looked mischievously in my direction, to see how I was taking it. As she started to throw some water at me, I got out of the whirlpool and headed for the showers. A few minutes later she and Jessie installed themselves under the shower-head next to mine and started to soap each other's backs, heedless of the shocked faces of the nearby women.

"Do you want me to wash your back?" Claire asked me, all innocence and charm.

I cursed myself for not having predicted this turn of events, and was sure that the owner of the *sento* would ask us to never show our faces at his door again and preferably to leave the country.

Later that evening Claire came up to my room, trying hard to look contrite.

"*Alors*, hahaha, are you still mad at me or what?"

"Come on," she poked me in the ribs when I didn't answer, "it's not so serious. I'm sure none of the bathers died from the shock, hahahaha."

It was hard to stay mad at Claire, hard not to admire the strength of the life-force in her.

"Japan means nothing to you," I said finally, "but it means something to me. You have no reason to adapt, but I do."

"If you think you can become one of them, you're fooling yourself *royalement*—"

"There are things I want to learn from them, that's all. Like their patience, and their gentleness. I know you find their reserve intolerable, but —"

"Gentleness? Are you forgetting what these people did in Korea, in Nanking? It wasn't so long ago, you know."

That was a hard one to answer. I was surrounded with politeness and consideration, with warmth and curiosity behind the bashful facades. And yet I'd heard first-hand accounts, from a survivor of the Japanese occupation in China, of soldiers slicing babies' heads off while their mothers looked on. There was simply no way of reconciling such behaviour with what I saw around me every day, a courteous and peace-loving people who could be faulted for many things but not for their lack of kindness. I could only shrug my shoulders and drag out the old cliché that war made swine out of pearls, monsters out of men.

Claire and I shook hands, but I never did go back to the *sento* with her, and eventually she stopped asking. Nor did Joanne and I ever go hunting that winter — I wasn't much of a hunter anyway, and Joanne seemed to have run out of ammunition.

4

If Japan is the cautious introvert of the Orient, its sunny extrovert is most surely Thailand. Thailand is to Japan what a belly laugh is to a titter, a deep kiss to a bow. People who are drawn to Japan (aside from those who are in it only for the money or the easy sexual conquests) tend to be reserved, reflective, intense in a muted sort of way, people who value solitude as much as social intercourse. Thailand's champions, on the other hand, are relaxed and expansive, comfortable in their own skin, and not, as a rule, overly driven. There were quite a number of gaijin of this type living in Tokyo. They thought the Japanese uptight and anal-retentive. As soon as their store of yen was replenished, they would head southwest for a week or two of psychic recuperation. I considered Jessie to be in this category.

"You'll love Thailand," she told me. "The people there are so much more natural than the windup dolls who pass for people here. If you bump into somebody, you bump into them. None of this silly bowing and apologizing and *shitsurei* this and *shitsurei* that. I don't know how I ever get myself on the plane back to Tokyo after I've been down there."

Hot, friendly, noisy, lazy, smelly Thailand. Just out of the Bangkok airport, an ultra-modern affair that did little to prepare one for what the city was really like, I began almost immediately to cough. It was said that the pollution in Bangkok was so bad that if you wore white, it turned grey by the end of the day.

I'd travelled in France, Italy, Switzerland, Spain, Israel, Mexico, and always knew at least a smattering of whatever language was being spoken — enough, at least, to order a meal, book a room or ask the bus driver for directions. But here in Bangkok, speeding along in a cab with a splintered front windshield, I experienced for the first time ever the sensation of being completely unable to communicate. I showed the cab driver the handwritten directions, courtesy of Valerie at Tokyu BE, to the Shanti Lodge in the northern part of the city. He shook his head and started to laugh. "It's on

Samsen Street," I offered. "See here on my map? There it is, Samsen Street."

"Samsen samsen samsen samsen," he repeated.

Some of the street signs were in English as well as in Thai, and I tried to follow our course on the map, though the driver kept making inexplicable turns which caused me to lose my place.

"Go right," I instructed at one intersection. "I think you should go right here."

"Samsen samsen samsen samsen," he muttered while driving in circles.

Forty-five minutes later and no closer to our destination, I was starting to worry that the driver might not be as innocently confused as he appeared. Maybe he was plotting to wear me out and then take me to some deserted road where he would rob me, or worse. With mounting paranoia, I recalled Sylvana's incredulity that I would consider travelling smack in the middle of the Gulf War. Maybe this man was a hired guerilla ...

"Stop the cab and ask someone," I demanded. "Ask, all right? *Ask.*" Finally catching my meaning, he obediently got out of the car and consulted with a pedestrian, while I scolded myself for being so easily spooked.

Some fifteen minutes later I was finally deposited at the Shanti, relieved enough not to care that I would be sleeping on the top bunk of a creaking bed, one of four such beds in the small room.

The next morning I woke up alert and ready for action. I had breakfast in the courtyard restaurant right outside the lodge, pleasantly shaded by lush greenery of all sorts. The young waitress, all smiles and droopy eyes, had to be summoned three times before she agreed to take my order. She leaned her body chummily against my shoulder while I pointed to the "apple fritters" entry on my menu. (Only local exotica for me in Thailand, I decided.)

A thin man with very long and very straight hair was sitting alone at the table next to mine, with a pad of paper and a stack of envelopes in front of him. We made brief eye contact, after which he eased into a slow-motion smile.

"Where are you from?" I asked.

"Holland," he said, the grin never leaving his face. "You know," he drawled out after a long pause, "yesterday I had an almost perfect day."

"How so?"

"Well, I sat here all day long, doing nothing. No sightseeing, no shopping, nothing at all. The only thing I did all day was go to the mailbox to mail a letter. If I hadn't done that, it would have been a truly perfect day."

Such was Bangkok, as far as youngish Western visitors were concerned. Everywhere I turned I saw people who seemed to have been frozen in the late sixties, then thawed out a quarter-century later with their hippie looks and values intact. They were most concentrated on Khao San road, mecca of the tourist on a budget and reputedly one of Bangkok's prime drug-swapping zones. As I walked up the street and back down again, passing young women with flowing madras skirts and peace-sign earrings, gaunt young men with beadwork chokers and watery eyes, half-expecting to bump into Joni Mitchell, I was struck by how completely different a breed of malcontents were attracted to Thailand than to Japan.

For three days I wandered through the city, following the dictates of whim, taking the Chao Phraya express boat instead of the hot, smelly buses whenever I could, stopping at a streetside booth for a plate of richly spiced meat or vegetables whenever I felt hungry. It got so hot, in the middle of each day, that I threw common sense to the winds and allowed the vendors to put ice cubes in the beverages they served me, counting on my generally robust stomach to process the local water without incident.

And so it happened that I found myself somewhere in the Wat Pho maze of chapels, gardens and temples, face to face with two young men wrapped in brilliant orange robes — monks, I presumed. They smiled. I smiled.

"Naw spik English," one of them said.

"Wheh you fom?" said the other.

"Canada. But right now I'm living in Japan."

"Japan? Really? You spik Japaniss?"

At my nod, both monks looked at each other excitedly, and the first one started talking to me in the meticulous Japanese of a diligent but unpracticed student. "The two of us are currently learning Japanese," he stated. "Is it all right if we practice with you?"

For a moment I saw myself from a distance, and with a sense of the improbability of the situation — a large Canadian woman conversing in Japanese with two Thai monks under the scorching Bangkok sun — came that delicious upsurge of feeling, the Travel Orgasm, coursing through me from head to toe and then evaporating just as quickly as the other kind. This moment alone was worth the price of my plane ticket.

With engaging forthrightness, the monks told me that they had no spiritual aspirations whatever, that they were simply taking advantage of a system that provided free room and board to monks-in-training. Their real ambition was to go to Japan, work in an auto factory and make lots of money. I wished them good luck and continued on my way.

After three days of pounding Bangkok's torrid pavements, Ko Samet island seemed the perfect place to spend the rest of my holiday. Just a few miles long and barely a mile wide, the island was said to have the whitest, softest sand in all the country, and to be less built up than its more famous sisters of Phuket and Ko Samui. The truth turned out to be somewhat less idyllic — the mounds of litter and ramshackle lodgings didn't quite add up to untarnished beauty, though the absence of any highrise structures was a welcome rest for my city-sated eyes.

I decided upon the Naga resort as being the best value for the price, the romantic in me drawn to its wooden sleeping huts equipped with nothing but a mattress, mosquito netting and a naked bulb. After prepaying my fee for three nights' accommodation — about twenty dollars — I rushed to my hut, changed into my bathing suit and made a dash for the beach. No sooner had I settled on the hot white sand and closed my eyes than I felt a shadow upon me. "Massage, chipp, massage. You wan massage? Chipp massage? Only sixty baht."

I squinted upwards and saw a sarong-clad woman of about twenty. "Sure," I told her, thinking that for three bucks I was game for anything.

I didn't have a watch, so I couldn't be sure just how long she spent kneading my body, but I knew that the sun was still fairly high in the sky when she started, and had turned red and huge by the time she decided my time was up. She left me in a blissful stupor, already looking forward to repeating the exercise the following day, and the day after that.

Once again I felt a presence hovering over my roasting body.

"Are you stayink et the Naga?" This time it was the voice of a man, a German by the sounds of it.

He sat down beside me and offered me a Thai cigarette, which I accepted in the spirit of what-the-hell-I'm-on-vacation, though it was so strong and bitter that I put it out almost immediately. His name was Max, and he worked for Lufthansa as a flight attendant. He'd been coming to the Naga for years. "This year is kvite different from the other years," he sighed. "I came here to get leyt, and all I've done so far is eat ice cream." I smiled noncommittally — even though he was a German, and so officially out of bounds for me, I allowed myself to entertain the idea that theoretically, at least, anything could happen.

The Naga was owned by a husband-and-wife team, the wife being a sturdy blonde from England who had created a most unusual life for herself: running a bustling resort on a tiny, blazing-hot island off the southeast coast of Thailand, making lots of babies and shouting orders to her Thai husband.

In the evening she held forth to her entourage of fascinated guests.

"How do you do it?" someone asked admiringly. "Live out here, light-years away from anything resembling your own culture? What if your husband were to — "

"If my husband were to die tomorrow ... " she said cheerfully, while the man being discussed stood a few feet away tossing their young daughter in the air. "Will you stop that!" she yelled out at him, then turned back to face us. "Well, I suppose I'd be upset for a while, but then I'd just get on with it."

"You'd probably have men buzzing around you in no time at all," someone offered.

"I don't know about that," she said, "but I do know that I'm too damn busy to brood about things. That's what it's all about, I suppose — for me, anyway. Making your life crazy enough that it just *has* to go on, no matter what. Anyone for a game of trivial pursuit?"

Later, when the crowd had thinned out to just Max, myself and a couple of others, she waxed nostalgic about the year she'd spent in Japan.

"The most erotic experience I ever had," she told us, "was in Tokyo. I was seeing this Japanese man — he was engaged, you see, so it was strictly sex. He got together with his fiancée every Tuesday, with another mistress every Wednesday and with me every Thursday. The schedule never varied. We would meet in this expensive, dimly lit Japanese restaurant and spend the whole evening staring wordlessly at each other across the table. By the time we got to his place we were so charged up that we would rip each other's clothes off, and I mean that quite literally."

We all continued to stare at her. Max gave an audible gulp. I felt a twinge of envy. She glanced over at her husband, as though to remind herself of his existence, then went off to change her youngest son's diapers.

The following morning I strolled down the dirt road leading to the souvenir shops at the near end of the island, in search of postcards. The road sloped upward, and when I got to the top I saw a small black dog about fifty yards ahead, one of the hundreds of sickly-looking dogs strewn like rugs all over the island. Most of them were bone-thin, had half their fur missing, and appeared to spend their days just lying around miserably, probably too hot and weak to do much scavenging. All of a sudden, this particular dog got up, pointed his nose in my direction, and shot toward me with the speed and purpose of a homing missile. Pausing only briefly at my ankle, which he lustily bit into, he continued past me on his helter-skelter way. I looked back at the receding ball of fur, then down at my ankle, which was spurting blood like a busted fire hydrant.

"My foot, my foot, my foot!" I yelled inanely. Attracted by my cries, a child of about five peeked over a fence. Moments later he was at my side.

"My foot, my foot. Look, bleeding," I told him, as though he were capable of understanding my English if I simplified it enough. "Foot, bleeding. See?"

The little boy pointed his index finger toward the road in back of me. I turned around and saw the black dog, who now stood panting at the bottom of the slope.

"Yes, yes," I said excitedly, "that's him. He's the one that bit me."

With stunning composure, the boy took my hand and led me (clearly the real child in this scenario) to the island infirmary, which happened to be just a few paces ahead. He spoke briefly with the doctor on duty, then waved goodbye to me and went on his way.

The doctor led me to a tiny room and motioned for me to lie down on the raised platform against one wall. His movements seemed as unhurried to me as those of the waitresses in Bangkok.

"Can't you put something around it?" I said urgently. "I'm losing all this blood. Can't you — "

The doctor took my foot and inspected it carefully. "Tsk tsk tsk tsk," he said, shaking his head.

"What? What's wrong?"

He continued his leisurely inspection of my wound, eventually covering it with a gauze pad.

"Aren't you even going to clean it?" I asked stupidly. "Would you please tell me what's going on?"

"Tsk tsk tsk tsk," he said again. "Wei here, okay? Wei here."

He disappeared for a few moments, then came back with a stocky young woman dressed in white.

"He no spik English," the woman told me. "He say you have to go back to Bangkok for rabies shot."

"What are you saying? Does that dog have rabies?"

"Lil boy tol us you bit by black dog, rye? Some dog have owner, some no owner. We no sure bout dah one. Anyway, you have to go back to Bangkok."

A choppy boat-ride and several buses later, I arrived in Bangkok and found my way to a hospital. While stuffing my wound with a brownish jelly and wrapping yards and yards of gauze around my ankle, the doctor told me, in broken but understandable English, that I was very lucky indeed, since one of the bites had come within a half-inch of a major artery. He told me not to swim or to put any kind of pressure on my foot.

I went back to Ko Samet that same evening, and spent the rest of the week eating, chatting, writing letters, and fending off Max's advances. On the last evening he upped his pursuit, buying me dinner and drinks, massaging my foot, and blowing smoke from his pungent Thai cigarettes in my face while he complimented me on my "long, sturdy body." Perhaps because I hadn't received that kind of attention in all the months I'd spent in Japan, I found myself thinking that he was quite a charming man, and not half-bad to look at, and I'm on vacation on a different planet, so why *shouldn't* I ...

"My cabin's number twenty-three," he said huskily when I announced I was ready to retire. "What's yours?"

"Nineteen."

"Is it far?"

Reason suddenly prevailed. "Yes, very far," I muttered, then limped away from the dinner table, feeling that I had narrowly escaped a situation I would have deeply regretted. For all my detachment from the religion of my birth, sleeping with a German was where I drew the line. In some tiny way, it seemed, I was a Jew after all.

On the Air India jet the next day, I found myself looking forward to the refined, compulsively ordered world I was returning to, and thought, Thailand is a very nice place to visit, but I'm awfully glad to be living in Tokyo.

5

With her uncanny perceptiveness, Susan smelled out my secret — or maybe I was simply more transparent than I thought.

Eager to put my mended foot to good use, I'd gone on an organized hiking trip to the Tanzawa mountains as soon as the doctor gave me the go-ahead. One of the other hikers in the group, a tall, bony man from Denmark (whom I privately dubbed the Great Dane) had taken an interest in me. He was a perfectly nice fellow — friendly and articulate — but I'd somehow managed to lose the scrap of paper on which I'd written his telephone number.

"I'm not surprised," Susan said when I told her the story. "You're not going to *let* yourself fall in love with a gaijin while you're in Tokyo."

"What makes you say that?" I asked in surprise.

"You *need* a Japanese man," she answered, "in order to get to know Japan the way you want to. And until you find one, nothing else will do the trick.

In half a year, I hadn't even had a nibble. The men I encountered were either too shy, too young or too married. They called me *bijin*, "beautiful woman," but made no moves. I conducted an informal survey with my IHI class one evening, asking them what they thought about men having relationships with older women. While three-quarters of the students approved of the idea in principle, only one person said that he himself would consider doing it. My heart sank as the statistics rolled in.

I'd even gone as far as to ask Hitomi if she "knew anyone," a request that seemed to make her slightly uncomfortable. A few weeks later, eyeing me across her rosewood table with that concerned, maternal look I'd come to know so well, she was finally ready to give me her answer.

"I remember what you asked me," she said earnestly. "I searched and searched in my mind, but couldn't find any man I thought might be suitable for you. I'm sorry."

My inexplicable craving for a Japanese lover reminded me of one of my former neighbours in Toronto, a German woman whose long-standing attraction to India included an attraction to its men. She confessed this to the leader of her religious group and he proclaimed that in order to cure herself, she would have to go to bed with twenty-one Indian men. She never told me if his advice had worked or even if she'd followed it. I wondered if the principle could be applied to Japanese men, though at the rate I was going I would be well into my next incarnation before I got to twenty-one. Besides, it wasn't in men that I was interested, just in one man — the man I was sure lay in wait for me somewhere, preparing himself to enter my life and change it forever.

With March just around the corner, I decided it was time to take matters into my own hands. I placed an ad in the personals section of the Tokyo Journal, describing myself as a tall and attractive woman who was looking for a tall, attractive and educated Japanese man for conversation exchange, friendship or more. When my four-line ad appeared in the journal, surrounded by blurbs like "Attention Japanese women: look no further!" and "Finally! Gaijin-sized condoms," I had no idea what to expect. Would I get two telephone calls? Six? None?

When I got home the evening after the issue came out, there were eleven messages on my answering machine. The next evening, twenty. The evening after that, thirty-five. And so it went every day for a week. The following week I left my phone off the hook.

Who were all these men? Suddenly Tokyo seemed filled with lonely men, hundreds and hundreds of lonely men ... Since I wasn't about to return two-hundred calls, I chose about ten callers on the dubious basis of their tone of voice. The first man I talked to was Oda-san, a dentist. He told me he was tall, attractive and successful, and that he "understood Western women." That should have been a warning.

Well, maybe he's *successful*, I told myself when we met two days later at the Kinokuniya bookstore in Shinjuku. He certainly wasn't tall or attractive. In awkward silence, we made our way to a sober Italian restaurant at the top of the *Keio* tower, the streets of Tokyo receding to a blur of neon and blackness as the glass elevator shuttled us skyward.

No sooner had I opened my menu than Oda-san thrust his index finger on it and started pointing to various entries.

"This is spaghetti, this is a fish dish, this is — "

"I'm not very good at reading katakana yet — " I forced a smile, " — but I'd like to give it a try."

"This is chicken cacciatore, this is sole Florentine, this is — "

"Excuse me, but I'd like to order for myself, if you don't mind."

"Well, I thought you might have trouble reading the menu. This is minestrone — "

"Excuse me, but I can read katakana."

"This is — "

"I *said*," I cut in, my patience exhausted, "I can *read* katakana." Meeting his gaze head-on, I yanked the menu away from his pointed finger and made my selection.

During our meal he talked about how successful, ambitious and driven he was, then segued into a lecture on the psychology of Western women. Women like me, he said (looking very pleased with himself), were self-centred rather than selfish. "But there's nothing wrong with that," he hastened to add. Undaunted by my finger tapping and curt nods, he steered the conversation to what was obviously his favourite topic — teeth. Cavities were preventable, plaque was preventable, dentures were preventable, Japanese materials for fillings and caps were superior to Western ones, and didn't I think Americans made too big a deal about straight teeth? *Is this what I got divorced for*, I thought in a moment of panic. Then, out of spite and boredom, I took to answering his questions ("Did you know that Japanese people eat their rice plain, with no sauce or vegetables mixed in?") with dripping sarcasm ("No, I've never noticed. How interesting."), to which he seemed genuinely oblivious. He suggested drinks after dinner but I mumbled something about expecting a long-distance call and quickly fled.

The next man I agreed to meet was a self-proclaimed poet and playwright, four years younger than I was. Wary after the previous fiasco, I was taken aback by his youthful good looks — poreless skin stretched taut over fine features, spikey haircut and shy smile — and long, graceful body. "Call me Kimura," he said. He refused to tell me his first name, which he claimed was unsuitable for an artist.

We took the subway to Harajuku and spent the afternoon walking — it was a sparkling day — back and forth through the thick crowds of teenagers, clothing racks and crepe vendors on Takeshita street, then up and down Omotesando road with its modish boutiques, Sunday strollers and gaijin street vendors (shifting sand sculptures enclosed in glass seemed to be the rage that day), finally stopping for a bite to eat in a trendy-looking pasta joint.

Kimura-san was one of those Japanese who appeared to have swallowed an English dictionary whole — he probably knew more English words than I did — but became all flustered and tongue-tied when it came to having an actual conversation, so we ended up speaking mostly Japanese. He took care to point out my every mistake, as I'd told him to do, and seemed to take pleasure in coaching me.

Although he thought of himself as a playwright, he paid the bills by teaching Japanese literature in schools. He seemed reluctant to discuss his work.

"Do you enjoy writing plays?" I tried.

"No."

"Then why do you do it?"

"Because I must."

I chuckled. "You must?"

"Yes."

"And why is that?"

"Nobody else is capable of writing the kinds of plays I write." He said this in a flat, emotionless tone, with not a hint of conceit in it. I almost believed him.

He was knowledgeable about Western books and movies, conversation flowed smoothly, and his face lit up when he smiled. *Great,* I thought hopefully, *this guy has potential.* But when I tried to steer the conversation to more personal matters, he stopped smiling.

"So what made you answer my ad?" I finally asked point-blank.

"I wanted to practice my English," he said simply, the words sounding suspiciously like "let's just be friends" to my ears.

Though we saw each other occasionally after that and carried on lengthy phone conversations (which consisted mainly of him recounting some play or foreign film in painstaking detail and me interrupting to ask the meaning of a word), he never made a move. Probably gay, was my sour-grapes conclusion.

Then there was Hideo, a law student at Keio University, friendly enough but so trembly and shy that I was tempted to take his hand and say, "There there, it's OK, I'm not going to bite you." Presumably out of nervousness, he kept pointing to things and naming them in English. "Oistaaah," he said, pointing to the deep-fried oysters on his plate. "Neon right," he said, pointing outside. "Taigaaah," he said, pointing to the gold tiger appliqué on my pullover. Another winner, I thought with a sigh. When we parted at the station, he asked me if I wanted to see him again.

"Well ... " I hesitated.

"Please be honest with me," he said.

"OK, I don't think I want to see you again."

"Is it because I'm not masculine enough?" He had a point there.

"It's not that, but ... "

"Please tell me the truth," he said earnestly. "Then I can change my personality to make it more suitable for women."

My heart went out to him, though not enough to make me want to see him again. Thinking it too cruel to tell him what I really thought, I opted for evasiveness and told him he was fine the way he was, just not my type. We shook hands, and I bounded up the stairs to the Chuo-line train platform three at a time.

The next one, Akira, seemed more promising. He'd spent two years in California where he'd obtained an MBA. He was thirty-three, friendly and casual, tall and long-haired. But over lunch he described himself as lazy and wishy-washy, and surrounded me with clouds of cigarette smoke as we spoke. He was a two-pack-a-day man, which was a bit more than I was willing to tolerate. And he was right about being wishy-washy: he couldn't make up his mind about whether or not to quit his dead-end job, whether or not to get married, whether or not to quit smoking, whether or not to get his grey teeth capped ("I know a good dentist," I was tempted to say). He complained about his boss, who liked to go out to karaoke bars every night. "Do you have to go with him every time?" I asked. "Two out of three times," he said right away. "The rule in Japan is that you can refuse your boss's invitation only one out of three times." This might have been true, but I saw it as further evidence of his lack of spine.

And so it went. I met six men altogether, but except for Kimura-san I found all of them wanting. Though I longed for a Japanese lover, clearly not just any old lover would do.

6

There isn't a Western hotel that I know of where you can unwind as thoroughly as you do in a top-class *ryokan*, such as the one Miki selected for our long weekend in Hakone. It isn't cheap — about $150 a day for each person, including dinner and breakfast — but it's well worth the money. Staying at a good *ryokan* is like crawling back into the womb.

You return to your room after a long soak in the *ryokan's* private hotsprings, and the low table is set for tea: little earthenware cups, a thermos of scalding water, a bowl of tea leaves, glazed rice-crackers, *omanjuu* bean cakes dusted with frosting sugar, one beside each cup. While you're sipping, an attendant taps on the sliding door, you say *hai hai* and she pokes her head inside, just to see how you're doing. Then she retreats, and you're left with the memory of her anxious smile. Later in the evening you're back in the hot pool, watching your breath escape (it's early March and there's a bite in the air), submerged to the tips of your ears. Your body and thoughts turn to jelly under the bleeding sky. Just five minutes after you get back to your room, the attendant knocks on your door again and asks if the esteemed guests might be ready for their supper. She comes back with a tray piled high with wooden boxes, each one guarding a secret: a smoked fish of some kind, a square of green tofu, strips of *konnyaku* jelly, eggplant tempura, squishy things, gelatinous things, crunchy things, unnameable things. By the time she is finished, you have about twelve dishes laid out in front of you. She chats with you for awhile, and her exclamations about your *pera pera* Japanese don't sound phony at all. You start to eat, all tension evaporates, there is only food, sake and laughter, the lingering warmth of the *onsen* vapours in your bones. Build a few *ryokan* in North America and psychiatrists would be out of business.

We were three — Miki, Chiemi and I. Naomi had wanted to come too, but a sick uncle had claimed her conscience at the last minute. With our stomachs distended by too much good food and several cupfuls of sake coursing through our veins, we unrolled our three mattresses on the tatami floor, lined them up so they faced the full-length window at one end of our room and lay down on our backs. We gazed out onto the town of Hakone Yumoto and the blackening sky.

Miki broke the silence. "*Chotto kowain'dakedo* ... It's a little scary, but I've decided that it's time for me to go to Sweden. Ten years of dreaming is long enough, I think."

Chiemi sucked in her breath and I held mine, not sure whether to congratulate her or to try and dissuade her. The Sweden of her imagination had steadied her course for ten years, like a distant star whose light never faltered, and I wasn't sure if the real Sweden could measure up. "I gave my notice at work last week," she was saying, "and for the next few months I'll do nothing but study English. I'll spend the fall in Stockholm, do lots of sketching, learn about designs for the handicapped, then come back to Japan and hopefully put my knowledge to use." She sounded earnest, purposeful — not a peep about Stefan Edberg.

"How would you feel about renting an apartment together?" she asked, rolling over to face me. "I need to learn English in a hurry, and it would also be good for your Japanese, don't you think?"

"It sounds like a great idea," I said immediately, "though I'm not sure it would be fair to you, since we seem to have gotten into the habit of speaking only Japanese to each other."

"I've thought about that," she said. "We'd have to make some rules, like English on Monday, Wednesday and Friday, Japanese on Tuesday, Thursday and Saturday. Or English during the day, Japanese in the evening. I've heard about some people who tried it."

It seemed very Japanese to me — a cozy set of rules, which we could both pretend to follow. "Let's do it," I said. She flashed me her warm Kyushu smile and I showed her how Westerners shook hands on a deal.

"I'm so jealous," Chiemi said suddenly. "I wish I could join you." Chiemi's parents were well off and in perfect health, but they'd told her that if she wasn't going to take care of a husband, she would have to stay home and take care of them. It was a duty she never considered shirking, much as she might wish things were otherwise.

Early the next morning we went down to the *onsen* again, a U-shaped pool nestled in a garden of rocks and trees. It was a *rotemburo*, where mixed-sex and even nude bathing was permitted, though none of us felt brave enough for that. As soon as we stepped inside — two trim Japanese women and an oversized gaijin, all wearing modest one-piece bathing suits — the five or six men at the other end of the pool all stood up together, wrapped their loins in white towels and scurried off to the men's showering area. A few minutes later, we too went to wash ourselves. As we walked away from the springs I saw the men making their way back outside. When Miki and I returned to the pool (Chiemi stayed behind to wash herself some more), the men jumped out, wrapped their shivering abdomens in towels again and hurried back inside. Was I imagining it, that they were avoiding me? They hadn't seemed bothered by any of the other women in the pool. It occurred to me that that they too might have heard about gaijin-sized condoms and were afraid I might be comparing. The spell of the *ryokan* was broken, momentarily. I was back to being an outsider, a big bad gaijin who scared grown men away.

We went back to the showers and watched Chiemi as she soaped, and soaped, and soaped herself — tenderly, as though she were her own child. "I'm *nagaburo*," she told me when she finally came out. "At home I spend at least an hour a day washing myself, sometimes two." It didn't surprise me that the Japanese, with their love of baths, would have a special word for people who took their time in the tub.

On our way back to our room, we ran into the squat, heavy-set owner of the *ryokan*. His face tensed up all of a sudden and he started to mutter something, half to himself and half to me. I couldn't make out what he was saying except for the occasional *damè* and *ikenai*. No good, no good.

"What is it?" I asked Miki in alarm. She listened more closely to his muttering.

"You wearing *yukata* the wrong way," she told me in English, "and he mad about that. He say it's not Japanese-style." He was scowling at my bathrobe. "Don't worry about it," she whispered in Japanese, "You couldn't have known that."

But I did know. I knew that women were supposed to fold the right side over the left side when they put on a kimono or *yukata*, men the opposite. Only at her own funeral was a woman dressed left-over-right. I was normally quite careful about that sort of thing, but it was true, this time I'd done it wrong. The owner continued to glare at my misplaced lapels.

"This is a traditional *ryokan*," he growled, more distinctly this time. "We can't have people running around with their *yukata* on backwards. We're traditional people here, we follow traditions. Mutter mutter mutter, traditional, mutter mutter."

Miki spoke up for me. "But Mr. Owner, she's just a foreigner, she hasn't been in this country for very long — "

"This is a traditional lodging, a traditional town, mutter mutter," he repeated stubbornly.

I was mortified. I'd committed the ultimate social taboo — dressing like a dead woman. Back in our room, Miki tried to calm me down. "Even

a Japanese could have made that mistake," she told me. "It's a dying custom, and many younger people wouldn't know about it." I wasn't convinced. "*He's* the one who should be ashamed," she persisted. "How can he
expect a foreigner to know all the conventions? Besides, you're the guest. It's
his duty to be hospitable."

For the rest of the day, he sulked and muttered and glared at me whenever we crossed paths.

"Should I apologize?" I asked Miki.

"Leave it to me," she said.

When the attendant served us dinner that evening, Miki told her the
story, emphasizing that I was very sorry for what I'd done and that the
owner was being a little unreasonable about the whole thing. "We really like
this *ryokan*," she added diplomatically, "and we're thinking of coming back,
but ... "

"I'll talk to his daughter," the attendant said.

"Why not to the owner himself?" I asked Miki after the woman had
left.

"The difference in status is too great," she told me. "He wouldn't listen
to her."

So Miki told the attendant and the attendant told the daughter and the
daughter told the father and the conflict was resolved, Japanese style, without anybody losing face. The next morning the owner was all smiles. Before
we left he asked Miki to take a picture of him and me together, with the
ryokan signpost in the background. I knew it was just good business on his
part, rather than genuine contrition, but I posed for the picture and
promised to send him a copy.

7

True to her word, Miki gave me a call a few days after we returned from Hakone. "You want look for apartment this Saturday?" she asked. I dreaded the procedure. Throughout the fall and winter, I'd occasionally walked into one of the dozens of rental agencies around the train station. There would be a sign on the window advertising a single-room apartment, five minutes' walk from the station, only ¥60,000 per month. Perfect, I'd think. I'd step in, ask the agent about it in my best Japanese, and invariably the place would be unavailable. I would look into his eyes and he into mine, and we'd both know that the other knew. But there was nowhere to lodge a complaint, no civil-rights agency that dealt with this sort of thing.

I had come close, once in late November. The agent had called the landlord who'd said that yes, he was willing to rent to gaijin. We went to see the place — tiny, of course, but on a hill and looking out onto the winding canal that ran through the northern part of Nishiogi. My new home, I thought as I stepped across the six-mat room and out to the balcony. No sooner had the agent and I walked down the hill than we heard galloping footsteps behind us. It was the owner, with a pained expression on his face. "Sorry, I changed my mind. I can't do it." Then he wheeled around and scampered back up the hill. As we walked in silence, the agent gave me a sidelong glance and saw the tears of frustration in my eyes. I wanted badly to get out of Esther House and into a Japanese environment, and at that point it seemed hopeless.

Around that time, Tom Koyama was in town for a Yamaha directors' meeting, and we met for lunch. He listened patiently while I ranted and raved about the bigotry of his people. "I see your point," he said finally, "but I don't think it's actual prejudice on their part. The Japanese are very shy, as you know. They want peace and quiet in their lives. They're deathly afraid of having to speak English, and they're worried that a foreign tenant might not understand their instructions about sorting garbage or paying bills, or that he'd get an important notice in the mail and be unable to read it. Then they'd have to confront him if a problem arose, and you know how the Japanese feel about confrontation. So they tell the agents to refuse foreigners."

"But I speak the language," I said. "I always address the agents in Japanese, so that couldn't be the problem."

But then I recalled how shopkeepers would sometimes cross their hands and tell me they couldn't speak English even after I'd made my request to them in Japanese. I concluded that Tom was probably right.

When it came to Asian foreigners, though, I knew that the landlords' attitude was more a result of prejudice than of shyness. Wary landlords circulated stories of holes gouged in walls, grease splattered on ceilings, cigarette burns in tatami mats, prayers wailed out at the crack of dawn (with the devotees presumably facing Mecca), and a variety of other frightening smells and sounds emanating from windows.

There was a vicious circle at work: young Japanese, even those with a limited education, were turning their noses at employment they considered to be "3-K": *kiken, kitsui, kitanai* (dangerous, strenuous, dirty). The solution for manufacturing companies was to import labourers from all over Asia. Indians, Thais and Filipinos were more than willing to take on menial jobs at rock-bottom wages. To make it possible for them to send money home, they had to crowd together in tiny apartments — as many as half a dozen in a six-tatami room. Naturally, no owner would consider renting a small room to six people, so what often happened was that after one person secured an apartment, his friends "came to visit" for an indefinite period of time. Understandably enough, owners got angry, and nasty rumours proliferated.

Miki was unwilling to consider living anywhere except Nishiogi, and that was fine with me — I'd grown attached to the place myself. I was hoping that the agents' anxieties would be dispelled when Miki and I showed up together.

"You're not sisters, right?" asked the first agent we went to see. Was she blind, or what?

"*Hai*," Miki said politely, confusing me for a split second until I remembered that in Japanese you answered "yes" to indicate agreement. "Well, we have a policy ... We only show apartments to individuals or married couples. The only way we'd consider female roommates is if they're sisters."

"May I ask why?" This was from me, of course. The Western Why.

"Owners feel that friends are not as stable as siblings. They might have an argument, one of them might leave, and then who pays the rent?"

"But we're *good* friends," I tried. "We both have steady jobs, and we can give you references." Miki let me gush on, knowing it was useless. Smiles were exchanged and then we left.

Considering the ratio of people to space in Tokyo, refusing to rent to roommates seemed a little crazy to me, but most of the agencies we went to had a similar policy.

Over the course of the day, we did come across a few agents who were willing to show us apartments. I let Miki do the talking, contenting myself with a few *ah so desuka's*. On one occasion we were led to a tenth-floor apartment which had two decent-sized bedrooms with good views, although the kitchen was the size of a cat's forehead. I nodded eagerly to Miki. Then, with mounting astonishment, I listened as she embarked on a lengthy negotiation with the agent, which went something like this:

Miki: This place has a nice atmosphere, a nice feeling.

Agent: It does, doesn't it? But it's a bit small.

Miki: Yes, a bit small, but it's new, it's clean, and ...

Agent: It's a little old, but it's not too far from the station.

Miki: Yes, the location is very convenient. And the view is lovely.

Agent: It gets a little noisy during rush hour, but ...

Miki: The landlord may not be willing to rent to us. If we were siblings ...

Agent: It's true, he may not. I'll give him a call and see what he says.

Miki: Thank you. It's a great apartment, although the kitchen is a little on the small side.

Agent: Yes, that's too bad, isn't it? Otherwise it's a nice place, good price too.

Miki: Yes, good price, considering how close it is to the station. It's too bad about the kitchen ...

Agent: Yes, it's a shame.

Miki: Yes. Well, if you might be so kind as to show us another place ...

Agent: You're right, the kitchen is just a little ... Well, it's not a good time of year to go apartment hunting ...

Miki: Yes, it's a bad time of year. Maybe you won't have anything else to show us.

Agent: Maybe not ... I'll give you a call if I do.

Miki: Thank you so much for going to the trouble of showing us this apartment. It has a really nice atmosphere ...

What was all *that* about, I asked Miki when we left. It turned out that she'd never had any intention of taking the place, after seeing the kitchen. But she didn't want to make the agent feel as though we'd wasted her time, especially since she was one of the few who hadn't turned us away. The agent, in turn, didn't want to appear too boastful about "her" apartment, so she took pains to belittle it. The scene made me think of two large animals — elk, perhaps — face to face and both in a submissive stance, each wishing to reassure the other that it posed no threat.

Then there were the flirts.

"*Me ga oookiiiii*," said a rental agent with permed hair, peering into my eyes.

I didn't answer. I'd never thought of my eyes as being particularly biiiiig. "How old are you?" His eyes travelled down my face and stopped a few inches lower. He seemed to like things that came in pairs.

"We're looking for an apartment — " Miki tried.

"How tall are you?"

"One hundred and seventy-eight centimetres."

"You're very pretty," he told me. "Are you married?"

"Do you have an apartment available for two people?" Miki asked.

"Your eyes are biiiiig," he repeated.

"And yours are smaaalllll," I said with a sudden burst of chutzpah, looking right into his peepers.

Miki nudged me. "Let's get out of here."

We continued our search over the next few weeks, though with less and less heart. Even when an agent was willing to show us a place, it turned out we could never agree. Miki wanted to be close to the train station, even if the apartment was on a noisy street. I wanted quiet and a nice view. Miki was concerned with the size of the kitchen, I with the size of the bedrooms. We seemed to have reached an impasse.

At the end of March, I was no closer to my dream of living among Japanese, still sandwiched between Ariel's machine-gun laughter and Tyler's heavy breathing.

A FLASH IN THE PAN

"To feed the remainder of life with one hour
of fulness and freedom!
With one brief hour of madness and joy."

Walt Whitman

—— 1 ——

There they were. I had read about them, imagined them, heard stories about them, seen pictures of them, waited eagerly for their arrival, and there they were, finally, everything I had hoped for and more. Knowing that they would be gone in a week made them seem almost painfully beautiful. Trembling pinkly against the sky, they gave messages of hope and sorrow both. People said they were larger in Kyushu, more brightly coloured in Yamanaka, but as far as I was concerned there could be none more beautiful than the Tokyo blossoms, milky white with just a breath of pink. They made you want to give up all worldly ambitions and spend the rest of your days penning *haiku*. Or blowing into a *shakuhachi*. It was not only what they looked like, but what they stood for. More than any other icon, the cherry blossoms said Japan.

The Japanese are meticulous in charting the progress of their blossoms, from *ichibuzaki*, meaning ten-percent blooming, through *gobuzaki*, half-blooming, and culminating in *mankai* — full bloom. In Tokyo, *mankai* comes in early April and can be as short as a day. All it takes is a gust of wind and the petals start dropping off, all too willingly, and pretty soon the earth beneath the trees is smeared with pinky whiteness and the trees are shivering again, though a close look reveals the tiny buds of leaves, protruding like tongue-tips.

Mankai fell on a Wednesday that spring. I had some free time in the afternoon and headed over to Inokashira park, famous for its blossoms and just a short walk from Kichijoji station, the one after Nishiogi. If you walked south to the Marui department store and rounded the corner, you suddenly found yourself on a narrow, carless road called Nanabaishi-dori, Bridge of Seven Fountains Street, flanked by coffee shops and craft stores and spilling right into the park — sensuous, romantic Inokashira park with its glassy pond, arched wooden bridge, lovers pushing yellow pedal-boats, smell of fresh earth, and cherry trees. It was the perfect refuge when Tokyo got too manic and huge.

Inokashira means fountainhead, and legend has it that the Shogun Tokugawa Ieyasu used the mineral water from the park's fountains to make tea when he came to Edo, as Tokyo was then called, for a holiday of falcon hunting. The last of the park's seven fountains ran dry about thirty years ago and the water is now pumped up from the earth.

During the cherry blossom season, it is common practice for one or two members of a company department to take the afternoon off and reserve a space under a cherry tree. The rest of the group shows up at the end of the work-day, food and sake is passed around, and the annual ritual of blossom viewing (which in most cases means drinking to oblivion) begins. As I strolled through the park I saw several such squatters, dozing under cherry trees on the giant plastic sheets they'd laid out for their blossom-viewing parties. It was a cool day, with just a touch of wind and a white, sunless sky. I stopped near the bridge and let the whiteness engulf me — the white reflections of the blossoms in the pond, the white petals against the white sky, almost invisible except for their fluttering movements. The sky's pale colouring was even more fitting, somehow, than would have been a brilliant blue. As I gazed out into the whiteness, I wondered how many more *mankai* I was to experience in Tokyo.

A few days later I was sipping coffee in the Donatello's ice-cream parlour at the end of Nanaibashi-dori, sitting at the counter that looked out onto the park. The wind had done its work — there were more petals on the ground than on the trees. I put down the book I was reading and stared outside for a few moments.

Sitting to my right was a man poring over a Japan Times. I let my eyes travel to his face, along the pinched nose and up to the hair, thick and wavy and just beginning to grey at the temples.

"Do you often read English newspapers?" I asked him. He turned toward me and took a few seconds before answering, as if to bring me into focus. His eyes were not quite black, not quite as narrow as most Japanese eyes.

"I try to read one article every week," he said, "but I'm not always successful."

His accent was quite good, for a Japanese, and I asked him if he was taking English lessons. He said that he didn't have time for lessons, but he listened to F.E.N. Radio every day.

"Is that how you learned your English pronunciation?"

"Yup."

"Do you live in Kichijoji?" I asked.

"Nope," he said. "I live in the next town."

"Mitaka?"

"Yup."

"Do you come here often?"

"Nope."

He told me he was a doctor and didn't usually have free time during the day, but he'd just made a house-call in the area and was stopping for a short break before going back to his office.

"What kind of doctor?"

"A saahjon."

Somehow it pleased me that he mispronounced the word, that he sounded Japanese after all. I asked him if he'd spent any time abroad. He told me he'd been to China for a few weeks to study acupuncture and to Florida for a two-week holiday, but that was all.

"Is that where you learned to say yup and nope?"

"Yup," he said, a flicker of amusement in his eyes as they met mine.

"You haven't told me your name," I said.

"I'm sorry, I forgot to introduce myself. My name is Takeyama. Tetsuya Takeyama."

What a beautiful name, I thought. Takeyama. *Bamboo Mountain.* I told him my name and he gave me a Western-style handshake. Not quite firm enough, I thought, but that was only to be expected.

"Mr. Takeyama," I said on impulse, thinking *please don't be married and make me look like an idiot,* "would you like to get together again sometime?"

He looked surprised but pleased. He stood up from his chair, fished into his coat pocket and produced a business card.

"Here is my work number," he said. "I don't have a phone in my apartment but you can always reach me at work. The best time to call is either in the early afternoon or after eight in the evening." I gave him my number and told him where I lived, thinking there was an appealing symmetry in our having met in Kichijoji, right between his town and mine.

He was tall, I noticed, a good two inches taller than me. And there was something graceful in his movements as he slung his jacket over his shoulder and walked out the door.

2

Stay in Tokyo long enough and you start to make *konè*, the Japanese English word for "connections." One thing leads to another and pretty soon you're turning down most of the work you're offered, accepting only the juiciest plums. A plum came my way in mid-April via the Tsuda institute, where I was studying Japanese. One of my teachers told me of a job opening at a junior high school in northwest Tokyo. The carrot was the $70-per-hour salary and the compact schedule — four consecutive classes on Fridays. She gave me the name of the person to contact and said that she'd put in a good word for me.

The interview was conducted entirely in Japanese. I dug deep into my brain in order to remember and use the proper respectful forms. Mr. Nakajima, the head English teacher, took a liking to me and hired me on the spot. I'd be teaching first-year students, he said, seventh graders. Three of my classes would be students who'd never had an English lesson in their lives, and one was a so-called returnee group — kids who'd spent time abroad and had to be reintegrated into the Japanese school system. At the end of the interview he told me that I was forbidden, absolutely forbidden to use Japanese in my classes. This took me aback — I'd assumed that he'd interviewed me in Japanese to find out if I spoke it well enough to communicate with the beginner students.

"But how will I explain things to students who don't speak a word of English?" I asked. I understood the value of language immersion but this seemed a little exaggerated.

"Use your imagination," he said. "Gesticulate, draw pictures on the board, do whatever it takes, but no Japanese. Under no circumstances should you let the students know that you speak it. If they address you in Japanese, give them a blank look and pretend you don't understand. If the students find out they can communicate with you in Japanese, they'll come to rely on it." It seemed to me that he would have been better off hiring a teacher who didn't speak Japanese at all rather than one who had to double as an actress.

Mr. Nakajima said he would sit in on my classes the first day, so I asked him if I could start off with an English song and have him translate as we went along. It was a song I'd composed several years earlier for my Yamaha students. He was enthusiastic about the idea and even procured a little electric keyboard, so I could accompany myself while singing.

> There's a worm, there's a big worm, in my apple now
> There's a worm, fuzzy wuzzy worm, in my apple now
> But I think I will eat it anyhow.
>
> Hello worm, hello big worm, why don't you say hi
> Yummy worm, yummy yummy worm, you taste good as pie
> Maybe I will try crunching on a fly.

The students bubbled with delight as Mr. Nakajima translated, just as my five-year olds had done at Yamaha. "Eewwwww," they said, and "How disgusting!" By the end of the first day, I hadn't taught them very much but had them firmly on my side.

The teachers all ate lunch together in a small, stark-looking cafeteria. At lunch I was asked to give an introduction speech, as was the custom in Japan whenever a new employee joined an organization. "Seven months have elapsed since I first set foot in Japan," I started, trying to impress them with my formal Japanese. The teachers whistled in admiration. Ashamed of my boast, I lost my concentration. "I hope to make a bombitrution, uh, contribution ... "

We sat down at the table, the other teachers untying the cloth napkins that secured their lunchboxes and I unwrapping my egg sandwich. They asked me about life in Canada and taught me Japanese proverbs. "*Tsutta sakana ni wa esa o yaranai,*" Mr. Nakajima volunteered with a chuckle. It translated to "You don't have to give bait to a fish after catching it," and was most commonly used in the sense that a man didn't have to be attentive to a woman after securing her as a wife. Mr. Nakajima assured me that the proverb was equally applicable to women and their husbands.

There was a problem — a rather serious one — with the returnee group. Two of the eleven students spoke no English. One had lived in France, the other in Germany. The other nine students were fluent. I discussed the situation with Mr. Nakajima and he said that the definition of a returnee was a student who was reentering Japanese society after living abroad. By that definition, the German girl and the French boy were returnees and should therefore learn English with the returnee group.

"But this is a language class," I said, unconvinced by his reasoning. "How am I supposed to plan a lesson for nine fluent students and two who can't speak the language at all?"

"Use your imagination," he said. "Have the students teach each other, give the beginners separate work sheets, vary the level of difficulty, and remember — don't ever use Japanese as a shortcut."

When I asked Mr. Nakajima why he couldn't switch the two beginners to one of the regular English classes, he explained that the returnees' English period didn't coincide with any of the other ones. This made little sense to me, as it would have been a simple matter to juggle the schedules around. But I say nothing.

My task was made easier by the fact that the returnees were a delightful group — eager, rambunctious and saucy — but the problem still remained. In spite of my best efforts to "use my imagination," the German girl and the French boy quickly lost interest and spent most of their time with their heads plopped on their desks, while the other kids joked and laughed and learned words like "ambivalent," "conspicuous" and "indecisive."

The regular classes were equally frustrating. "Repeat this word," I would ask the students, getting forty blank stares in response.

"Repeat, repeat," I repeated. Still there was no reaction.

"Say it again — a-gain," I tried. "Say it after me."

I pointed to myself and then to the class. "Me, you. *I* say, then *you* say. Understand?" By this time they were breaking up into giggles.

"*Kurikaesu-tte?*" one boy ventured. Yes, yes, I thought with relief. But then I remembered that I was under orders to play dumb. I couldn't nod my understanding to him without revealing that I knew *kurikaesu* meant "repeat." So I put on my best poker-face and continued the charade.

All the loud talking and frantic gesticulations had me dog-tired by the end of each class. It seemed to me that it would have been a lot simpler for me to say a word or two in Japanese and get on with the lesson, rather than spend half the class playing guessing games.

And yet my students were learning, if less efficiently than they might have been. We played "What's your favourite?" to practice words like book, food, drink, sport, rock star. "What's your favourite subject in school?" I asked one morning, after having explained the different subjects by way of elaborate illustrations on the blackboard, as though we were playing Pictionary. They all answered at once. "History!" "Science!" "English!"

"Does anybody like mathematics?" I asked. Several boys raised their hands but not one girl. Unable to resist the opportunity to slip some feminism into my lesson, I asked the question again, raising my own hand as I spoke:

"Does anybody like mathematics? Any boys, any girls?"

This time, along with the boys' arms, one girl's arm went up timidly. It was one of the very few instances, in all my hours of teaching in Japan, that I felt I'd accomplished something useful — not by imposing math on the girls but by giving one of them the courage to admit that she liked it.

At the end of the spring semester Mr. Nakajima called me into his office. "The students tell me they are enjoying your class," he said, "and they seem to be learning something too. You have been successful so far and I'd like to thank you. But there's a problem — several students suspect that you speak Japanese."

"But I never said a word — "

"You probably reacted when you heard them speaking Japanese. Maybe you nodded your head, raised your eyebrows or otherwise showed you understood. Please be more careful in the future. The students won't learn any English if they know you speak their language."

Why tamper with success, I thought to myself, but knew better than to argue.

3

"A home of one's own." The phrase did not have the mystical overtones for me that it seemed to have for just about everybody else I knew. The way I saw it, owning a home was not only a mundane achievement — millions, after all, had succeeded in doing it — but an insidious drain on one's personal freedom. Under the rule of the despotic Mortgage, homeowners devoted long hours to jobs that gave them little pleasure, and spent what little time they had left plugging leaks or fixing patios, whistling cheerlessly as they went along. I could never figure out what all the fuss was about.

The Japanese, I was disappointed to learn, were just as captivated by the American dream as the Americans, even if they were far less likely to achieve it. They had even coined a word, *maihomismu,* for their collective passion. Couples who couldn't afford standard mortgage payments were sometimes granted mortgages of forty, fifty or sixty years, with the understanding that the payment schedule would eventually be passed down to their children, in whose *maihomismu* the parents and loan officers presumably had absolute confidence.

For all my rejection of the dream, I was itching to put down some sorts of roots in Tokyo. Esther House, with its assortment of cackles and yelling matches and beds creaking under the strain of hurried sex, was becoming more and more of a prison to me. It was a travesty of the kind of life I had come here to live. I knew I had to get out, but I seemed to have exhausted the possibilities. Miki and I had tacitly reached the conclusion that we were not destined to be roommates, and my solo efforts were getting me nowhere. "We'll call you if anything comes up," the rental agents always told me, but nothing ever did.

On Susan's advice, I placed a want ad for a Japanese roommate in the Japan Times. I got a single response, from a twenty-nine-year-old office worker called Eiko, and we arranged to meet at the McDonald's in West Ikebukuro. She was a tiny woman, pleasant enough if a bit gushing (I *love*

English, I *love* foreigners, I *love* Western food), and she seemed excited about the idea of having a gaijin roommate. We flip-flopped from English to Japanese without any awkwardness, and by the time our McChicken burgers were eaten, concluded that we were compatible enough to be roommates. But the next time we talked on the phone she was much more reserved.

"Is anything wrong?" I asked her.

"Well," she said, "there's one small request I have, if we're going to live together. You might think it's strange, but I'd like us to have separate phone lines."

That meant an extra ¥80,000 deposit. "Why? Do you get a lot of phone calls?"

"It's not that." She paused to clear her throat. "You see, my mother — well, ah, she's just not used to foreigners. She doesn't know how to behave with them. It's not that she has anything *against* you, or against me living with you. But I know she'd get flustered if she called me and, ah, you answered instead. I hope you understand ... "

"And what if she wants to visit you?" I asked. "Would you expect me to keep out of sight?"

"No problem," she said right away. "I would arrange for her to come when I knew you weren't going to be in. I hope you understand ... "

I did and I didn't. In the end I decided that I simply wasn't comfortable with such an arrangement. We said our goodbyes, and once again I cursed the housing gods for having placed a red herring in my path.

And then, just a few days later, I got a phone message from a rental agent whom I'd gone to see several weeks before. "Come and see me right away," was all she said. I rushed over to the agency, a cluttered four-mat room that called itself Happiness Real Estate, and listened to the details. A one-room apartment had become available, less than five minutes' walk from the Nishiogi train station. The building was four years old, clean and quiet, and each apartment had its own heater and air-conditioner. Best of all, the owners had no objections to renting to foreigners. "They even rented to a black man once," the agent offered.

The two-storey whitewashed building was on a narrow side-street off Shin Midori. Its name of Cosmos (in keeping with the celestial theme that prevailed among Tokyo's newer apartment buildings) was especially charming in a building of such modest proportions. The agent introduced me to the landlords, a retired couple with kindly faces, and we all shuffled up the iron staircase leading to the vacant unit. I fell in love with it immediately — with its translucent sliding doors, its tiny verandah overlooking treetops and rooftops, even its *wan-unitto* bathroom which was not much larger than a telephone booth. "I'll take it," I said right away, hardly giving a thought to the fact that I would soon be parting with the equivalent of about $4,000, two-thirds of it non-refundable, for the privilege of moving in.

There was one problem. Before I could sign the lease, I needed to find a guarantor. By law, every tenant had to get either an employer, a relative or a personal friend to sign a document stating that they would take financial responsibility for the tenant in case the rent didn't get paid. The guarantor had to file the document in the town hall as well as cosign the lease. It was quite a big favour to ask of a friend, but I had no choice. I decided on Teruko, since she lived close by and time was of the essence — if the lease wasn't signed within forty-eight hours, the landlords had the right to rent to someone else.

A lot had changed since I'd last seen Teruko. Her husband had finally expired, which theoretically made her a wealthy woman. But things had gotten complicated. While we sat on the floor drinking tea from her grease-rimmed cups, she filled me in on the details.

"My husband's family — I've never gotten along with them, as I think I may have told you — anyway, they're trying to cheat me out of my inheritance. Apparently my husband told them that he and I had been living apart for the past several years. Not in different houses, but *apart*, if you know what I mean. Not sleeping together. Now they're claiming that I wasn't really a wife to him, so why should I inherit all his houses and restaurants? They've all ganged up against me, and I have to hire all these *royaahs* ... " Even though she was speaking Japanese, she said "inheritance" and "lawyer" in English, as she always did when talking to me.

This wasn't a good time to bring up the guarantor question, but I had to move fast. I cautiously put the request to her, stressing that it was only a formality since I would never actually need her financial assistance.

"But what if you get sick?" she asked. "What if you're in an accident? As your guarantor I'd be responsible, you know. The landlords would call me. I still don't know how much money I'll get from my husband's inheritance — maybe nothing, if my greedy in-laws get their way."

I told her that if anything happened to me, she could call my brother in Canada and he'd take care of it.

"And how do I know that the owners of your building are honest people?" she pressed. "Maybe there are hidden costs you don't know about. Maybe the previous tenants left the place in bad condition, and the landlord will try to get you to pay for the repairs."

"Look, if you don't want — "

"I'm not joking," she said. "A friend of mine once rented an apartment to some Asians — Indians, I think it was. After they left, she went to inspect the apartment and found stains on the tatami mats." She leaned forward a little. "*O-shikko* stains."

"Pee stains?" I let out a chuckle. "How could your friend know they were pee stains?"

"I don't know, I guess she smelled them."

"Didn't the apartment have a bathroom?"

"Yes, of course."

"Why on earth would the tenants have peed on the tatami mats when they had a perfectly good bathroom to use?"

"I don't know why," she said stubbornly, "but they did."

"You and your prejudices," I muttered, hoping she knew I wasn't really offended.

"But it's true," she said. "Come on, let's go to the town hall."

The following day, kneeling solemnly at the low table in the landlords' dining room, I signed the rental agreement with its elegant columns of scripted Kanji. Teruko countersigned it, Mr. Kijima stamped it with his florid red seal, then we all exchanged bows. I had no idea what I had signed, of course, but it was the prettiest lease I had ever seen.

The previous tenant had left behind his refrigerator, hot plate, washing machine and vacuum cleaner. Mrs. Kijima told me that he was moving to the North of Japan, and didn't want the hassle of bringing the stuff with him or disposing of it. I could hardly believe my good fortune — as a rule, refrigerators, stoves and even light fixtures came and went with each tenant. The day I moved in, Mr. Kijima appeared at my doorstep hugging a bright red television. "This is for you," he said. "Hirose-san gave it to us when he left, but we already have two ... "

Cosmos was a four-and-a-half minute walk from the train station, so I knew that if I left my apartment at nine thirty-five with the second hand on the six, I'd have my foot on the platform just as the nine forty train was rolling in. Every time. And when I got back home in the evenings, the first thing I did was take a chair out to the verandah, where I would sit for a few minutes with the warmth of the May sunset on my face. *This* was my world now, this jigsaw of whitewashed walls, bent *obaasan* wheeling pushcarts, futon mattresses drying on laundry rods, trimmed hedges with dark waxy leaves and everything in miniature. I felt absurdly proud of my new surroundings, as though I'd created them myself.

A home, I discovered, was not so much a property as a state of mind.

4

Half an hour after I got my phone reconnected at Cosmos, the tall doctor called.

"I wanna see you again," he said simply.

"Sure," I told him, a bit shaken by the timing of his phone call. I waited for him to say something else, then finally added, "So when would you like to meet?"

"I can't make it on weeknights," he said in Japanese. "As you know, I work until eight or nine in the evening. And this Friday I have to do some hospital work. On Saturday — well, I usually work on Saturdays, but about once a month I play golf. Three friends and I made reservations for this Saturday a long time in advance, so I can't really cancel. And in the evening I have a wedding, one of my friends from junior high. And Sunday I have to go to a medical meeting."

"Well," I laughed, "How about next week, or next month?"

He seemed not to have heard this. "I really wanna see you," he said again.

I'd noticed this before about him, the way he had of deflecting questions without seeming to notice he was doing it. When we finally settled on Sunday evening, I had the impression that he'd stretched himself in some way, that he'd bent some rule he normally lived by.

I arrived at Kichijoji station at the appointed time, and immediately spotted his large head poking through the cluster of other heads as he stood leaning against the square pillar where we'd arranged to meet. I had almost cancelled our date, since I was still recovering from a bout of high fever I'd woken up with the previous morning. While tossing around in my bed that day, I'd chanced to thumb through my Lonely Planet guide to Thailand. *Ko Samet Island still has a bit of malaria*, I read, and suddenly remembered the hand-painted sign I'd seen at the entrance to the island, warning visitors about malarial mosquitos. I also recalled that I'd been erratic in my use of insect repellent, and that my sleeping net had let through a mouse, so would have posed no problem for an insect. Convinced that I'd contacted the disease, I'd dragged myself to the Nishiogi hospital and requested to be tested. But by Sunday evening the fever was almost gone.

Tetsu's eyes were on me as I approached him, and in some transient, almost imperceptible shift in his features — nothing approaching an actual smile — I read his pleasure at seeing me again. With hardly a word between us, we set out through Kichijoji's twilight landscape, around corners and down alleyways, into a tall building and up an elevator, Tetsu leading the way without telling me where we were headed, which turned out to be a movie theatre.

The featured movie was Awakenings, transmuted to *Renaado no asa* (Leonard's Morning) in Japanese. Throughout the screening, Tetsu kept his legs spread apart — they were too long to fit comfortably in front of him — so that they came within a hair's breadth of touching mine but never actually did. (Whoever said that first dates give many clues about the tenor of a relationship knew exactly what they were talking about.) I was thinking *it's perverse, but I like the way you led me here mutely, as though I were a small child, or a cow.*

And then, just as inexplicably as I'd found myself in the movie theatre with this odd, bulky, quiet doctor, I found myself walking at his side along the narrow pathways of Inokashira park, whose cherry blossoms were now fat with leaves that hadn't quite darkened to summer colouring. And he was asking me questions, lots of questions.

"Who's your favourite actor?"

I was never good at this kind of thing. I tended to have favourite roles rather than actors, books rather than authors, songs rather than singers.

"Mine's Robert De Niro," he said when I didn't answer.

"Why is that?"

"Just because." After a pause, he added, "Because his acting doesn't *show.* You think 'what an interesting character' rather than 'what great acting.' "

The protruding root of a cherry tree caused me to stumble, and for a split second I felt his hand on my shoulder.

"How about singer?"

"What?"

"Singer? Who's your favourite singer?"

"What is this," I laughed, "an interview?"

"Mine's John Lennon."

"And why is that?" I was secretly disappointed, having always thought John Lennon's songwriting talent overrated.

"You probably won't believe me," he said intently, "but I think his music has a *message*."

I believe you, I heard myself thinking. *Whatever you're about to say, I believe you.*

"Other songwriters develop a style," he continued, "and then stick to it for the rest of their careers. But John Lennon's music was always changing — every album was different, right up to his death."

He went on to tell me that he (like a million other Japanese adolescents) had been a big Beatles fan as a teenager. He'd formed a basement rock band with some friends, and they'd concentrated exclusively on Beatles songs. They'd even got a spot on television once, with him singing the lead. I had trouble picturing this man, with his restrained and soft-spoken manner, belting out Hard Day's Night into a microphone, and felt my interest quicken at the incongruity.

We continued to walk back and forth through the crisscrossing paths, then made our way to the arched wooden bridge that stretched over the pond, where we paused to take in the cherry trees bowed over the water and the yellow pedal-boats gliding through it. I was telling him about my fever the previous day and how I was afraid I'd contacted malaria.

"If it were malaria," he said right away, "your temperature would have reached forty degrees. And it would have lasted a lot longer than a day."

"How long?"

"Oh, maybe three or four days."

A couple and their young son walked by us, all three wearing red bandannas around their necks. The son pointed his finger at me, and in his clear child's voice, said "Look, a foreigner."

Because I was pleased that Tetsu hadn't reacted to this, and because I was also pleased at his knowledge of things, esoteric things like the symptoms of malaria, I forgave him when, a little further along, he reverted to the naïve questioning ("Is the word 'fuck' used a lot in everyday life, like it is in in the movies?" or "Have you ever smoked marijuana?") that so typefied Japanese men of about his age.

Back at Kichijoji station, I asked him if he'd ever been to Nishiogi.

"Yes, a couple of times."

"And? How did you like it?"

"I was very moved."

I forgave him his handshake (this time because of my pleasure at his poker-faced humour, and because he was a Japanese and couldn't possibly know the proper way to shake hands), which was somewhere between a weak grip and a caress.

The following morning I got up early for a job interview at an international patent office called Shiga. I'd spotted their employment ad in the Japan Times — Wanted: part-time English editor with a science background and some knowledge of Japanese — the previous Monday, and called immediately to schedule the interview. Mr. Murasaki, the editorial director, led me to a small cubicle where we chatted amiably for about fifteen minutes. Although I'd never worked as an editor, hadn't opened a science book in twelve years, and knew nothing at all about patent law, he told me that my background was exactly what they were looking for (this sort of thing could only happen in Japan) and offered me the job on the spot. I walked out of the office in a daze, hardly daring to believe that I was finally, finally off the English-teaching treadmill, that I would be working in a bona fide Japanese office, clocking in and out with a punchcard like a real Tokyoite.

That same evening there was a message from Tetsu on my answering machine. "You looked very good tonight, buddy." I smiled at his choice of words, knowing that he was simply trying to sound colloquial. I had the sense, all of a sudden, of being pulled into Japan's belly, of becoming intertwined with the lives of its people in a way that would change us all.

Things were definitely starting to happen in Tokyo.

5

I was on my way home from Kichijoji, trying with difficulty to balance a broadloom carpet on my shoulders, when I practically bumped into Ariel, studiously coiffed and clothed to give the illusion of careless chic, and a new spring in his stride which I took to be a reflection of his recent good fortune: after months of moping in his room and eating *ramen* noodles, he had finally managed to secure the lead part in a real-estate commercial and a role as a gaijin buffoon in an educational video for foreign students.

"Did you *hear*?" he asked me without preamble.

"Hear what?"

"I guess you didn't. Tyler's dead."

I almost let go of the carpet. It was true I'd hated his guts, but dead? "How did it happen?" I asked. "I thought he was supposed to be in Thailand."

"He was. It's quite a bizarre story, actually, and the Thai authorities haven't released all the information, but it seems he was murdered by some peasants."

I tried to imagine it, Tyler the musclebound stud stabbed to death by a band of hill tribesmen. The story that Ariel had been able to piece together was indeed bizarre. It appeared that Tyler had gone to Thailand to avenge the murder of his brother, who'd been travelling through the northern part of the country some two years earlier. While visiting Chiang Mai he'd inadvertently stepped into a drug-related gang fight and gotten himself killed in one of those oops, sorry, got the wrong guy scenarios. Tyler was hoping to catch the killers, presumably to exchange an eye for an eye, but was beaten to the finish line.

Listening to this far-flung tale, I suddenly recalled the fragments of a conversation between Tyler and Sumiko I'd overheard a few nights before moving out of Esther House. There had been crying, yelling, pleading, whispering, something about getting a girl into trouble, about losing a job, the threat of a lawsuit. I'd heard him tell her that he would be going to Thailand for a couple of weeks, to take a break from the nightmare his life had become. Tyler had seemed at the end of his rope, and I wondered now if he had really been murdered or if he might have died by his own hand instead, OD'd on some cheap Thai barbiturate he'd taken to forget his troubles.

Whatever the cause, Tyler's death affected me more than I would have expected. He was a lousy housemate, but he was no stranger. After five months of sharing a rickety wall that let me in on his darkest secrets, we'd developed an odd sort of intimacy. I knew the sound of his cackle, his curses and his pillow talk. He was thirty-one to my own thirty-four, too close for comfort.

Ariel and I chatted some more. I asked him about the modelling business in Tokyo. "It's sleazy," he said. "You're told that your net profit will be a certain figure, and after doing the gig you find out it's your gross."

"Are you sure it's not a language problem?"

"Positive. I ask them, is this the net figure? And they nod their heads vigorously and say *netto, netto*. Then they keep half of it. The last time this happened, they told me it was because my work had been unsatisfactory, although they'd seemed pleased enough during the shooting session. The worst part is that there's nothing you can do about it, nowhere you can go to file a complaint. It's the Dark Ages here, is what it is."

After dropping off the carpet at my apartment I headed straight to Esther House, hoping to find Susan or Mark there and hear their version of the story. I found Mark in his room, tinkering with his most recent acquisition, a Nikon. He couldn't tell me much more than Ariel had, except that he'd talked briefly to Sumiko, who was shaken up but in control. She'd packed up Tyler's things and left a presumably well-intentioned note to Warren, the manager of Esther House and himself an Aussie: " ... Tyler was very clean, not like most foreigners ... " It was hard to say whether she'd been spared a worse or a better fate than the one she was likely to have now, getting hot baths ready for her Mitsubishi man and shuttling the kiddies to cram school.

"To change the subject," Mark asked me, "Are you making any headway in your, uh, search?"

"Too early to tell," I said. A picture flashed briefly in my mind, the tall, bulky doctor with the gentle eyes.

Mark cleared his throat and shifted in his chair. "Do you mind if I tell you a bit about mine?"

"*Your* search?" I wasn't sure I wanted to hear this. Mark and Susan were a couple to whom no harm was supposed to befall, who laughed at each other's jokes and gave each other daily back rubs. I'd always assumed they were one of those charmed pairs whose bond was immune to time, place and circumstance.

"I don't quite know how to put it," he said, "but it looks like I've caught the bug." I had no idea what he was talking about.

"Damn it," he said angrily, "I can't tell you how disgusted I am with myself. It goes against everything I've ever said about Japan, against everything I believe in. I wouldn't have thought it could happen to me." He gave me a sheepish look.

"Sorry, Mark, but I'm not following you."

"It seems," he said wryly, as though he were talking about someone else, "that I'm longing for the affections of a Japanese woman."

It was as though he had kicked me in the gut. Wasn't this the man who looked upon Japan as a giant cockroach, who went on and on about its moral bankruptcy, self-serving politics, sexism, ageism, materialism, slave mentality, antiquated thinking, and more to the point, its airhead women? If Mark could fall, then nobody was immune. Let this be a warning to all you Western women who come to Japan with your spouse, partner or boyfriend: you're taking your relationship into your own hands.

"What about Susan?" I asked when I found my voice again. "How does she feel about all this?"

"She's very hurt, naturally. She's thinking of getting her own apartment, though we haven't decided anything definite yet."

"But you and Susan seemed so ... like you brought out the best in each other, somehow. Are you telling me you're ready to throw all that away?"

"I don't know," he said, studying his fingertips. "I just don't know. There's this friend of ours, Michiko, and all I can think of day and night is what a treat it would be to have a woman like her. I know it sounds ridiculous, it goes against all my feminist ideals, or what I *thought* were my feminist ideals, but there's something about the softness of these women, the way they focus on their men, that makes me crave the experience firsthand. I've become obsessed with the idea, and I hate myself for it." He had a pleading look on his face, as though he were hoping I'd give him my blessing. It occurred to me that all his talk about the "infantilism" of Japanese women might have been an attempt to deny, even to himself, that he was gradually falling under their spell.

I wondered if Corey might have had anything to do with it. Corey — aptly described by Susan as having his brain between his legs — had moved into Esther House a few weeks earlier. He was a sunny blond boy from California, engaged to be married to a sunny blond girl from California with whom he exchanged I-miss-you's over the trans-Pacific telephone lines.

He'd come to Japan with a surfboard and an indefatigable libido. "I'm not married ... yet," was how he justified the sexual conquests he was accumulating in Tokyo. I knew that he'd taken Mark with him on some of his expeditions to the Roppongi disco-jungle, and maybe it had been too much for Mark, seeing all those nubile young things buzzing like flies around his friend while he looked on from the sidelines.

There could be no doubt about it — somebody had put a curse on Esther House. Not only was Tyler dead, Mark and Susan's marriage on the rocks, but I also learned that Fredrik had become an object of rivalry between Jessie and Claire, who were no longer on speaking terms. Clearly, I'd left Esther House just in time.

6

In a twist on the standard desert-island question, I asked my IHI students which one they would choose if they were marooned on a desert island for a year: books or television. Without exception, they chose television. "We'd want to keep up with what was going on in the outside world," they all agreed. I challenged them with a Zen aphorism — "when the work goes well, the outside world doesn't matter" — but it didn't strike a chord. They wanted news, information, action, and television was how they wanted to get it. Not without pride, they told me that according to national surveys, the Japanese watched every bit as much television as did Americans. This meant that in relation to their free time, they actually watched more.

During my seven months at Esther House, I had enjoyed the simplicity of a TV-less existence. Nevertheless, I was eager to start watching my little red television, both for the language practice and because I thought it would give me another angle on the culture.

A staple of Japanese programming is the *dorama* (from the English word drama), roughly equivalent to the American soap opera but generally lasting only one season rather than decades. This type of program suited me just fine, since my Japanese wasn't quite up to documentary or even sitcom fare. There were a couple of hour-long *dorama* to choose from every weekday evening, along with a fifteen-minute quickie at eight o'clock in the morning.

I went through a few weeks of trial and error before settling on a favourite, *Wataru Seken Wa Oni Bakari*. The title sounded rather ominous in translation — "In the world that we pass through, there are nothing but ogres" — and nobody was able to tell me exactly what it was supposed to mean. The plot revolved around an aging couple and their five daughters, each with her own family or budding relationship. The central theme was the modern woman's dilemma of work versus family. "My life is my work!" the prettiest daughter cried to an unwanted pursuer. Later, when she met the man of her dreams (at the office), she declared that she was ready to quit working and get married. Another daughter was being torn between her desire to work outside her home and her devotion to her son. The I-can-have-it-all option didn't seem to exist for these women, as it did for women in American soapland.

There were other differences, little details that gave away how distinct the sex-roles were in Japanese society, even in this doramatized world that struggled valiantly to present a contemporary face. When the *Wataru* patriarch came home after a long day behind the counter of his noodle-shop, his two live-in daughters would rush to his side, remove his slippers, fan his face and place a bowl of hot soup in front of him. At his cry of "*biru, biru!*", his wife would scurry to the refrigerator and fetch him a bottle. And at the end of each day, he would sink into the bath prepared by his wife while she darted around the bedroom, laying out futons and nightclothes for the two of them.

Subservient though they were, these women seemed more believable than the American soap heroine who, in the midst of raising her four children, decides she needs some personal fulfillment, dusts off her old Brownie camera and in a wink of an eye, becomes an acclaimed portrait photographer.

Another mainstay of Japanese television is the game-show. Here too, I discovered, there was a departure from the American format: instead of being rewarded for getting the right answers, contestants got punished for getting the wrong ones. Buckets of water rained down upon their heads, or cream-pies or sacks of flour, while the studio audience gave shrieks of delight.

Gaijin made occasional appearances on these shows, where they were known as *tarento*. Their talent was the ability to speak Japanese fluently, which was unusual enough to enthrall audiences and to make me green with envy. I also caught glimpses of foreigners on the soaps and detective shows. They would dance across the screen with toothy grins and spastic arm movements. TV gaijin were always manic — a somber or pensive gaijin was as improbable as a bashful car salesman.

Gaijin, of course, dominated the freak shows. There was the Belgian woman with the world's largest breasts (which the host stretched out on a plank and measured with due solemnity), the American man with the world's longest tongue ("good for kissing," he said), the man with the most body hair, and a woman of average height who was married to a midget ("He's a *great* husband," she enthused).

Immediately following *Wataru Seken* on Thursday nights was the Yamada Kuniko variety show. Miss Yamada was a national celebrity, a writer of romance novels as well as a TV personality. Her manner could be described as butch and was certainly as un-Japanese as I'd ever seen in a female. She had a throaty voice and raunchy laugh, and was built like a fire-hydrant. It was easy to see how she was a source of fascination to more run-of-the-mill Japanese women.

The show began with some bantering between Miss Yamada and three other panelists. Following this, a "situation video" was aired. The situation was usually based on some romantic conflict (for example: woman is neglected by lover, woman finds new lover and starts seeing him on the side, liaison is discovered by first lover) and the four panelists had to decide whether the protagonist was *yuuzai* (guilty) or *muzai* (innocent). While they deliberated, the studio audience cheered them on and waved placards. *Yuuuuzai! Muzaaaai! Yuuuuzai! Muzaaaai!* It took several minutes before a verdict was reached and several more minutes before the audience calmed down.

The scene then shifted to the interior of an opulent house, where one of the panelists was shown interviewing a member of the resident family, usually the *o-josan*. An *o-josan* can be defined as a young woman who makes a career out of being rich. There is a lively interest in *o-josan* in Japan, reminiscent of Britain's fascination with its aristocracy. (How do you know if you're an *o-josan*? If you refuse at least two dates out of three, if you get chilled easily and if you've skied in the Alps — the Swiss ones, of course.)

"What's that in your back yard?" the interviewer would ask the bored young lady, pointing to the window.

"A swimming pool."

"A *swimming pool.*" The interviewer would turn toward the TV camera. "What do you think of that, folks?"

I had to remind myself, while rolling my eyes, that a private swimming pool was probably as uncommon in Japan as a backyard golf course in America.

The commercials were as entertaining as the programs. If it was a shampoo that was being advertised, a fresh-faced young woman would appear on the screen, sigh a few moody words (it's Spring ... I feel so light, so restless ...) and depart with a wink. If it was a car, or a washing machine, a fresh-faced young woman would appear on the screen, sigh a few moody words and depart with a wink. To my Western eyes, these commercials seemed naïve, amateurish. I was surprised to learn that two of my SECOM students who'd lived in America felt exactly the same way about American TV commercials. "American commercials are so literal," they told me. "Some silly man in a lab-coat comes on-screen and rattles off statistics about comparison tests or scientific data. There is no mood created, no atmosphere. It's hard to understand how such ads can be effective."

One evening, I came upon an animation program in the popular mystery-drama genre. The language was easy to follow, so I watched on.

A young housewife, alarmed that her husband never came home until midnight, called up a detective agency to help her find out how he was spending the evening hours. The agency put two of their detectives on the case, a man and a woman. After a few days of sleuthing, the detectives informed the housewife that her husband could be found every evening at the same *izakaya*, eating dinner and chatting with his buddies. The wife was mystified. "Why wouldn't he want to eat my home-cooked food?" she asked the detectives, shedding grape-sized cartoon tears.

The detectives had a brief tête-à-tête, then asked the woman if she wouldn't mind letting them watch her cook. "Of course," she said, and showed them to her kitchen. "This is my pasta-making machine, and this is my blender. I use it for making pesto and Hollandaise sauce. This is my kneading machine, which I use for making onion loaf and croissants." She pointed to her collection of international cookbooks. "Before I got married," she said, sniffling all the while, "I took courses in French cooking, Italian cooking and Viennese pastry-making, just so I could make my husband happy. A lot of good it's done me. Waaaaah!"

The detectives had another tête-à-tête, then announced to the woman that they'd solved the case.

"Really?" she cried. "What do you mean?"

"Your husband has been going to that *izakaya* because they serve traditional Japanese dishes there. He doesn't like all this rich, fancy food you've been preparing. He wants the kind of food his mother used to make — simple, nutritious, traditional Japanese meals."

The woman looked dubious. "Come on," the female detective told her, "I'll help you. Let's make some hot soup with *ramen* noodles and vegetables. It's almost midnight now, and your husband's due home any minute."

In a flash, the two women chopped up the ingredients and put them into a bowl of steaming broth, just as the front door swung open. In walked the grumpy husband, heading straight for the stairs to his bedroom. All of a sudden he stopped in his tracks, wiggled his nose and broke into a smile.

"*Ramen* soup?" he said in astonishment. "Could it be?"

His wife led him to the dining room, where the soup was waiting for him. He dove in with great gusto, making loud slurping noises. He was then shown walking up the stairs to his room again, but this time not alone. The housewife glanced back at the detectives and gave them a wink.

Was it because I was an outsider, I wondered, that I could do little except roll my eyes at this message to Japanese women? I pondered the impossibility of looking objectively upon another culture, the tendency to see good cheer and naïveté where complexities lay.

7

We met in East Shinjuku under the giant, madly flickering screen of the Alta building (where at least five hundred other people were waiting for their other half), and bushwacked through the neon frenzy until we reached the restaurant he'd picked out for us, a cozy Korean Barbecue joint with do-it-yourself grills embedded in the tables. I let him order for me, finding it oddly pleasant to sit back and have him take responsibility for what I would be putting into my mouth. A few minutes later our waitress returned with mountains of beef tongue, calf liver, chicken and pork cut into paper-thin strips, along with a platter of raw vegetables and two mugs of beer.

"Am I doing it right?" I asked Tetsu as I placed a strip of tongue on the hot grill and sprinkled *shoyu* sauce over it. I'd only been to this type of place once before, with a pack of gaijin, so I wasn't sure if I was cooking, seasoning or handling the meat properly. I didn't want him to think me uncivilized.

"What's right?" he shrugged.

"I don't know," I answered. "You tell me."

"Just eat it the way you want," he said, sounding a little annoyed.

"Tetsu-san," I pretended to be hurt, "don't get angry with me."

"I'm *never* gonna get angry with you," he said immediately, with an intensity that seemed to come from nowhere. "Never." The "gonna" stuck in my ear, incongruous in his carefully enunciated speech.

"What I meant was," he continued in Japanese, "there are so many *rules* in our lives. The proper way to eat, to greet people, to dress, to bow. I have no choice when I'm working, but in my private time I try to forget about all these rules." He looked at me intently. "Let's forget about rules when we're together, OK?"

"No rules," I concurred. "Fine with me." What I was thinking was: It's been four dates and he still hasn't touched me. Is there a rule about *that*, and is he following or breaking it?

He was in a drinking mood tonight. After a couple of beers he switched over to whiskey, in keeping with the classic drinking pattern of Japanese businessmen, downing the glasses so quickly that I hadn't a hope of keeping pace. He went back into his interviewing mode: Who was my favourite author? What was my favourite book? Favourite sport? Favourite flavour of ice cream? His own favourite author, it turned out, was Yukio Mishima. That would make him either a romantic, a reactionary or a homosexual. I hoped it was the first.

"What's the most dangerous thing you've ever done?"

I thought for a moment. "Probably skydiving. How about you?"

"See that scar on my forehead? I was playing catch with a friend in high school, not with a ball but with a javelin ... "

One inch lower and it would have been his eye. "You were very lucky," I told him.

"Yup," he said. "Just like tonight."

"Like what?" I wasn't sure I'd heard properly.

"Just like tonight," he said again, causing me to flush with surprise, though I couldn't be sure if his words came from the heart or from the eighty-proof. His face said little — you had to look at the eyes to know if he was smiling or serious, earnest or joking.

For the first time since we'd met, he seemed willing to talk about his family. His parents, it turned out, were just recently divorced although they'd been living apart for years. He had an older sister who was married to an American and a younger brother who still lived with his mother in Chiba Prefecture. His father, also a doctor, had been rather difficult to live with, a choleric type with the nasty habit of throwing dishes around when his temper got the better of him. "At you?" I asked incredulously. "Nope," he said, "at my mother." It was an *o-miai* marriage, he told me, and there had never been much fondness or even civility between them. "But I have a lot of respect for my father," he said. "Aside from his violent temper, which I can't comprehend at all, he was — still is — a good man and a very good doctor." It surprised me that the composed, soft-spoken Tetsu would have emerged from such a harsh childhood landscape.

There were nine empty glasses on our table, most of them his. He studied the glasses for a while.

"Let's not have any more to drink," he said suddenly.

"Why not?"

"It's good luck if we stop now."

"Good luck?"

"You've had three drinks and I've had six. That's nine altogether. My favourite numbers," he said earnestly, "are three, six and nine."

I'm falling for this man, I thought to myself, charmed that a grown man would state his favourite numbers with such conviction, like a child.

Though he seemed to be loosening up a little, on the subject of his work he remained the artful dodger. Whenever I brought it up he would deflect my question with a joke or a shrug. How was your day at the office? Long. What kinds of patients do you see? Many. What do you enjoy the most about your work? The end of the day. I didn't press the issue, sensing that he wanted to keep his work and his time with me in separate compartments. I knew, from hints dropped by students over the months, that the Honey-you'll-never-guess-what-happened-at-the-office style of dinner-table conversation was not too common in Japanese households, even assuming that the husband made it home for dinner. Many of my students had only the sketchiest idea of what their husbands did after they stepped into their suits.

We'd fallen into a pattern of switching from one language to the other in our conversations — four or five sentences in English, the next few in Japanese. Though he wasn't exactly fluent, he spoke English with care and took great pains to sound authentic, with his yups and nopes and pop-song contractions like "lemme" or "wanna," which I supposed were remnants of his years of devotion to the Beatles. He was straining for informality, I could see, English being the best weapon against his natural reserve. I, on the other hand, was all caught up in the romance of affixing the respectful "san" to his name and asking him if he would be so kind as to pass me the salt, something I couldn't get away with in my own language.

He suggested a walk to the new city hall in West Shinjuku. Outside again, we made our way through the booze-blurred tapestry of neon and noise. There was something monstrous and marvellous about the way Shinjuku sprang to life after the sun went down, like a giant sequined cockroach. Amusement halls, shot bars, dens of sin, at every doorstep the exhortations of stereo speakers ("Welcome, welcome, just for tonight we're offering gobbledee gobbledee gobbledee ... "), the flash of chrome everywhere, elevators shooting up and down inside their glass casings, the entire visible spectrum of blinking, twinkling, popping colours and not a tree in sight in this revenge of the urban gods. We came up to the pedestrian overpass that led to West Shinjuku and its skyscrapers. At the top of the stairs we stopped for a while, surveying the scene.

"*Te?*" he said, offering me his hand.

And at that moment — the shock of pleasure, surprise, hope all mixed together — it seemed to me that a thirty-four-year-old longing was put to rest, that I'd finally made a connection, not only with Tetsu but with the freedom I'd been vainly courting over the years. For the first time ever, there was no distance between where I wanted to be and where I was — in mad, mad Shinjuku, hand-in-hand with this tall, quiet Japanese doctor who touched a part of me that none of the men before him ever had. Far away from the shoulds and shouldn'ts of my own society (you *should* love your job, your culture, low interest mortgages, two-week vacations, Liberal politics, have a child and your restlessness will evaporate), I felt free to love for the first time.

"People will stare at us," I said, trying to hide my pleasure and thinking of what an outsize couple we made.

"No, they won't," he answered. "And if they do, who cares?"

We walked all over West Shinjuku, his hand never letting go of mine even as we clambered up and down pedestrian walkways, dodged passers-by and stopped at a vending machine for an *aisu kohii* break. We talked about nothing in particular — flying cockroaches, gum-chewing gaijin, noodle-slurping Japanese. And as we continued to walk I felt a twinge of sadness, knowing that in a sense the best part was already over — that no matter what lay ahead, no matter how steamy the sex or heady the pillow-talk, nothing would rival the pointed beauty of that one moment, *Te*, the intimacy it promised and the mirrored hallway of possibilities it revealed.

It was also from that moment that I began to dream up a script for a one-act play called My Life, Part II, in which Tetsu had the leading role.

CHASING RAINBOWS

"Why are we burdened with the duty to destroy
everything, change everything, entrust everything
to impermanence?"

Yukio Mishima

— 1 —

As the weeks turned into months and the months into seasons, I began to understand why my students were making so little progress. I came to see that they didn't want to learn English as much as bask in its atmosphere. English was not only a language, it was a stepping-stone to a world of vigor, excitement, frankness, a world inhabited by men of action like Indiana Jones and cleansed of all the niceties and duties and restraint that the younger Japanese were starting to resent. In a word, it was freedom. In English you could answer no to questions, you could admit to disliking your job, you could be daring, outrageous, tell it like it is, man, instead of all the dodging and evading and blurring that made up the bulk of communication in Japanese. I never met a Japanese person under thirty-five who didn't claim to prefer talking straight to talking in circles, even those who were thoroughly incapable of it. Time and again my students would tell me how they felt freer expressing themselves in English than in their own language, even if the most they could express was "yesterday I go mobie *Die Hard*, very exciting, I think."

English was freedom, something every self-respecting parent wanted for his children. In a modern twist to the lullaby, one of the businessmen in my new Microsoft class, eager that his infant son learn English properly, put earphones on his one-year-old head every night and played him English conversation tapes until he fell asleep. "I read article people learning most well when they relaxing," was his rationale. Another new father decided to name his daughter Reika instead of the common Japanese name Reiko, because "it sounds more English." I imagined the alteration was probably as peculiar as changing Lisa to Liso or Katrina to Katrino, but he was unfazed: "If she want to go America, she have name sounds more natural." I also knew of a Japanese couple who was raising their daughter entirely in English, even though neither of them spoke the language well and they had no intention of leaving Tokyo.

One product of the English craze was the institution known as a conversation lounge, a no-frills type of bar where Japanese and gaijin got together to converse in English. Some of the lounges had strict rules: if you were caught speaking Japanese once, you got a warning; one more time and you were asked to leave. There was usually a cover charge of around ¥500, though in an effort to attract more English speakers the fee was often waived for non-Japanese.

I found myself in the Takadanobaba district one evening and happened to walk by a lounge of this type. I'd seen it advertised in the Tokyo Journal — Come to Mickey House, as informal as you are — and decided to go have a look. It was a small room, informal to the point of being run-down, and all of its dozen or so customers were gathered at one long table where a fortyish Japanese man was holding forth, throwing his hands in the air and shaking bits of paper at his audience. The proprietor gave me a warm welcome, and when he saw I was alone, led me to the table where all the customers were seated. I declined his offer of "many choices of American beer" and ordered a Kirin Dry.

The man who was holding everybody in thrall stuck out his hand as soon as I sat down.

"Hi, I'm Shigeharu," he said, giving me a vigorous handshake. "I speak thirty-three languages."

He produced a typewritten page and showed it to me. It was a list of languages, with a qualifying word next to each one: good, fair, fluent, passable. There were entries like Swahili and Basque. I wondered if he carried the sheet with him wherever he went, and thought that if he really did speak all those languages (in a country where speaking more than two caused people's jaw to drop) he could hardly be blamed for wanting to show off a little.

"We've just been discussing my theory of life, which I call the options method," he said excitedly, eyes darting behind thick square lenses. Surveying his mute audience, mostly young Japanese women and a couple of scraggly gaijin men, I thought the "we" a little imprecise.

"You see," he said, waving a diagram-filled sheet at me, "at every stage in life you've got to look at your options, right? It's very simple, really. Once you know what your options are, you simply choose the best one. If more people used this approach there would be a lot less unhappiness in the world, I'm sure of it."

His English was not only flawless but he was talking so fast I had trouble following him.

"Take marriage, for instance. Four years ago I was divorced, right? So I sat down and drew a chart." He pointed to one of the diagrams. "There are four options, right? The best one is married only once, next is widowed or divorced then remarried, third is widowed or divorced but not remarried, and last is never married. So what did I do? I looked at the chart, crossed off the first line, which was no longer an option for me, then I sat down and designed a strategy for moving up from option three to option two."

He adjusted his glasses and pointed to his empty beer mug, trying to catch the eye of the proprietor. "Now, four years later, I'm engaged to a wonderful woman, right? Chinese, I might add. Mind you, I didn't just pick the first woman who came along. But I didn't sit in my room and feel sorry for myself, like so many people do. It's all a matter of knowing your options, I say. Sorry, what was your name already?"

I introduced myself and asked him where he had learned to speak English so well.

"Lived abroad, lived abroad. Now, does anybody have any questions?" He surveyed his audience with flashing eyes. He had that genius-or-madman look about him, arms and eyes in perpetual motion and brain cells crackling audibly.

"What if person don't *want* getting married?" a young woman ventured.

"*Everybody* wants to get married," he said, pointing to his chart for emphasis. "Or at least, everybody wants a life partner of some kind. You see, there are three things people need in their lives. Someone to come home to, something to do, and something to look forward to." He paused to let this sink in. "If you have nobody to come home to, that's a maximum of two out of three." He wrote a large 2 on the page. "Two out of three, right? So you won't have maximum happiness." The woman said nothing. "It's all a matter of knowing your options," he added as an afterthought.

"What about love?" I asked, half-hoping that this madman, who appeared to have solved the puzzle of life once and for all, might shed some light on my excitement about Tetsu.

"Love? It's very simple." He tore out a blank sheet from a notepad. "Romantic passion," he said, drawing a pair of graph coordinates and scribbling "passion" near the y-axis, "is all a question of *hope* (he wrote "hope" at the left end of the x-axis) and *doubt* (he wrote "doubt" at the right end). He hastily graphed something that looked like Mount Fuji. "You see, all hope and no doubt means no uncertainty, no mystery, no passion, right? And too much doubt and not enough hope means fear, jealousy, anger, and the passion deflates like a flat tire." He made a noise like air hissing out of a tire and a matching gesture with his hands. "But the right balance between the two," he pointed to the top of Mount Fuji, "and you have love."

"I don't believe in love," a graying gaijin said, a Brit by the sounds of it.

He was surrounded by empty beer mugs. "I'm a cynic," he added, looking at me conspiratorially as though he presumed me to be an ally.

"So you've never loved a woman?" I asked him.

"I did once," he mumbled, almost to himself. "God, did I fucking love her. And do you know what she told me?"

"What?"

"That the *timing* was wrong." He said this in a mock-whiny voice, as if recalling how she'd sounded. "Can you beat that? We had this fan-fucking-tastic thing going, great sex and communication and all that, and she tells me that the *timing* is wrong."

"When did this happen?"

"Two fucking years ago." He shook his head in disgust. "I'll never love anyone like that anymore."

"You see, you see?" Shigeharu cut in excitedly. "A perfect example of somebody who needs to use the options method." He started scribbling again as he talked. "The four options are: fall in love and never lose it, lose love and find it again, lose love and don't find it again, and never love, right? So what you need to do," he said firmly, "is move up from option three to option two, just like I did." He tore off the sheet and handed it to the Brit.

"And how do you guarantee that he'll find love again?" I asked, drawn into Shigeharu's diabolical logic in spite of myself.

"Guarantee? There are no guarantees. What you have to do is maximize your chances, right? You take a piece of paper and make a list." He tore off another blank sheet and inscribed "important qualities" at the top of it. "So," he said to the Brit, "tell me some of the qualities you look for in a woman."

"It's OK," the Brit told him. "I'm not looking for love anymore, just sex." He scanned the circle of young Japanese women, but there seemed to be no takers.

I looked at all the sheets littered on the table and at the Brit's sour smirk, hoping I'd never have to choose between the two modes of living. Still, it was good to meet someone like Shigeharu once in a while, someone who was none of the things a Japanese was supposed to be: vague, wary of logic, wary of absolutes.

When I got home there was a message on my answering machine. "I ... miss you." It was Tetsu's voice, soft and hesitant. I played the message again, hardly believing what I was hearing. "Japanese men don't express feelings to women" was something I'd heard many times from friends and students, and I hadn't expected Tetsu to be any different. I wondered if using Harrison Ford's language was making him bolder — wondered, for an instant, if it was me or English he was courting.

Lying in bed that evening, unable to find sleep, I swung back and forth between hope (he said he missed me) and doubt (maybe he thinks that's what Western women like to hear), and thought, that madman in Mickey House was no fool.

2

Charlene's life in Tokyo had evolved rather differently from my own. When we met one Sunday afternoon at the World Restaurant in Shinjuku, she proudly told me that she'd managed to survive nine months without learning a single word of Japanese, not even the numbers from one to ten.

"But how do you shop?" I asked her. "What if you want to get, say, five chicken-breast filets at the meat counter?"

"I have fingers, don't I?" she said coyly. "And if the shopkeeper is too *moronic* to count fingers, I simply write down the number in my notepad and show it to him."

Charlene was a shameless Anglo-supremacist, believing that it was the rest of the world's business to learn English and to hell with them if they didn't. She was openly scornful of the Japanese, thinking them slow and stupid and constitutionally incapable of learning a foreign language.

"I mean, when I was learning French in school," she told me, "I made an *effort*, at least, to get my verb tenses right. But no matter how many times I remind my students to use the future tense for tomorrow and the past tense for yesterday, they just can't seem to get it into their skulls. The following week they're back to saying 'Last night I go to sheeatre.' I mean, are they missing a *gene* or something?"

I had heard her speak a few words of French at Kimi, and her pronunciation was so hard on my ears I'd been tempted to block them, but I said nothing when she complained about her students' atrocious accent and declared the Japanese incapable of imitating sounds.

I had never seen Charlene look less than perfectly groomed, and that Sunday was no exception. Blood-red lipstick, nails that shone like teardrops, dark sunglasses worn as a pendant, fitted red jacket and linen city-shorts — the weekend look of a dress-for-success'er. She was now a curriculum planner as well as teacher at Bilingual, and claimed to be thrilled to have turned her back on her law career. To me she seemed every inch a lawyer, and though I wouldn't have asked her point blank, I wondered what on earth she was doing in Japan. During her free time she watched American shows on her bilingual TV ("Don't want to lose touch"), read books on every subject except Japan, plotted her next Club Med vacation, ate Haagen Dazs ice cream straight from the container and occasionally went out with her friends (all gaijin, naturally) for an all-night drinking bout in Shinjuku. She'd been no slouch in the sex department, having racked up five encounters with other Bilingual teachers or staff members, and she now had her eye on a sixth prospect. "There's a lot of sexual tension between us," she told me. "Something's gonna happen any day now, I can feel it." She confessed that staff meetings were getting to be a little tense for her, with so many ex-lovers gathered together in one room. It was hardly surprising that her all-time favourite story should be *Dangerous Liaisons*, which she'd seen three times on screen and once in the theatre.

As usual, she spent a few minutes heaping scorn on Western men who took up with Japanese women. "I see these couples on the train," she told me, "and it's nauseating. The women can't get through a full sentence in English and make gurgling noises like one-year-olds. Don't these men want *communication*? Don't they want *intelligent* women?"

I was a little hesitant, under the circumstances, to tell her about Tetsu, but she was more baffled than outright disapproving. "What on *earth* do you talk about?" she asked me, sincerely wanting to know.

It was hard to get offended. She wore her bigotry with style, like a mink-clad diva wading imperiously through a crowd of anti-fur demonstrators. For all her disdain of things Japanese, she seemed to be enjoying herself in Tokyo, removed as she was from the pressures of fulfilling people's expectations of her. She was free to pursue her own brand of hedonism for which, with tongue only half in cheek, she'd coined the term Charlenism. And she knew how to bring me down to earth when I started rhapsodizing about the virtues of Japanese women, about their grace and patience and lack of complaining. "That's all very charming," she would retort, "but it all comes down to sexism, pure and simple. The women are not treated as equals in this society, either at home or in the office, and they've been brainwashed to believe all that crap about how it's unladylike to put your foot down." And to my protestations that Japanese women seemed at least as content as their Western counterparts, she countered that a happy slave was still a slave. Conversations with Charlene were never dull.

Hungry for concrete information about Japanese-style romance (to help me put Tetsu in cultural perspective), I consulted with Hitomi. "Consider yourself lucky," she told me. "It's very rare for a Japanese man to use love talk. Do you know that Kazuo hasn't once, in all our years of dating and marriage, told me he loves me? Or even that he appreciates me, or finds me attractive?" On the subject of touching during courtship, she disclosed that Kazuo had waited two full years before holding her hand. Judging from the Kazuo I knew, who was nothing if not a sensual guy, I found it hard to believe that his sixteen-year old self would have been content to rub shoulders for two years, but she insisted it was true. "Although," she said shyly, "maybe ours was not a typical case. Why don't you talk to some of your younger friends?"

Acting on her advice, I gave Miki a call one evening, remembering that she'd had two serious relationships before declaring herself free of men.

"*O-noroke,*" she said when I'd finished my breathless description of Tetsu.

"What does that mean?"

"It's a word we use when someone is boasting about their new boyfriend."

I winced. She was right, of course. I apologized as best I could, and she, well trained in the art of defusing tension, replied that *ie ie*, no no, she'd only been kidding.

"Where does he live?" she asked. I told her he lived and worked in Mitaka, only two train stops away. And that he always called from work since he didn't have a phone at home.

"Doesn't have a *phone?*"

"That's what he told me."

"I hate to say this, but it sounds a bit suspicious. Sounds to me like the guy is married."

In my gut I felt this wasn't true, that a lie of such import had never passed Tetsu's lips. Still, Miki's words made me uneasy. The circumstantial evidence was undeniably strong. A doctor, obviously not hard up for money, with no phone at home ... If he was married, I thought in alarm, then he couldn't play his part in my script.

By the following evening I was in a state of full-blown panic. Against my better judgment I gave him a call at work. I told him about my conversation with Miki, told him that even though I didn't doubt his honesty, it was risky, in a foreign culture, to rely on intuition alone.

"Please, Tetsu, if you're married, tell me *now*," I said urgently.

"I'm *not* married," he answered firmly.

"Are you living with any other people?" I asked, meaning a woman.

"I live alone." He sounded puzzled.

"What I don't understand," I pressed, "is how people can get in touch with you when you're not at work. Say we'd planned to meet and I had to cancel for some reason, how could I let you know?"

"I carry a beeper with me," he said. "It starts beeping whenever there's a message on my answering machine at work. Then I go to a payphone and listen to my message from there."

"But what if it's an emergency?"

"Would it make you feel better," he asked after a pause, "if I had a phone installed in my apartment?"

"That's not what I meant," I told him, flattered nonetheless that he would consider it. "I just wanted to confirm that my fears were groundless."

As soon as we hung up I started to panic again. What on earth had possessed me, interrogating him like a vice-squad cop? I cursed myself for my lack of restraint, feeling sure I'd blown it. But two days later he left me a friendly telephone message and all was well again. Weak with relief, I vowed to breathe deeply and count to ten the next time I had an urge to hurl accusations at him. If you're going to keep this man, I told myself sternly, you'll have to be more careful.

The next time I spoke to Charlene, asking how things had progressed with the sixth object of her lust, she admitted that she'd completely misread the signals this time. It turned out he was a very active homosexual who knew Shinjuku's gay district like the back of his hand. But that was OK with her, since she was *definitely* not in the market for love and all its discontents.

3

On the first Sunday in June there was a fine drizzle over Tokyo, a hint of the rainy season to come. I was waiting for Tetsu in front of the Mitaka post-office, starting to worry a little even though he was only a few minutes late. I never saw him approaching from a distance when I waited for him — he had a way of materializing right before my eyes, as if he'd rounded some invisible corner. There was always the sense that he lay hidden somewhere.

A navy blue Nissan sports car pulled up at the traffic light and I saw his face inside it, eyes intent and hair very black against the white upholstery, my tension evaporating as soon as I met his gaze. He pushed the door open and I got in, sensing that a charmed day lay ahead. Much later, I would look back on that day and wonder if I'd dreamed it.

I remembered asking Hitomi about the "san" suffix, when to use it and when not to. She told me that as two people got closer, there came a time when the "san" fell away naturally, like an old skin. It wasn't anything you could explain — you just *knew* when to drop it.

"Good morning, Tetsu."

"Sorry I'm late," he said. "I was up until two o'clock last night."

"Work?" I asked.

"Yup."

We were headed for Yokohama. As we sped along the highway I watched his hand on the stick-shift, noting the sureness with which he drove, the sporty way he changed gears and wove through the traffic.

"You drive well," I told him.

"I love cars," he said simply. He told me he'd bought his first car at eighteen, with money he'd earned by working in a *soba* restaurant on weekends. It had taken him four years to save up the money. This man has never stopped working, I thought, wondering where all the drive came from.

Our first stop was Sankei-en, the famous Japanese garden in the Honmoku hills, mixture of nature and artifice. I felt a rush of pleasure at the way Tetsu wordlessly took my hand when we got out of the car, as though he now owned it. With his other hand he held a large checkered umbrella above our heads. Though the park had a reputation as a *dehto-spotto* (place to go on a date), the rain seemed to have persuaded most couples to go elsewhere. We walked past lily-dotted ponds and pruned trees bent over wooden bridges, thickets of overgrown bushes and teahouses with curled rooftops.

"How do you like it?" he asked.

"I *love* the greenery," I told him, wondering if he understood I meant him.

We walked hand in hand, our talk sparse but playful, he calling me *ameonna*, woman who brings the rain, and I poking fun at his yups and nopes, his earnest attempts to talk like a tough Western dude ("fuck," as he tripped over a branch), which sounded about as menacing as a chihuahua bark.

"What do you mean, *muko no hito*?" I protested when he used that phrase to refer to foreigners. "*People from the other side.* What other side? And what side are *you* from?"

He laughed — a short laugh, only three or four ha's, but hearty. His laughter didn't come easily, and it felt like something I'd earned.

I teased him about his compatriots' naïveté about foreigners, their flat-footed questions. "And your TV shows," I accused. "Why are TV gaijin always so silly?"

"I wouldn't know," he said. "I don't have one."

"No TV?"

"No TV, no phone." He hesitated. "You probably think that's strange."

"Not at all." I glanced up at his face and saw a flicker of something, maybe relief.

"I'm a bit of a *kawarimono*, actually," he said after a few moments.

"A what?"

"*Kawarimono.* Strange person."

I laughed. "I've always liked strange people," I told him. And it was true. I was a sucker for eccentric types. If a man lived in a hut in the wilderness, or refused to vote, or didn't know what a megabyte was, my interest was piqued.

As we zigzagged through the park I waited for the right moment to ask someone to take our picture. I wanted to get us on paper, to make us official. And when the moment came — without effort, like everything else that day — I got into position in front of the water-lilies and Tetsu put his arm around me just as the camera went click, and after that we walked not hand in hand but arm in arm and I was thinking that I wanted this day to go on and on and on, just as it was. Sex could wait. Just having come this far seemed miraculous. Just being close enough that I could feel the warmth seeping out of his body.

The rain was now stopping, now starting, now stopping again. We sat down at a roof-covered picnic table and took out the sandwiches I'd brought along. He ate with gusto, an egg and a cream cheese and two roast beef. I, on the other hand, had no appetite.

"Do you like the sandwiches?" I asked.

"They're delicious," he said without smiling. "Delicious because you made them."

We left Sankei-en and drove to another parking spot. I had no idea where he was taking me, nor did I much care. He was leading me everywhere, down to Yamashita park and the waterfront, up and down Motomachi street, up a steep hill past the Foreigners' Cemetery where over four thousand gaijin were resting in peace. He was telling me that he'd been quite serious about music as a teenager, that he'd hoped to make it his full-time career. But his father had been adamantly opposed to the whole thing and eventually persuaded him to give it up. Now he was toying with the idea of using conducting as therapy for arm injuries.

We found ourselves on a deserted strip of land, flanked by a cliff on one side and an old rusted train on the other, frozen in its tracks. "Whenever I see an old train I think of my uncle in Yamanaka," he said. "He used to tell us stories about the Pacific War, about having to ride on a train for an hour in order to get food for his family." Pacific War. It sounded so benign, like a war for flower children. It occurred to me that I ought to tell him I was Jewish, though I couldn't think of any good reason why. Soon, I thought, but not yet.

Walking up another steep hill, we came upon the courtyard of a small shrine, hemmed in by a web of trees. By some silent agreement we stepped in, found a bench and sat down. It was starting to drizzle again. He leaned his umbrella against the bench so that it covered both our heads. I kept my eyes forward, feeling like a virginal schoolgirl all of a sudden, waiting expectantly for the scene to unfold. We sat quietly for awhile and listened to the tapping of the raindrops. Pretty soon I felt his hand around my neck, his fingers massaging the back of my ear.

"It feels wonderful," I murmured.

"It's a technique I learned in China," he said. "If you ever have trouble going to sleep, repeat this motion — " he applied pressure and made a circle " — one hundred times."

I reached up to his ear and tried to copy his movements.

"Like this?" I asked.

All of a sudden his face zoomed in on my own and I felt the pressure of his thick lips against mine. I drew myself up to him, surprised at how familiar it all felt. It surprised me that a Japanese kiss would be no different than a New York kiss or a Vancouver kiss. The warmth, the pressure, the movements were all the same. What was different was that I didn't want it to stop. That I wasn't secretly thinking *you're not my type* or *I wish you liked Chopin* or *I can't breathe.*

Slowly I disengaged from him, not wanting him to think me too eager or too experienced. Almost Japanese by now in my awareness of age, I was all too conscious of the four-year gap between us. I wanted him to forget the fine wrinkles around my eyes, forget that I'd been married, touched, kissed by other men. I wanted him to know that none of the others had been real.

We made our way back to the parking lot, huddled together under his umbrella as we sliced through the drizzle, not saying too much. When we got into the car he didn't start it right away, and we sat tensely for a moment. Then his face rushed in on mine again. There was something odd, after all, about his kissing. He would draw back every few seconds and smile. Kiss and smile, kiss and smile. I'd never seen him smile that way before, with his lips fully parted and teeth showing. He fumbled with the buttons on my blouse, a splashy print I'd bought in Thailand. I closed my eyes and buried my face in his hair. It was a full five minutes before I realized that my breasts were in full view of the passersby.

"Tetsu," I pretended to be shocked, "everybody can see us."

"*Kimochi ga ii kara, basho to kankei nai,*" he said softly. The feeling is good, so the place doesn't matter. But he pulled away.

I asked him if he was tired, remembering how late he'd been up the previous night.

"If I thought I was going to be tired today," he said, "I'd have cancelled our date." He was still close enough that I could feel his breath tickling my face. "When I'm with you," he continued, "I want to be with you one hundred percent. I've never liked it when people get together and then complain about being tired. If I'm tired I stay at home and rest."

He wouldn't let me pay my share of the gas, or of the dinner we had on our way back to Tokyo. "From now on," he said, "let me pay. I don't want to have discussions about who owes who three-hundred-and-fifty yen, do you?"

I laughed. The only words I'd really heard were *from now on.* So there would be a next time, and a next.

A waltz in perfect step, I wrote in my journal that evening. And I hardly dared believe the words on my answering machine the next day ("I care about you ... "), or the way he kissed the picture of us I gave him, calling it his treasure. It was all too much for me. By the end of two weeks I'd lost ten pounds and memorized all of Kevyn Lettau's love songs.

All this should have happened to me at seventeen. At thirty-four, first love is much more dangerous, like the measles.

4

Uneventful though it was, my first day at Shiga International Patent Office was a milestone of sorts: I finally had a *real* job in Japan, a job that had nothing to do with teaching. I savoured it all — battling for breathing space in the elevator, punching my time-card, exchanging bows with my new colleagues, wolfing down a plate of *yakisoba* at a lunch counter, watching half the office rise for the three o'clock calisthenics break, getting acquainted with the NEC and Macintosh computers on my desk, punching out and joining the hordes of commuters headed for Tokyo station. I felt an absurd pride in having finally become a part of the mad scramble, a link in the gears of Tokyo's workaday world. More than ever, I felt I belonged.

The novelty soon wore off, of course, and by the end of the first week I was already starting to have private gripes. The hardest thing to get used to was having three co-workers' heads within a couple of feet of my own. I couldn't even chew a nail without several people knowing about it. The working area consisted of one large room, with desks arranged in typical Japanese office style: about ten sets of double rows, each one made up of six adjacent desks pushed up against another six. Two, sometimes three personal computers sat atop each desk, along with stacks of documents which occasionally lost their balance and toppled over. In order to clear away a work space on my desk, I had to perch my computer keyboards on their respective monitors and transfer several books and folders to the floor.

Reiner, a lapsed physicist from Heidelberg, sat at the desk facing mine. He was taut and muscular, handsome if a bit pallid-looking, and monstrously intelligent. His interests ranged from international politics to mathematics to Thai music to Chinese characters, for which he had an eidetic memory. He took an instant liking to me, possibly because I was, as he put it, "easy to tease." I'd often catch him staring at me with a half-mocking, half-kindly gleam in his eye, and even with my head bent over my papers I could tell when his don't-bite-your-nails look was fixed on me.

Reiner made it clear that he wasn't the rules-and-regulations type. He disappeared for stretching breaks several times a day, went for lunch when he felt like it (instead of the standard twelve-thirty to one) and was the only employee who ducked the compulsory Monday afternoon meetings. He would often interrupt my work and challenge me to find the solution to a math problem or a logical paradox.

"Do you know the one about the three rooms?" he'd ask innocently, just as I was getting started on a new assignment.

"What?"

"There are three rooms with closed doors numbered one, two and three. One of the rooms has a red Porsche inside. Let's assume you're trying to maximize your chances of getting that car, OK?"

"OK," I'd say, all too willing to be distracted from my work.

"So pick a number."

"Number three."

"Good. I'll keep that door closed for the time being, and open the door to another room that *doesn't* have the car in it. Now, I'll give you the option of changing your selection to the remaining door, or staying with your original choice. Statistically, which way are you better off?"

"It shouldn't make a difference, right? Either way I have a fifty-fifty — "

"Aah ... " he'd cut in with a knowing smile, "that's one of mathematics' great paradoxes. If you think about it, you'll see that if you change your selection, you have a two-out-of-three chance of getting the car. If you stick with your original selection your odds are only one in three."

I hoped this wasn't his way of flirting. Not that he lacked charm, but he *was* a German, and the timing couldn't have been worse, of course.

Mr. Murasaki, our supervisor, didn't seem to have any objections to Reiner's freewheeling style. He would often walk over to Reiner's desk and engage him in an hour-long discourse about some esoteric physics or engineering problem. I suspected that he considered Reiner brilliant and consequently exempt from petty duties like working.

Ted, a lapsed chemist, sat to my left, and on my right was Tom, a lapsed doctor. Further down the row of desks sat Hozumi-san, a lapsed geologist who'd lived in Canada for most of his sixty years and was perfectly bilingual. The impish, wise cast of his features made him a favourite among the young female employees. "He's so cuuute," I'd hear them croon. "He'd make a perfect grandfather, *neh?*"

Almost all of the dozen or so foreign employees were lapsed scientists of one kind or another, which made them a rather interesting bunch. Someone who had the brains and staying power to become a scientist but the imagination to opt out wasn't likely to be dull. Tom, the ex-doctor, wore what was left of his hair down to his shoulders, jeans that looked like something the cat dragged in, and a baseball cap with a long blond ponytail pinned to the back — presumably to make up for what nature had taken away from him.

Birgit was a young Biology major from Sweden who showed up in halter tops and shorts that barely covered her ass and a look of studied innocence, as though it had never occurred to her that such garb might be inappropriate. I was frankly surprised that Mr. Murasaki never raised any objections to her or Tom's sartorial choices, or to the fact that the foreign employees spent a good portion of each day in idle chitchat. Evidently, he believed that gaijin functioned better if they were allowed complete freedom in dress and work habits.

I was given a number of books and articles on international patent law. After two weeks of reading, I was considered knowledgeable enough to begin working as a patent editor, a specialized career that might take several years of study in Canada or the States. "Fix up this patent application," Mr. Murasaki would tell me, handing me a document about a new method for treating fertilizer or controlling the lubrication of car parts. "The claims are too broad. You need to make them more specific, otherwise the application will be rejected again. Also, see if you can improve on the logical flow of the information." I would spend the next few hours poring over the document, trying to make sense of the mishmash of technical language, graphs, equations and legalese. When I'd reached a peak of frustration, I'd look up from my work and find Reiner baiting me with his mirthful stare. I'd have no choice but to ask him to explain the document to me, which he usually did in short order. As a reward, I would allow him to steer me into a lengthy discussion about prime numbers or Thai rock groups.

Oddly enough, Mr. Murasaki seemed perfectly satisfied with this state of affairs. I felt guilty every time he told me what a valuable employee I was, and guiltier still when I received my absurdly generous paycheque every two weeks. As far as I could see, the only real value I had to the company was my ability to write letters in French, since Shiga did business with several patent agencies in France and Switzerland. I lived in fear of the day when Mr. Murasaki would finally realize that I was clearly in over my head with this job.

Every Monday at one o'clock in the afternoon there was a general staff meeting, which only Reiner had the nerve not to attend. A stand-up microphone was brought out and placed in the middle of the large room. At a prompt from the P.A. system, everybody got up and stood at attention beside their desks. The president of the company walked up to the microphone and said a few words about new policies, changes in patent law or upcoming company events. Following this, two or three of the employees, who'd been designated in advance, took turns providing us with "instructive or amusing anecdotes." The president then announced that the meeting was over, there was a round of applause, and everybody sat down to resume the business of being or looking busy.

Keiko was a shy young woman who worked as a translator and administrative assistant. When she learned that it was her turn to speak the following Monday, she worried herself sick for the rest of the week. On the fateful day, she came to the office looking miserable. We were all rooting for her when she walked up to the microphone, eyes glued to the ground.

"I'm going to talk about an experience I had last year," she said in that forthright, determined way of the very shy when under duress. "As some of you know, I'm still not married." She took a deep breath. "Well, last year one of my friends suggested that I enrol in dance classes as a way of meeting eligible bachelors. Why not, I thought. I registered for a ballroom dancing class at the school my friend had recommended. On the first evening of instruction, I found myself surrounded by people who looked like they were in their sixties and seventies. Don't worry, I told myself, the younger folks are probably rushing over from work, so they'll be a little late. But ten minutes into the lesson, I knew I was in trouble. The youngest of the other participants was about thirty years older than me." Several people chuckled, and Keiko seemed to relax a little.

"The last thing I'd expected was to be doing the polka with senior citizens. To tell the truth, I didn't find the lessons very enjoyable, and there were a lot of Tuesday evenings when I'd have preferred to stay at home with a book. Under the circumstances, though, I had no choice but to stick it out for the rest of the year. So, the point of my story is that it's worth your while to do some thorough research before acting on the advice of a friend."

After the meeting was over, I walked over to Hozumi-san's desk and pulled up a chair beside his. "I don't understand," I told him.

"What? You mean Keiko's story?"

"Yes. I don't see why she felt compelled to waste a year of Tuesday evenings taking lessons she didn't enjoy. Why didn't she simply quit, when it became obvious to her that she wasn't going to find what she was looking for?"

"It's a matter of saving face," Hozumi-san said instantly.

"What do you mean?" Ten months in Japan and I still didn't get it.

"Think about it for a minute," he said, as though quizzing a child. "Who recommended the dance school to Keiko?"

"A friend of hers."

"That's right. So if she quit partway through, her friend would feel terrible."

"But her friend had no way of knowing that only senior citizens would sign up."

"Doesn't matter," he said. "She would still feel responsible, and the friendship would be strained. So Keiko decided it was better to save her friend's face and pretend that all was going well."

"I still say it's a waste of time," I countered. Hozumi-san simply shrugged his shoulders and gave me one of his grandfatherly smiles.

5

A commonplace truth about being in love is that physical imperfections and even character flaws become part of the loved one's appeal. If that was indeed a sign of love, then it was not only Tetsu but Tokyo itself I'd lost my heart to. No longer eyesores, the clusters of vending machines at every street corner looked bright and cheerful through my rose-tinted lenses. While I'd initially regarded them as products of the convenience mentality, I came to see them as blessedly convenient. There was a set of vending machines at the beginning of my street, and on my way home I would sometimes stop to buy a can of *aisu kohii*, thanking the Japanese for having anticipated my thirst and placed this colourful oasis in my path. A few steps further on Shin Midori street was another machine that dispensed cold sake and beer. When the spirit(s) moved me I walked over and bought myself a glass or two of sake. Then I would go home, turn on the air conditioner (which cooled down my tiny room in two minutes flat), sprawl out on my sofa and take slow sips of the drink, listening to Kevyn Lettau's songs and letting my fantasies swirl around me like curls of smoke.

At five o'clock every morning I was wide awake, bursting to give expression to my elation. I would jump out of bed and go for a walk, exulting in the perfection of my surroundings: asphalt gleaming as though a hundred dogs had licked it clean overnight, compact houses with obsessively well-tended hedges, spanking new apartment buildings called Luna or Milky Way, the streets empty except for a few insomniac *obaasan*, they too perfect in their tidy walk and softly creased faces. Sometimes they even smiled back at me.

About once a week, usually in the afternoon, the paper-waste exchange truck drove through the neighbourhood, stopping at every intersection. Since I was often at home during the day, I had the pleasure of hearing the driver's repeated exhortations, amplified through his megaphone:

"Once again I am humbly grateful to serve you. Should any member of your esteemed family be in possession of paper items that have outlived their usefulness and turned into garbage, such as old newspapers, magazines or cardboard boxes, in quantities large or small, kindly allow me to exchange them for toilet paper or facial tissues according to your preference."

Tokyo was my lover now, so even its crowds, its goofy after-eight salarymen, silly with liquor, its pomp and circumstance about toilet paper, were part of its allure. Tokyo and Tetsu were becoming inseparable in my mind — one was weaving into the other and both were taking root in the subterranean layers of my fantasies.

Superstitions began to crop up in my behaviour. If I knocked on wood nine times before calling him, it would be a good conversation. If I burned the clipped ends of my toenails (like my mother used to do), our romance would continue to burn brightly. If I was meticulous about sorting the garbage properly, I might be entitled to stay in Japan (with him).

I was still teaching about four hours a week, and during one of those classes I brought up the topic of superstition. I asked the students to break up into small groups, discuss Japanese superstitions among themselves and designate group leaders who would report their findings to the class.

Most of the superstitions, I learned, revolved around death. When passing a *kichuu* (In Mourning) sign, closing the fingers of your hand around the thumb was a way of protecting your parents from death. It was bad luck if you were summoned to a dying person's house and your shoelaces came undone on the way there. You were also supposed to avoid cutting your nails at night, because the words for night and nail put together sounded like a word that meant evening burial. Seeing a funeral car, on the other hand, was good luck. A student from Aomori Prefecture told of a local belief that if a crow circled a sick person's house three times, that person was going to die. Another student said something that made my heart miss a beat. She'd read about it in the newspaper, a warning to couples that if their first date was in Inokashira park, they'd eventually split up. Not only was my first date with Tetsu in Inokashira park, I thought anxiously, but we ended up there almost every time we met.

"I find that hard to believe," I said to her, trying to conceal my personal stake in the matter. "Lots of couples go to Inokashira park on their first date, and surely they're not all going to break up."

"But it's true," she insisted. "If first time dating in that park, is bad luck. Newspaper say it, even they do survey."

This is ridiculous, I told myself, you don't believe in that sort of nonsense. Nevertheless, I felt vaguely uneasy for the rest of the day.

Tetsu and I found ourselves in Inokashira park again that weekend, engaging in a long round of kisses. Kiss and smile, kiss and smile.

"Shall we go to your place?" he mumbled in between kisses. I hadn't expected the question to pop up so soon. He'd always given me the impression of being in no hurry and I was reluctant, almost, to put an end to the suspense.

"I'm not sure, Tetsu," I muttered.

"You don't trust me?"

"It's not that, but ... " What I feared was some unwanted piece of reality breaking through my web of fantasies. The child in me wanted things to stay just as they were, on the brink of consummation, the hope and doubt in perfect balance. But I also wanted Tetsu.

"OK," I said finally, "let's go. But promise me you won't leave quickly."

And as we stepped into my apartment, as he took me into his arms, removed my clothes and then his own, kissed me all over and reached down between my legs, I was surprised again by how international it was, the way a man touched a woman. Somehow I'd imagined that a country whose school-children bowed to their teachers every morning, a country whose trains always rolled in on time and whose lovers held their trysts in hotel-rooms with Lone Ranger or Mickey Mouse themes, that such a country would have produced a different kind of lovemaking.

"Tonight is for you," he declared, pinning my arms above my head and saying *ikenai* when I tried to wriggle free. It was absurdly erotic to me, being made love to in Japanese. He covered me with kisses, holding me down so I couldn't move and making my body sing with pleasure. But he wouldn't let me reciprocate. "No rules," he said. "Remember?" He wasn't the least bit shy about touching me, but when I tried to move my hand along the inside of his thigh, he pleaded shyness and gently pushed my hand away. "Tonight is your night," he kept saying. A flicker of worry went through my head. Why didn't he feel any urgency?

He gave me an elaborate face massage — a technique he'd learned in China, he said — then insisted on doing the rest of me. "You have a lovely body," he told me. But his was the beautiful one. I was surprised at his hairiness (having been under the impression that all Japanese men came hairless), his thick legs and torso. He was bulky enough to make me feel delicate, which was no small feat. "I think I'll call you Grizzly," I told him, afraid to ask why he insisted on giving everything and taking nothing.

We lay on the bed as the pre-dawn light filtered through the sliding door, his unmoving face in the crook of my arm.

"What are you thinking about?"

"I'm thinking about today's happiness," he said quietly, "and the next happiness."

The word "next" caught in my ear and I held my breath. Was it possible that he wanted the same thing I wanted? Did he lie in bed, as I did, imagining our future together? As always, his words were full of promise but left me guessing.

A few days later, on one of my early morning walks, I came upon a large sign inscribed with the words "Selfish Restaurant" in bold cursive lettering. I chuckled to myself, wondering if the sign was meant to describe the customers or the staff. Peering inside through the restaurant's window, I saw Selfish menus, Selfish paper napkins and Selfish matchbooks. Then, taking a closer look at the sign, I noticed the characters for *kairyori*, the Japanese word for shellfish. On my way home I passed the grounds of a small *jinja*, and on impulse turned back and went in. There was a hut-like structure at the foot of the shrine, four pillars and a tiled roof from which hung a bell with a pullstring. I stood in front of the hut and prayed that Tetsu would be more selfish the next time. I prayed that Tokyo and Tetsu would continue to romance me and that I would do nothing to disappoint them.

6

There is Jewish hospitality, all warmth and informality and inducements to eat. (Hev enudda matzoh-ball — what, yuh dieting? Yuh skin and bones, fuh heaven's sake.) There is Italian hospitality, much the same as the Jewish variety except for the types of foods being offered. The French will ply you with wine and sparkling conversation. Spanish hospitality might include a singalong around an acoustic guitar. But Japanese hospitality is a breed apart. When the Japanese put their mind to playing host, you will come away feeling awestruck and just a little uneasy, as if you owe them favours well into your next incarnation.

Hitomi had given me a taste of it with her minutely orchestrated dinners, but it wasn't until I spent a full weekend in a Japanese home that I understood just how serious this business of hospitality could be in Japan. It wasn't so much that pleasing a guest was a pleasure, but that *not* pleasing one was a shameful disgrace, to be avoided at all costs.

Naomi, the thirty-six-year-old Japanese teacher I'd first met at Miki's sukiyaki party, had become a friend of mine in her own right, and we often met in Shinjuku for a stolen hour of lunchtime chitchat. For several weeks she'd been toying with the idea of having me come and spend a weekend at her parents' *besso*, or summer cottage, in the mountainous Chichibu district west of Tokyo.

In a society where the difficulty of owning even one home is matched by the unanimous longing for one, having a second home put the Saito family in a much-envied social stratum. I was curious to see how cottage life unfolded in rural Japan, so when Naomi's invitation took concrete shape at the beginning of July, I eagerly accepted.

"I afraid you think it's boring," she told me as we rode the westbound express train. "This weekend only my mother and aunt over there. They're, uh, how you say ... chatterboxes, right? *O-shaberi*. Typical Japanese women. My mother is Yoshiko and my aunt is Toshiko. Confusing, *neh?*"

The cottage was located in a small town called Ogose, in the foothills of the Chichibu mountains. The two women met us at the train station, almost falling over at the sight of me, and drove us to the house. Though they didn't — much to their credit — say a word about my height, they were clearly beside themselves with excitement. It wasn't often that an elongated *hakujin* woman appeared at their doorstep, and a Japanese-speaking one at that.

The cottage was half-hidden by a profusion of disheveled greenery — trees, shrubs, bushes of all sizes, and overgrown grass. Its wooden exterior walls were faded to a dull grayish-brown and didn't seem quite vertical, though it was hard to pinpoint where they slanted. The inside was just like the outside — disorderly and homey. Too many lamps, too many slightly crooked pictures on the wood-panelled walls, too many knickknacks, a gilded miniature shrine recessed into one wall, and a blaring TV that nobody seemed to be watching, added up to a welcoming whole. This was clearly a place where one didn't have to worry about sneezing or unfluffing the sofa cushions.

"It's not fancy here, but I hope you'll feel comfortable," Yoshiko blustered, ushering me toward the TV and handing me a remote control device. "I'm afraid you'll be bored here."

"Not at all," I said as I installed myself on the large square cushion she was pointing at.

"You can watch anything you like," she told me. She yanked the remote from my hands. "Here, I'll show you. There's channel eight, from Tokyo. Oh look, there's a talk show. Do you like talk shows? And channel ten is from Osaka — "

"Mother, stop!" Naomi said impatiently. "You didn't even ask her if she *wants* to watch TV."

Yoshiko turned to me in sudden concern. "Do you want to watch TV?"

"Sure."

"You see, she does. Here, take this, and choose whichever channel you like."

Obediently, I took the remote and started flipping. I had no idea what my next move ought to be, what was expected of me as a good guest. I finally settled on the talk-show and started watching intently under Yoshiko and Toshiko's anxious gazes.

"Can you understand what they're saying?" Yoshiko asked, then grabbed the remote from my hands again. "Here, let me show you. Oh look, a program about animals. Maybe you'd prefer to watch this. What do you think?"

"Sure."

"How do you know she likes animals?" Toshiko asked.

Yoshiko shot me another worried look. "Are you enjoying the show?"

And so it went, until Naomi announced in forceful tones that she was going to take me on a bicycle tour of the area. We departed in a hurry, urged on by the two sisters' cries of "Show her the temple!", "Show her the statue on the hill!", "Show her the pond, you know the one I mean?"

Rural Japan always cast an eerie spell on me. If I were the New Age type, I would conclude that I must have lived one of my past lives in Japan, because there was an undeniable sense of connection, of belonging, every time I found myself passing through the Japanese countryside. The most obvious reminder of my foreignness, as we pedalled through the rolling foothills, was that the bicycle Naomi had lent me ("Adult model," she'd assured me) was about the same size as the one I'd received for my eighth birthday.

Back at the cottage, the air was alive with the sizzle of oil and the intoxicating smells of frying tempura — eggplant, squash, green peppers, onions, and even apples, which Yoshiko explained was a local custom. While we ate the tempura, washing down the food with home-made plum wine, Yoshiko ran the hot water in the large wood-panelled bathtub. She insisted that I be the first to take the evening bath after dinner, matching my protests ("No, no, *you* should go first") with more forceful counter-protests ("Out of the question — it wouldn't be right if we made our guest wait") and handing me a blue-and-white checkered *yukata* as she shooed me in.

After a half-hour soak in the deep square tub, sleep came easily. And when I told Yoshiko, the next morning, how comfortably I'd slept in the *yukata*, she insisted I keep it as a souvenir. Amid my feeble protests, she snatched the garment from my hands, ran up the stairs to my bedroom and laid it on top of my suitcase. It wasn't every day that she had the honour of playing host to a Canadian, she told me on her way back down the stairs, as though that explained everything.

Fortified with a breakfast of ham, eggs, toast and jam, salad, potato-salad, mixed fruit salad and ice cream, we piled into Yoshiko's hatchback and went on our way, the two sisters arguing about where to take me first.

"My relatives talk too much, don't you think?" Naomi told me *sotto voce* as we cruised along.

It was true that the two sisters never stopped talking. Every cottage we passed, every farmhouse or stream, set their jaws in motion. But possibly because they were speaking Japanese, and because they weren't *my* relatives, I found their small talk charming rather than irritating.

Our first stop was a *wasshi* paper-making factory, where we were shown how the translucent, coarsely textured paper was stained and hung out to dry. The last room in the mom-and-pop operation was a boutique, where finished products such as *wasshi*-bound notebooks and *wasshi* hairpins were displayed and sold.

"Nice, isn't it?" I said to Naomi as I fingered a delicate pink hairpin rimmed with gold metal wiring. The next thing I knew, the pin was wrapped, paid for and in my hands ("Just a little gift to show how much we appreciate your visit"), courtesy of Yoshiko and Toshiko, who once again were arguing about what sights to show me next.

That was pretty much the way the rest of the day went — the two ladies inundating me with food, gifts and compliments, and I trying to find an artful way to deflect their generosity without hurting their feelings. The opportunity came when we stopped for lunch in a cozy restaurant high up in the Chichibu mountains, where customers could observe the making of fresh *udon* noodles. While the other three women were in the bathroom, I surreptitiously paid the bill, then dragged them out of the restaurant before they had a chance to protest, feeling smart for having finally outwitted them.

We spent the afternoon at the roof-covered outdoor market in Chichibu City, the largest town in the area. As we strolled through the maze of tiny kiosks where vendors were displaying their wares — clothes, jewellery, packaged foods and gift items such as plastic turtles that gurgled when squeezed — the delicate pink of a woven scarf caught my eye.

Spotting me as I touched the scarf, Yoshiko rushed to my side. "Do you like it?" she asked.

"It's pretty, isn't it? The colour reminds me of cherry blossoms."

I should have known better. No sooner had I turned around than the scarf was in my hands, wrapped in clear plastic and a pink bow.

"Yoshiko-san!" I said, trying to sound stern. "You're spoiling me too much. You don't have to — "

"But you *said* you liked it," she retorted, with the logic of a born giver.

A little farther along, I ran my hand along the surface of a brightly coloured futon pillow.

"It's nice, isn't it?" Yoshiko asked as she walked by.

This time I only nodded, but the result was the same — Yoshiko waited until my head was turned, scurried off to the cashier with the pillow in hand, then presented it to me as a *fait accompli*.

Eventually I figured out what I had to do. For the rest of the afternoon, the conversation between Yoshiko and me went something like this:

"Do you like this T-shirt?"

"No."

"But don't you — "

"No."

"How about these earrings?"

"No."

It was only by being downright rude, I discovered, that I could prevent her from making a gift out of every item I happened to touch or look at.

All too soon it was time to return to Tokyo. After a quick supper of grilled eel on rice, we drove to the Ogose train station where we bowed our goodbyes to each other. Unable to resist, I gave both women a big Western hug. They giggled nervously but looked quite pleased.

"Wait!" Yoshiko called out as I turned toward the approaching train. She walked up to me and handed me a small envelope. "Don't open it until you get home," she instructed. "Promise?"

As soon as I stepped into my apartment that evening, I opened the envelope and pulled out four crisp ¥1,000 bills along with a carefully hand-written note in English: *We ashamed to let our guest pay for udon lunch, so please accept this money. Love, Yoshiko.*

Once again, the foxy lady had beat me at the game of giving.

7

In a romance between two people of different cultures, there is always the suspicion that the culture gap is the binding glue. I sometimes wondered if Tetsu was in love with me or with or the novelty of whispering endearments in English, the status of having a gaijin woman on his arm, the thrill of kissing in public, just as they did in the movies. I wondered if it was me or the language he was courting. "Damn it," he would say when he stubbed his toe or popped a shirt-button, with the satisfied look of a child who'd just learned to tie his shoelaces. I saw the earnestness of his efforts to sound like an American ("I forgatt to tell ya ... "), the pleasure he took in using expressions like "pain in the neck" or "gut feeling" or "gimme a break." His years of listening to F.E.N. radio were finally paying off.

For my part, I couldn't deny that being romanced in Japanese had a unique appeal. As much as Tetsu liked saying Wish I could see you tonight, I thrilled to hear him say *Aenakute samishii naaah*. And there was something uniquely Japanese, it seemed to me, in the way he used words — sparingly, suggestively, to evoke rather than explain. "Let's spend a day in Izu sometime," I learned, meant "I'm sorry for showing up late tonight." He never told me he was tired or under stress, only that the weather was strange. The straightforward, tell-all style of my previous lovers seemed crude by comparison.

The rainy season was now in full swing, and it wasn't nearly as oppressive as the locals had led me to believe. The days were light grey, drizzly and windless, sometimes brightening up for a few hours — nothing at all like the brooding skies that hung over Toronto throughout the month of November. From my window at Shiga, I would look down at the umbrellas bobbing along the sidewalk in an continuous stream, so close together they sometimes overlapped, and feel a surge of affection for the city.

"How long does the rainy season last?" I asked the old grouch in the stationery store on Shin-Midori street.

"It ends on July twentieth."

"How can you know the exact date?"

"*Tsuyu* is from June tenth to July twentieth," he said flatly.

"You mean to tell me it stops raining on the same date every year?"

"*Tsuyu* is *tsuyu*," he grumbled as he gave me my change.

One Saturday in late June, I invited Tetsu to my apartment for a home-cooked meal. It was one of those *tsuyu* days that I loved — pearly sky, and a drizzle so fine that you had to put your ear against a leaf to be sure it was raining. I'd opened the sliding door so that Tetsu and I could watch the sky grow dark while we ate.

With my little table in the centre of the room, there was barely enough space between my sofa-bed and the far wall for us to sit comfortably. I watched anxiously as he tasted the pseudo-Chinese dishes I'd prepared — broccoli beef, ginger chicken, vegetable-fried rice. I had briefly considered making a Japanese meal but gave up the idea after Hitomi told me a few recipes, which sounded impossibly complicated.

"*Oishii*," he told me as he looked up from his plate.

I wanted badly for him to like the food. I wanted him to think *hmmmm, I could get used to this.*

A few days earlier, I'd asked Hitomi if she thought the four-year gap in our ages would make Tetsu less likely to regard me as a potential wife. "It's true," she'd told me in her tactful way, "that some Japanese men don't want to get serious about a woman over thirty. But if he already likes you ... " A few years back, she said, two baseball superstars had made headlines by marrying older women — one five and the other ten years older — and as a result, attitudes toward women in their thirties were starting to change. "It's case-by-case, I think."

The rain was coming down harder now, and the rooftops of the neighbouring houses were glinting dully in the fading light.

"Is it true that the rainy season always ends on July twentieth?" I asked Tetsu.

"I think it's gonna end a little later this year."

"What makes you say that?"

"You're a rain-woman, remember?"

Ever since our trip to Yokohama, he'd taken to blaming me for all the rain that fell over Tokyo.

"At least you're not playing golf tomorrow," I said.

"I was supposed to," he deadpanned. "I cancelled it because I knew you'd bring the rain."

I kicked his foot under the table. "What is it you like so much about golf, anyway? I mean, is it really worth thirty-thousand yen to chase after a little white ball for a few hours?"

"You're not gonna believe me if I tell you."

"Tell me anyway."

"I know it sounds strange," he said, "but I think of golf as a kind of personality test. I've noticed that when people play golf, their true character shows through."

"In what way?"

He cleared his throat. "Nervous people, for instance, can pretend to be cool and calm — they can hide their real temperament. In most situations, they can get away with it. But when they play golf, excitable types end up showing their frustration."

It occurred to me that I'd never heard him raise his voice, not even in jest or excitement.

"And which type are you, Tetsu? I can't imagine you'd ever lose your cool on a golf course."

His eyes grew serious. "I try not to," he said. "At the very least, I try not to let it show if I do." He was looking at me intently as he spoke.

"Do you never get angry or impatient?"

"Somebody once told me that it's better to keep one's anger inside," he said in that quietly urgent tone he sometimes used. "It was someone I respected, so his words made an impression on me."

We ate in silence for a few moments, then he looked up from his plate again.

"I'd like to take you golfing sometime," he said.

Just then there was a knock on my door. I got up to open it, wondering who on earth would be visiting me so late on a rainy Saturday night. It was Sugako, my next-door neighbour. Her eyes widened as she caught a glimpse of Tetsu.

"Oh, sorry, sorry," she stammered. "I didn't know you have friend here. Sorry, I didn't hear. I came bad time." Her face turned four shades of red. "*Sumimasen*, I come back later. I just wanted to give back English book you borrow, ah, lend me. I'm so sorry. Here, take book. Sorry I interrupt."

She gave a quick bow and hurried away before I could introduce her to Tetsu. And now it was my turn to blush as I saw Tetsu's eyes fall on the book I was holding, an English translation of Yoshiko Ariyoshi's *The Doctor's Wife*.

"So how's your English reading coming along?" I asked quickly. "Do you still read the Japan Times in the afternoon?"

"Nope," he said. "I've been too busy these days. Right now I'm reading a medical book called *Nihonjin no Honè*. Japanese Bones, I guess."

"Japanese Bones?" I started to laugh. "You're the only person I know who would read a book called Japanese Bones." I reached over and put my hands around his neck. "Can I read it too, Tetsu? I'd *love* to read Japanese Bones."

In answer, he got up from his chair, picked me up by the waist and carried me the yard's distance to the bed. He made growling noises as we undressed each other. "I'm a grizzly bear, remember?" he said, pretending to bite off my fingers, ears and nose. "A Japanese grizzly bear." All at once he grabbed me by the arms and turned me over on my stomach. "Doggie-style," he said as he rubbed himself against me, almost causing me to laugh. And then he turned me over again, sank his teeth into my neck and sucked hard. "Say something in Japanese," I told him as I slid my hand up his leg.

"*Damè*," he said tersely. "*Sawaru na.*" He pushed my hand away.

"Why, Tetsu? Why won't you let me touch you?"

"'Cause I'm a big bear," he said, "and I'm attacking you."

He spread my legs apart and held them down at the knees, making growling noises all the while. Again I tried to touch him, and again he moved my hand aside.

"I'm a big, dangerous bear," he said in Japanese.

I forced a laugh, but inside I was starting to feel anxious. Something was wrong here, though I wasn't sure what. Was he simply nervous, or tired? Or was a sturdy, broad-shouldered gaijin woman too great a departure from the pint-sized Sumikos he'd slept with in the past?

All at once he stopped growling and rolled over to my side. He stared up at the ceiling, his features locked in an unreadable expression. I put my head on his shoulder and watched the hairs on his chest as they rose and fell softly.

"Tetsu," I said after a while. "Is anything the matter?"

He didn't answer.

"Is there anything you're afraid of?"

"Like what?"

"Like diseases, or getting me pregnant ... "

"No," he said. "I trust you." He kept his eyes fixed on the ceiling as he spoke. "I don't wanna have a child right now, though. I wanna have one in March, so it will be born in December."

I could hardly believe my ears. "Why December?"

"I don't know," he said vaguely. "I just think it's good luck, that's all."

We lay in silence for a while, side by side under my thin quilt. So he wants a child in March, I thought in amazement. But which March? And with whom?

After a few minutes I felt his fingers tracing circles around my nipples. I let my hand trail softly down his chest, and this time he didn't push it away. Suddenly, as if making a decision of some kind, he climbed on top of me and entered me quickly. Pinned down by his bulk, I watched his face grow strained on top of mine. And then his eyes rolled upward and his body caved in, and I felt a gush of warmth between my legs, and I marvelled at the newness of it all, the flood of tenderness toward another human being, the rock-hard knowledge that I would never leave him.

Early the next morning, he shook me awake and told me he had to go.

"Where?" I asked groggily.

"To my meeting. Remember?"

I watched him as he got into his clothes, wondering if other Japanese men rationed their free time so stingily. I wished that just once, he would say *to hell with the meeting, I wanna spend the day in bed and fuck you doggie-style until you're blue in the face.*

"What's that?" I asked him. He'd taken something shiny out of his pants-pocket and was about to put it back in.

"My key-ring."

"Can I see it?"

I took the ring into my hands and stared at it in astonishment. It was about four inches in diameter, and there were at least fifty, maybe a hundred keys on it. I wondered why I'd never noticed it before.

"Tetsu," I said, "what on earth do you have so many keys for?"

He let the question hang. Again I felt it, the reluctance to probe any further, and find out ... what?

After he left, the questions lingered in my mind. I stood in front of the sliding door and looked out at the rainwater trickling down the glistening rooftops. No rules, he'd said, yet there seemed to be a lot of them. We could never see each other on weeknights, or make plans in advance, or spend a leisurely weekend together. And we were not to discuss his work. Our encounters were like the notes in a *shakuhachi* piece, tense and full of promise, then fading back into silence.

8

Tokyo sense.

The phrase popped into my head on the way back from a Sunday stroll through Yoyogi park. I'd brought my camera along, something I hadn't done in months, and clicked away at the gyrating members of the Rude Crash rock band and the teenaged girls bobbing up and down around them, at a self-styled poet giving an impassioned reading while shaking his fist skyward, at the giant hoop earrings and sequined vests being hawked by enterprising Israelis, finally stopping to rest on a bench where I segued into a conversation with a man from Iran whose nose resembled a dromedary's back.

Just two days after arriving in Tokyo, the Iranian told me, he'd walked into a Roppongi discotheque and caught the eye of a young Caucasian woman who'd been born and raised in Japan. She became his girlfriend. Through her various contacts she managed to find him a room in the house of a wealthy proprietor. The rent was only ¥20,000, and he had access to the whole house when the owner was away, which was almost every weekend.

Three months later, he still had the room but no longer the woman. "I found another one," he admitted. "It's more serious this time. Unfortunately, her father is having a hard time getting used to me. But he will," he added confidently. With the help of this girlfriend, he'd managed to get a successful import business going in just a couple of years.

"What about language?" I asked. "Wasn't it a problem when you were starting up your business?"

He grinned. "I chose girlfriends who taught me good Japanese."

Among the thousands of gaijin who poured into Tokyo, there were only a small number who had this sort of nose for it. Like rats in sewers, they knew how to squeeze the most nourishment out of the city, how to make it work to their advantage. They found the cushiest jobs, the best housing deals, the women who would give them not only their bodies but their connections.

At the other extreme were people like Vivian, my supervisor at INTEC. Though she professed to love Tokyo, she clearly didn't know how to make the city love her back. She worked like a dog but got neither praise nor promotions. In four years, she hadn't managed to learn more than a handful of Japanese words and hadn't made any real friends, either Japanese or gaijin. I cringed in embarrassment when she gushed on about how this or that colleague, ten years her junior, appeared to have a crush on her. The truth (drunkenly confessed to me over lemongrass shrimp one evening) was that she hadn't been touched by a man in all the time she'd been in Japan, discounting a *chikan* who'd assaulted her on her way home from work late one night.

I ran into her one afternoon, while window-shopping along Sakurada street with Hitomi and Yoko. She'd been walking with her head bent forward, and lifted it just in time to avoid crashing into me. There was something wild and hollow about the look in her eyes as she stood before us, all aflame in magenta and orange, dollops of pink lipstick staining her large front teeth. Hitomi and Yoko cast their eyes downward at the sight of her, and I too felt embarrassed, uncomfortable.

Equally lacking in Tokyo sense was Gordon, an older teacher who taught a class at SECOM on the same evening as I did. In the course of our weekly walks from the SECOM building to the bus stop, I managed to piece together the story of his life in Tokyo, which consisted of one mishap after another. Following the usual pattern for gaijin planning to work in Japan, he arrived without a working visa, quickly found an English school that was willing to sponsor him, then flew out to Hong Kong in order to receive his visa from outside the country. On his third day at the Hong Kong YMCA, his wallet was stolen from under his bed. It contained all the cash he had brought with him, about $3,000. Back in Tokyo, he "lucked into" a arrangement whereby he got reduced rent in exchange for ten hours a week of English instruction to the landlord. The trouble was, the apartment was a two-hour commute from downtown Tokyo, where he taught during the day. The result was that his entire day was spent in a train or in a classroom.

With a touch of smugness, I compared his situation to my own. The longest I ever had to commute to get to a job was half an hour, and my working hours left me large blocks of free time every day. I had kindly landlords, a steadily ringing phone, a growing circle of friends. On a deeper level, I felt that Tokyo had touched me, had changed me, in a way it hadn't touched Vivian or Gordon. I sometimes caught myself bowing on the telephone, or jerking my head in that bird-like way characteristic of Japanese women, or deflecting praise with a formulaic expression ("No, no, far from it, my Japanese is very poor"), all without conscious intent. People no longer stared at me on the train, the way they used to when I first arrived. Even Tom Koyama, who believed that adult personalities were set in stone, remarked that I seemed to be getting softer around the edges, more circumspect, more patient.

Another thing I was smug about was getting INTEC to sponsor me for a visa extension, even though I worked for them only two or three hours a week instead of the official requirement of twenty. My application was accepted, which meant I was entitled to stay in Tokyo for another full year after the anniversary of my arrival.

My weekly income was larger than ever, thanks in part to a "Music and English" program I'd put together for a group of twelve housewives eager to learn Western pop-songs. Nobue, the only one among them who had a piano, offered to host our sessions at her apartment, which was barely large enough for the thirteen of us to fit inside. After half an hour of diction and vocalization drills, I would sit down at the piano and accompany the ladies while they produced timid, wobbly renditions of the old war-horses they loved — Moon River, Feelings, My Way. I tried to challenge them with more lively numbers like The Girl From Ipanema, but the women proved incapable of hitting the off-beats. They breathed a collective sigh of relief when I gave up on Ipanema and started them on Somewhere Over The Rainbow.

To top it all off, of course, there was Tetsu. He rounded out a life that would have been vibrant and full even without him, made it shine like a polished pearl. I alternated between gratitude and pride, between thinking of him as a gift and an accomplishment. Unable to restrain myself, I sang his praises in long wordy letters to my brother, rhapsodizing about his refinement, his subtlety, his wisdom.

"Is it serious?" David asked.

I honestly didn't know. On the telephone, we carried on about how much we missed each other, as though we were separated by miles and mountains. But we only saw each other one night a week — this was an unspoken rule between us — either on Saturday or Sunday. On weeknights I had to make do with a quick phone call, or one of his whimsical offerings on my answering machine. I never questioned this state of affairs, never pressed for more time together, sensing that if I ever put him in a position where he felt he had to choose between me and his work, he would have no hesitation about ending our relationship. His work stood between us like a sacred cow, never talked about but always there, always blocking the way.

I was hungry for information about his past. It wasn't the unusual but the ordinary events that my curiosity fed on. I pictured him as a medical student, dissecting cadavers. At eighteen, parked near his high school with a bashful girl looking up at him from the passenger seat. Leaning against the brick wall of the school building, puffing on his first cigarette. Many years earlier, smiling with delight (before he'd learned to hide his smile in his eyes) at the sight of a *kappa* puppet. At eight, looking on in fear as his father hurled a plate across the dining-room table. As a small baby, speaking his first word. Sucking at his mother's breast. My imagination was shamelessly drawn to the mundane, the maudlin.

I brought his picture to a women-only party at Hitomi's house and showed it around. The women huddled around it and clucked their approval, sounding for all the world like Jewish mothers minus the *oy vey's.*

"He looks like a nice man."

"Yes, very nice man."

"A doctor, you said?"

"Handsome, *desu neh.*"

"What kind of doctor?"

"Have you talked about marriage?"

I evaded the subject and talked about his work, about how difficult it was to see him so infrequently.

"Typical Japanese man," one of the women said.

"But only once a week?" I asked. "Is that really typical?"

"Typical Japanese man," she said again.

"Even in a new relationship?"

"Typical Japanese man," three women said at once. I laughed, hoping they were right.

"Do you understand his work?" Yoko asked me, an ominous ring in her words. "Do you *really* understand it?"

Hitomi shot me a worried look. "Be careful," she said, clearly at a loss to figure out what a large, willful gaijin wanted with her country — wishing me well but possibly sensing trouble ahead.

More and more often, I felt myself drawn to the neighbourhood *jinja* I'd discovered a few weeks earlier. Pausing at the foot of the shrine, I would ask myself some difficult questions: Can I see myself living permanently in Tokyo? Can I see myself as the helpmate of this preoccupied, driven man? Preparing a bowl of hot *ramen* for him as he trudges up the stairs to our two-room apartment, weary beyond words? Over and over I ran the questions through my mind, and the only answer that came out was yes.

Tokyo sense — I was beginning to suspect I had it. In less than a year, I'd taken firm root in the city. I'd grabbed my life by the throat, shaken it, bent it out of shape, kicked it disdainfully, until finally a new pattern emerged.

"Pride goes before a fall," some dead relative must have whispered in my ear around that time, but not loud enough for me to hear it.

AN EARTHQUAKE AND A TYPHOON

"There is only work and love."

Sigmund Freud

—1—

We are sitting at a table for two in a posh steak house in Kichijoji, the kind of place where waiters glide around like ghosts, glasses get refilled by invisible jugs and candle lights flicker softly against dark walls and starched linen tablecloths. The hushed elegance is a perfect balm for the knot of tension in my gut, and I am grateful to Tetsu for sensing my mood and bringing me here.

"You seem tense," he says. "Is anything the matter?"

It's *you*, Tetsu, I sigh to myself, it's you I'm tense about. You treat me like a queen, whisper intoxicating phrases into my ear but never talk about tomorrow. "It's been a long week," I tell him. "New things to learn at work, overtime, that sort of thing."

"Forget about it, whatever it is," he says to me. "We don't have much time together, so let's enjoy it, *neh*?" He takes my hand and gives it a squeeze.

It's true, I think glumly, we don't have much time together. But why not? Why don't you *want* to see me more often, if you care about me as much as your nightly phone calls and terms of endearment would suggest?

He has cut up his steak into forkfuls, American style, something he probably picked up from a movie. He lifts a piece to my mouth, then another one to his own. The steak is perfectly done, juicier and more tender than any I've eaten before.

"Actually," he says, "I used to be quite a tense person myself."

"You? I find that hard to believe."

"For example," he continues, "if a person caught me *not knowing* about something I'd get very anxious. I remember once when I was about twelve, I was sitting with a friend in his bedroom, listening to music, and he asked me if I knew the name of the band that was playing. It was the Beatles, and at the time I hadn't heard about them. My friend was incredulous. He kept teasing me about it, and I was very uncomfortable."

Me too, I am thinking, but curiously enough I don't tell him this. I am recalling the evening — I was also twelve — that my friend Sophia asked me if I knew who the Beatles were. "A kind of bug?" I'd said, to which she'd rolled her eyes. I too had felt uncomfortable. This has to mean something, I tell myself now — Tetsu and I, living at opposite ends of the earth and in radically different environments, having the same thing happen to us at the same age.

"Later on, when I was older," Tetsu is saying, "I used to read all the latest gossip about actors and singers, watch dumb TV shows, keep up with the stock market, just so I wouldn't be caught *not knowing.* None of that stuff really interested me, and all the effort was making me very tense. Finally I thought to hell with it, being well-informed isn't worth that kind of stress. If people seem surprised when I don't know something, I don't let it bother me anymore and simply ask them to fill me in."

So he too has felt it, the pressure to be *au courant,* to keep up with the information-gathering Joneses. I am startled by how alike we are.

Something about the atmosphere of the place is making us talk more openly, steering us to more personal topics. Maybe this is why I wanted to come here. I need to find out more about this man, this mystery man who makes me crazy and keeps me guessing, guessing, guessing.

"You work very hard, Tetsu," I say cautiously. "Do you ever ask yourself why?"

"Yup," he answers right away, as though he were expecting my question. "My plan is to work hard until the age of fifty, then retire and spend my time doing *yaritai koto,* the things I've always wanted to do. That's my dream, anyway."

I wonder what they are, his *yaritai koto,* but I don't ask him. Twenty years seems a long time to wait. There might be another Great Earthquake, and he could get killed. Or he could get sick, or simply lose his drive.

"Isn't it a little risky, putting off the things you want to do until the age of fifty?"

"I don't put them off entirely. I play golf, I see you ... "

Is *that* where I stand, I think with sinking spirits, on par with a golf game?

"How about you," he asks. "Do you have a dream?"

I can't tell him the truth, of course. "It's hard to say," I answer finally. "I suppose what I've always wanted is to do something well, to distinguish myself in some way. I don't know if that qualifies as a dream, though."

After the meal we take our customary walk in Inokashira Park, which tonight is bathed in swirls of low-lying fog, thick and fluffy as cotton candy. The light of the electric lanterns shines thinly through the haze, and the outlines of embracing lovers come in and out of view as we make our way along the footpath. It is an enchanting evening, Tetsu has his arm on my shoulder, but still I am tense, unsettled. We find a bench up ahead and sit down. There is a question hanging between us, and he seems to be waiting for me to ask it.

"You tell me the most wonderful things, you act as if you really care about me," I say to him finally, "but you never make any plans, never talk about tomorrow, or next week, or next month. I just wonder, sometimes, what this all means to you, if it's only a game, or — "

"I love you," he says simply, looking me straight in the eye. If Tokyo is indeed my Everest, then this has got to be its pointy peak. Wrapped in fog, hearing the magic words from Tetsu.

"I'm so happy to hear you say that," I tell him. "I love you too, of course. But you knew that, didn't you?" I start to give him a hug.

He moves away from me a little, rests his elbows on his thighs and stares down at the ground between his feet. He looks troubled.

"As for marriage ... " he says slowly. Here it comes, I think. The crack in my wall of fantasies.

"I've never given much thought to the future," he says, switching to Japanese. "I've always believed that if you take care of the present, the future will take care of itself."

How astonishing, I think to myself. Those very same words were spoken to me, some ten years ago, by my then-boyfriend Joel.

"I look at my friends," he goes on. "They get married, they have children, and even then they're not really happy. Their focus narrows, somehow. All they talk about is nice clothes, stereos, stuff like that."

I'm not sure I agree with his assessment of marriage, but I hold my tongue. Tetsu also falls silent and continues staring at the ground.

"Remember that movie we saw together, Awakenings?" he asks after a while. I nod. "Remember the doctor, the Robin Williams character, what was his name?"

"Dr. Sayer, I think."

"Well, he actually reminded me a lot of myself. Do you know what I mean?"

A scene from the movie flashes through my mind. The incredulous look on Dr. Sayer's face when Leonard asked him if he was married. "Me, married?" he'd exclaimed, as though the answer should have been obvious. I hope that isn't what Tetsu means.

"I used to live with a woman," he says suddenly, as though he's made up his mind to tell me something he hoped he wouldn't have to. "I was even busier than I am now, if you can believe it, so we hardly spent any time together. She asked me the same kind of question as you did, about the future, and I gave her the same answer. Then she found herself another boyfriend ... "

"While she was still living with you?"

"Yup," he says stiffly. "At first I thought he was just a friend, then one day I came home early and found out otherwise."

I hold my breath and say nothing. It's rare for Tetsu to be so voluble, and I don't want to do anything to stop the flow of his words.

"It was a huge shock for me," he continues. "I packed my bags the next day and moved into the place where I'm living now."

"How long ago was that?" I ask.

"Almost a year," he says. "Anyway, I came to the conclusion that she had never really loved me, that she was using me all along. I was paying almost all the bills while we were together ... "

He's got it backwards, I think to myself. It sounds to me as though he was the one who didn't love her enough. Not enough to make any time for her or to give her a commitment, according to what he just told me. But then, I consider, he must have cared about her if he was so hurt when she betrayed him.

So what is he trying to tell me? That things will fall apart if I expect too much from him? *You can have me if you want,* he seems to be saying, *but only on my terms.* Suddenly I have the sense that we aren't doing a waltz anymore, that I am doing a solitary dance around an iron maypole, round and round and round a rigid pole without daring to blink an eye or stop and catch my breath.

— 2 —

I had become obsessed with the telephone. When it rang, I would fall off my chair, trip, smash into things, anything to get to that phone as quickly as possible, to get my fix. As soon as his voice reached my ears I would feel my body exhale the tension and my heartbeat subside as though it were obeying the *rallentando* of a conductor's baton. The trouble with being an addict is that as time goes on it takes more and more of the drug to satisfy, and I seemed to be getting less and less of it.

In the middle of one of our phone conversations he asked me, clear out of the blue, to remember him always. My body went cold. Was he predicting the end, or what? But the next evening his tone was as warm as ever. "I'm gonna cry myself to sleep," my answering machine crooned, "because I haven't heard your voice tonight." Giddy with relief, I started to laugh, then stopped in mid-ha. Why were his most tender words reserved for a tape-recorder? And why did he carry on about missing me and pining for me, when we lived only two train stops apart?

My morning ritual was now firmly established: wide awake at four o'clock, jump out of bed, slap on a pair of shorts and T-shirt, head over to the *jinja*, stand in front of the pull-string bell and pray for patience, perseverance, poise, always words beginning with the letter P. Each time I thought of a new word I would yank on the string as a symbol of my request: perceptiveness, clong, persistence, clong, perspicacity, clong, providence, clong ...

Patience, I told myself when he cancelled dates because of "sudden work" or fatigue. A Japanese woman wouldn't complain, I kept telling myself, recalling Hitomi's story about how shortly after her engagement to Kazuo, he got so busy at work that he was unable to see her for a month and a half which she spent, unbeknownst to him, in tears of frustration.

It was in this state of mind — taut as an overwound guitar string — that I called Tetsu one evening to confirm our weekend plans.

"Are you ready for Saturday?" I asked sweetly when he picked up the phone. "I'm preparing a feast, so bring an appetite."

There was a strained pause. "Some friends have asked me to play base-ball with them on Saturday night," he said after a few moments. "Would you be angry if I accepted their invitation?"

"Of course not," I said reflexively. Not angry at all, I thought with sud-den fury. Calm as a cucumber, happy as a hummingbird, patient as a god-damned monk.

"Every weekend," I found myself saying in a barely controlled voice, "I wonder if we'll be seeing each other or not. You never make any plans until the last minute, and half the time you cancel them anyway." Words were crowding my throat and I was unable to swallow them back. "We haven't seen each other for two weeks, and now it will be three, or maybe four, five, six, right? I never said a word when you cancelled dates because of your work, did I? But this is not work, Tetsu, this is *baseball.*"

I waited for a reaction, but he said nothing and this infuriated me all the more. "So what about Sunday?" I asked shrilly. "Why can't we see each other on Sunday?"

"You know I have meetings on Sunday," he said quietly.

"All day long? Do your meetings go on from morning until night?" He didn't answer.

"You like *answering* machines more than people," I cried, startled by my own words as they poured out. Still he said nothing, as though he were waiting to see what further accusations I might throw at him.

"Look, Tetsu, I'm not going to force you to see me if you don't want to, but it seems to me that you just don't care."

"I care about you more than I can tell you," he said with sudden feel-ing. "I think about you when I get up in the morning, when I undress in the evening, when I brush my teeth, I think about you to the point that I can't even concentrate on my work. Even when I'm with my patients — "

"But Tetsu, what's the good of *thinking* about me if you never want to *see* me?"

The next day I found a long and garbled message on my machine: " ... I thought you understood me ... it's a shame ... " I tried to tell myself it was nothing, just a lovers' quarrel, but in my bones I knew something was very wrong. Monday, Tuesday, Wednesday went by and still he didn't call. A terrible thought started to form in my mind. I tried to push it aside but it came back, more insistently each time, pressing outward until I thought my temples would crack: what if I never see him again?

By Friday evening I was fit for the shredder. I kept vigil by the phone, sitting on my hands to prevent myself from calling him. Sleep was out of the question, so when it was clear he wasn't going to call I sprang out of bed, hurled my alarm clock against the wall and walked away the night.

When I got home from my Japanese class the next day, the first thing I did, as always, was check the phone. No messages. That meant yet another week we wouldn't be seeing each other. Three weeks in a row and counting. I sat on the edge of my bed and tried to calm down. *What if I never see him again?* Before I knew it, I had picked up the receiver and dialled his number.

"Tetsu, I *have* to see you and talk to you," I said breathlessly as soon he came on the line.

"I'm sorry, but I'm in the middle of a consultation with my accountant," he answered in Japanese.

"But I simply *have* to — "

"I expect I'll be tied up with work for the rest of the day." His tone was cordial and businesslike, presumably for the benefit of the accountant. "I'll get back to you at a more convenient time."

There's always something, I thought with mounting panic. Always something to get in the way of our seeing each other. If it's not an operation, then it's a meeting, or a golf game, or a baseball game, or a consultation, or it's a weeknight and he needs his beauty rest, or he's unreachable because he doesn't have a goddamned phone in his apartment.

And then it snapped, whatever it was that had been holding me together up to that point.

"If you don't come and see me tonight," I heard myself say in a shrill treble, "you're never going to see me again!"

"Oh my God ... " Gone was the businesslike tone. "Look, I told you I — "

"Tetsu, we *have* to talk."

He switched back to Japanese. "*Saikin kimochi warukunatta,*" he spat out coldly. "*Senshuu ki ga tsuita no wa o-tagai ni rikai dekinai.*"

"No, no, Tetsu," I cried, "the feeling *hasn't* gone sour between us, and we *do* understand each other."

"Only words," he said. "You don't understand me, and I don't understand you either." His voice was cold and hard. This can't be happening, I thought, not this. Only a week before he'd told me he cared beyond words. Such feelings didn't just disappear, did they? Here today, gone tomorrow, like a spot of the flu? My body was starting to shake.

"Tell me what time you're coming," I said between clenched teeth.

"Can we just end this conversation? I told you I'm busy right now."

"What time are you coming?"

"I can't come today."

"Then come tomorrow."

"Tomorrow I have a meeting, and — "

"*Fuck* your meeting," I blasted. "Just tell me what time."

"I told you I can't see you today."

"Just tell me what time you're coming."

"Look, I have to assist a friend in an operation tonight, and I don't know when I'll be finished."

"I don't care about your operation." I was starting to cry. "Tetsu, I just *have* to see you."

"*Kanjasan ga shindara?*" he barked. And what if the patient should die?

He was almost shouting now, and there was a tremor in his voice. This man who had told me he would never get angry at me, who valued self-control above all else, this steel-plated man was finally losing his composure. I'd pushed him to the brink, and for an brief instant felt a surge of power.

Come. No. Come. No. We continued our fruitless tug-of-war. I begged, pleaded, sputtered, choked. My words were coming out in gulping sobs. I could imagine the accountant's amazement as he listened to his client bellowing into the phone, embroiled in this astonishing bilingual melodrama.

"If I come," he said, "do you promise me you won't cry?" He sounded tired all of a sudden. "I want to see your smiling face, not your tears. OK?"

What on earth was there to smile about? And why was he so afraid of tears?

"I can't promise you I won't cry at all," I answered, "but I promise to stay calm."

"And do you promise not to do anything to yourself while you're waiting for me?"

"Tetsu, how could you think ... " I felt my cheeks grow hot with shame.

Finally he agreed to come. He had a responsibility to his patients, after all, and I'd just become one of them.

— 3 —

At eight-thirty the doorbell rang and I let Tetsu in. I showed him to the sofa and offered him a beer. I poured one for each of us, gave him his glass and sat down on the floor, facing him. A stagey solemnity hung between us as we faced each other silently, cross-legged and unsmiling. Finally I started to talk. I told him that the contradictions in his behaviour were making me crazy and that I still wondered, sometimes, if he might not be hiding something from me.

He sat without moving a muscle. When I asked him if he understood my frustration, he ignored the question and began to recite, in slow and measured Japanese, a speech which he'd obviously prepared in advance.

"There were two baseball teams," he said, "each with a different type of coach. The first coach would yell at his players when they gave a poor performance, and the second would convey his disappointment without saying a word. But neither of the teams was responding. The first team disliked being yelled at, and the second team got exasperated with their coach's stony silence. One day the league manager had an idea — he decided to switch the coaches around. From that day onward, both teams started to play much better."

He paused for a moment and went on. "There seem to be two kinds of coaches and two kinds of players. If a type-A coach is dealing with type-B players, or vice-versa, there is a communication gap. The players won't get the message, they won't be fired up for their next performance."

He looked into my eyes for the first time that evening. "Do you understand what I'm trying to tell you?"

It wasn't hard to understand. He had pegged me as type-A to his type-B. I a Western woman and he an Eastern man. All my efforts to curb my impatience, to read his mind, to perfect the art of wordless communication, had come to this — this spectacular failure.

"It's a shame," he mumbled, almost to himself. "I had thought we were a good fit."

"But Tetsu," I protested weakly, "People are not necessarily all-A or all-B. It's not as though I lose my temper every day. My behaviour today was an exception, a freak." He didn't answer. I could see that he'd already made up his mind.

"Do you know how many patients I've seen this week?" he asked suddenly.

I thought for a moment. "Seventy-five?"

"Over two hundred," he said tonelessly. "This may sound like boasting, but many of my patients come to me as a last resort, after they've been mishandled by other doctors. I don't have the heart to turn them away, even if my schedule is full." He kept his eyes fixed on his hands as he spoke. "These are desperate people, they think of me as some kind of a god and I can't let them down." At this I let out an involuntary chuckle.

"Laugh if you want," he said, "but it's true. I know I'm not a god, but the least I can do for my patients is give them my full attention."

"I'm not laughing," I said. "Your dedication surprises and impresses me."

"Even when I leave the office," he continued, "I can't get them out of my mind. Sometimes when I'm lying in bed, I'll suddenly remember a patient I may have seen three or four months ago. I'll start wondering how he's doing, if he's feeling better or worse than when he came to see me. When that happens, I know it will be quite a while before I get to sleep."

"Tetsu, I had no idea ... "

"To tell the truth," he said, "I was shocked by your behaviour. Didn't it ever occur to you that I need my concentration while I'm working? How am I supposed to concentrate on an operation after you've made such a scene? Didn't you ever consider that the last thing I need is more stress than I already have?"

Before that evening, he had never breathed a word about his work except to say that he had lots of it and that he looked forward to the end of each day. Was I supposed to have guessed, from such clues, what a heavy burden he was carrying? Would a Japanese woman have guessed?

"But Tetsu," I said as gently as I could, "I never objected to your work. What hurt me is that you cancelled our date to play baseball. It's not as though we see each other that often."

"I hadn't exercised in a long time," he said. "My body was crying out for movement."

Sex is movement too, I thought to myself. And you never wanted much of that, did you?

"Tetsu," I said quietly, "I won't ever again behave the way I did today, I swear it." I tried to get him to meet my gaze. Frozen in his cross-legged stance, he looked too stern for me to dare touch him.

"I love you very much," I continued, "and believe me, I have no desire to interfere with your work. I understand that your work comes first. I don't even care about marriage or commitment, but ... *Tetsu, anata no kodomo o umitai.*"

I was stunned by my own, completely unpremeditated words. Tetsu, I want to bear your children. There it was, the naked truth. I wondered if the words sounded as theatrical in Japanese as they did in English. He continued to sit motionless, his face unreadable as a Noh mask. Finally he unfolded his legs and got up. "I'm very tired," he said, "so I think I'll be heading home. I'll give you a call when I come to a decision."

He stepped outside and started to close the door behind him, then poked his head back inside. "In the meantime," he said genially, "have pleasant dreams." What cruel parting words, I thought, since we both knew what his decision would be.

A few days later he called. "I've made up my mind," he said curtly. "You made me do a lot of thinking, and I've decided that I never want to see you again."

His words hit me like a kick in the gut. I tried to say something but couldn't make a sound.

"The reasons are," he barked out in Japanese, "one, I don't want children right away. Two, work is the most important thing for me. And three, I've invited a male friend to my apartment."

"That's not true!" I said instinctively.

"Do you understand what I mean?"

I thought back to our infrequent sex. Could *that* have been the reason?

"I ... *think* I understand," I said slowly.

"No, no, it's not *that*. Forget it." What on earth could it be, I wondered, if not *that?*

"You're selfish," he said. "I can't stay with a selfish person."

"Me, selfish?" I cried. "Tetsu, you don't know — "

"Alright, so you're not selfish," he said sarcastically. "Feel better?"

"You're making a mistake, Tetsu. You're not even giving it a chance — "

"You don't understand me. You don't understand me at all."

"You didn't exactly make it easy for me, did you?"

"I don't want to talk about it anymore. I'm calling from a payphone and there's less than a minute left on my telephone-card."

"Just give me another chance," I choked. "Tetsu, we — "

"I never want to see you again," he said emphatically. And then, to my great surprise, he started to cry. "I'd like to thank you," he said in a shaky voice, "for everything you've given me."

"Given you?" I asked blankly, moved that the steel-plated man was able to cry.

"I'd like to thank you," he said again, and then the line went dead.

I hung up the phone and lay on the floor, thinking of the questions to which I'd never have an answer: the Sunday meetings, the key-ring with a hundred keys, the friend he'd invited to his apartment ... And then it hit me: my dream, shattered.

I spent the week in bed, thinking of various ways to devise my own demise. The dream had been so compelling, its brush with reality so seductive that I had little faith in my ability to carry on in its absence. I cursed my Western heritage, all the voices that had molded me over the years: "express your anger," "talk it out," "make sure your needs are met." Coming to Japan had been an attempt to shake off those voices, to try on a completely different self. My sense of failure was deep and wide.

At the end of the week I had a dream. There was an earthquake rocking the walls of my room and a thunderstorm raging outside. I was in two places at once: standing near the sliding door, watching the spasms of lightning in the sky, and lying on my bed, a sexual feeling welling up inside me, welling up up up ... When I awoke, I had no idea if there had been an earthquake or even if I'd had an orgasm. All I knew was that my heart was pounding and it was raining hard outside.

4

To stay or not to stay, that was the question on my mind. There were pros and cons in either direction. If I left, I would be giving Tetsu the power to drive me away from a country I'd come to love. If I left, I would be throwing away a damn good setup: an interesting job, a large circle of friends, lots of free time, and the chance to save a bundle of money. But I also knew I'd accomplished everything I set out to do in Japan. I'd solved the sticky problems of finding good housing and challenging work, learned the language, formed solid friendships, even had my storybook romance. At least a year, I'd promised myself at the outset, and I'd stuck it out. There was nothing more to be done. I didn't want to become like Vivian and so many other gaijin I knew, growing attached to a country that had nothing left to offer them.

Tokyo had become Tetsu, and with him now gone the city was skeletal, barren. The pedestrian walkway in Shinjuku where we'd first joined hands, our rendez-vous pillar in Kichijoji station, the Mitaka-bound trains, my answering machine that had been the purveyor of so much hope and illusion, all these things mocked me now. If I stayed too much longer, I feared I might start hating first Tokyo and then Japan, and I didn't want that to happen.

"Wait and see," my friends told me. "In a few weeks you'll be over the hump." But as the weeks went by, it was clear that I was getting worse, not better. My tears were starting to spill over at the most inappropriate times: on the train, at the lunch-counter, and to my great mortification, in the middle of a class. They spilled over the afternoon I went to pick up my mended clock at the local jewellery store. The owner's wife, one of my *kinjo no tomodachi*, listened patiently to my tale of woe and even offered to give Tetsu a call and try to patch things up between us.

"If I explain the situation to him, how much you love him and how sorry you are, maybe he'll give you another chance, *neh?*" If only it worked that way, I thought.

Hitomi did her best to comfort me. There was nothing I could have done, she said, to change his mind. "You know *bushido?*" she asked. The Way of the Warrior, code of ethics of the samurai swordsmen in feudal Japan. I told her I did. "Well, his mind is *bushido*, I think." She was speaking English, though she rarely did anymore. "After he make up mind, then he cut right away, not discussing anymore. That's like old-type Japanese, not like new more softer type."

I did a lot of reading during those weeks, and everything I read brought me right back to my failure. Pico Iyer, in his moody book on Kyoto, remarks that "Japanese women knew that the best way of attaining their dreams was by becoming dream objects themselves ... They told themselves they could not, or should not, get sad or angry or tired, and they did not." — words that stung me like pellets of freezing rain.

Reiner took me to a chamber music concert in hopes of distracting me, but it was no use, and he too was subjected to my tearful story as we strolled through the Waseda university grounds later that evening.

"When are you going to get it through you thick skull?" he said in exasperation. "These people are *different* from you and me."

"They're not," I protested. "I've made more friends here than — "

"I know your kind," he cut in. "You come to Japan, fall in love with the place and delude yourself into believing you can fit in." I had no answer for that.

"Look," he continued, "if you blew your stack at me, I'd bonk you on the head and that would be the end of it. Anger, confrontation, it's a totally different ball game for these people."

"But not all Japanese women are doormats. My friends tell me — "

"You're a logical person, right?" he cut in again. "If you wanted him so badly, you should have been calculating, scientific. You should have realized that your best chance of getting what you wanted was to keep your mouth shut. I'm not saying you'd have been successful, but you'd have increased the odds."

The impact of his words was softened by the warmth of his hand which he'd now linked to mine. "It's a shame," he said quietly. "If you were in a better frame of mind, I'd take you out a few times and sweep you off your feet." Yes, I thought to myself, and it's also a shame that your name is Reiner Schmidt and you're a German and it's nothing personal but (lapsed Jew though I may be) I just couldn't live with that.

Though my friends kept assuring me I was getting better, I sensed I was on the edge of some kind of breakdown. In my dreams I was falling off things (ladders, bridges, rooftops) or things were falling off me (fingers, legs), and every morning I would wake up leaden, taking a good three hours to get out of bed. I talked with my cousins in New York, amassing huge long-distance bills. It was unresolved grief, they all said, over the deaths of my father, mother and marriage, none of which I'd mourned properly. But Joel's view rang truer to me. "You were looking for a kind of perfection," he told me, "and you found it in Japan. An existential orgasm, you might say." (Joel was never at a loss for sexual analogies.) My experience of a perfect love in a perfect country was pure fantasy, he said, but the perfection was still there, even if only in my mind, so the ensuing crash was bound to be violent. Joel and all his wisdom — where would he take it next?

One Sunday morning around six o'clock I awoke with a galloping pulse and stabbing pain in my chest. My breath was coming in great big gasps. Not knowing what else to do, I dialled the three-digit emergency number. The man at the other end of the line listened calmly and patiently while I tried to tell him, between gasps, what had brought on this sorry state of affairs. I was certainly putting my Japanese to unusual use.

"Sounds like a panic attack to me," the man said.

"You've got to contact him," I pleaded like a maniac. "Please, please call him for me."

"What's his telephone number?"

"I can't tell you," I wailed into the mouthpiece. "I can't let him see me in this state."

"If you won't tell me, then how can I contact him?" he asked gently.

"But you've *got* to call him for me," I continued pleading.

"If you give me his number, I will."

"No, no, I can't do that."

"Well then," he said with a sigh, "why don't you give me your own address and phone number?" Which I dutifully did.

Five minutes later I heard the sound of an approaching siren and winced as I realized why the man had asked for my address. He'd probably looked it up in his procedures manual: What To Do In Case Of Phone Call From Gaijin Who Has Gone Off The Deep End. I felt like the world's biggest ass.

The ambulance attendant helped me to my feet and led me outside. I saw the landlady standing at the foot of the stairs in her nightclothes, her face a zigzag of worry lines. As I made my shaky way down the stairs, my own face burning with shame, I didn't dare look into her kindly eyes. I wondered if she would ever take a chance on a gaijin tenant again.

I was driven to a nearby clinic, shot up with tranquilizer and sent along my way. As soon as I got back home I booked a seat on the earliest available flight to Toronto. This fiasco had made it painfully clear that I had to get the hell out of Japan.

The next few days were a whirlwind of packing, saying goodbye to friends and undoing commitments. Murasaki-san was very understanding and didn't pry at all, but Vivian carried on a bit about how I was letting her down, which was quite understandable considering that INTEC had gone out on a limb for me with the visa extension. Hitomi took me to one of her favourite haunts, a tiny and impossibly charming French restaurant in the Ebisu district. Over langoustines and champagne and passion-fruit soufflé, we vowed to keep our friendship alive forever. I knew that she, at any rate, would keep up her end of the deal.

5

I am sitting in a pot-bellied plane, heading straight west, not quite able to concentrate on *The Gods Must Be Crazy, Part II*, longing to hijack the aircraft and tell the pilot to turn back, and wondering when I'll cross paths with my crescent-shaped lover again. Already I have fantasies of returning someday, maybe to live out my retirement years in a coastal village at the tip of northern Honshu, learn dialect from fishermen and confound the natives. But chances are I won't be back for quite some time, except as a visitor. I will have to love the country from afar, an expatriate mooning for my spiritual home.

When I woke up this morning the rain was coming down in long glassy sheets. It looked like another typhoon, one of the many we've had this season. Feeling an absurd compulsion to ritualize my exit from Tokyo, I picked up my umbrella and headed for the small shrine that had been the seat of my summer fantasies. There wasn't much I could think of praying for, so I just stood there for some time, trying not to think too hard about anything. For the last time I looked around at the immaculately trimmed hedges surrounding the shrine, the towering plane trees covering the four-pillar hut with the pull-string bell. For the last time I felt the presence of the spirit — that curious mixture of restraint, obsessive industry and genuine warmth — that had gone into building the shrine, neighbourhood, city and country, and wondered if I would ever look back on this moment with fondness untarnished by regret.

Sitting beside me on the plane is a youngish-looking Japanese man whom I eagerly engage in conversation, not knowing when I will get a chance to speak the language again. It turns out he is thirty-eight ("Can you guess my age?"), on his way to Detroit to try and sell automation equipment to some car-parts firms, and as we talk and order one, two, three Kirin beers, my story comes spilling out again. "Leave it on the plane," he tells me, then reconsiders and says, "leave *half* of it on the plane and take half of it with you." And for a beer-soaked instant I feel a ray of hope that there might possibly be life after Tetsu.

A bit the worse for wear, but still alive and kicking, I have no doubt that Tokyo gave me exactly what it promised. When you take a risk, I learned, you sometimes get more than you bargained for. But no matter how things turn out, you never regret it.

GLOSSARY

(a selection of characteristically Japanese words and phrases)

Aitai: I'd like to meet (see, date) you.

Akirame: Resignation, giving up. Traditionally considered to be more of a good than a bad quality.

Chikan: Pervert, groper, molester. Women are told to be on the alert for them in crowded trains.

Chotto: A little. Often used at the beginning of a statement in order to soften it or convey hesitation.

Damè: No good, wrong, can't do that.

Enryo: Reserve, restraint. While people encourage their guests not to exercise too much *enryo*, it is taken for granted that they will.

Gaijin: Foreigner, non-Japanese. Literal translation is "outside person."

Hazukashii: Bashful, embarrassed. A catch-all excuse for inaction.

Kankei nai: Nothing to do with it, no connection, none of your business.

Kimochi: Feeling, mood, atmosphere. The prevalence of this word might explain why the Japanese are so fond of using the English word "feeling."

Kokusaika: Internationalization — what the Japanese are supposed to be doing in the nineties.

Maihomismu: The Japanese dream of home ownership. From the English words "my," "home," and "ism."

Mazakon: An adaptation of the English words "mother complex." Refers to a grown man who is ruled by his mom.

Muzukashii: Difficult. Sometimes used in business negotiations as a polite way of saying "not a chance."

Nenrei ishiki: Age consciousness. Generally well developed in the Japanese, who make a sport out of guessing other people's ages.